7/02

WITHDRAWN

*Tell Them We Are Going Home*

# TELL THEM
# WE ARE GOING HOME

*The Odyssey
of the Northern Cheyennes*

JOHN H. MONNETT

UNIVERSITY OF OKLAHOMA PRESS : NORMAN

Also by John H. Monnett

*Massacre at Cheyenne Hole: Lieutenant Austin Henely and the Sappa Creek Controversy* (Boulder, 1999)

(ed.) *Action Before Westport, 1864,* by Howard Monnett, 2d ed. (Boulder, 1996)

*The Battle of Beecher Island and the Indian War of 1867–1869* (Boulder, 1992)

*Cutthroat and Campfire Tales: The Flyfishing Heritage of the West* (Boulder, 1989)

*A Rocky Mountain Christmas: Yuletide Stories of the West* (Boulder, 1987)

(with Michael McCarthy) *Colorado Profiles: Men and Women Who Shaped the Centennial State* (Boulder, 1987)

Library of Congress Cataloging-in-Publication Data

Monnett, John H.
    Tell them we are going home : the odyssey of the northern Cheyennes / John H. Monnett.
        p.  cm.
    Includes bibliographical references and index.
    ISBN 0-8061-3303-1 (alk. paper)
        1. Cheyenne Indians—History—19th century.    2. Cheyenne Indians—Relocation.    I. Title.

E99.C53 M65 2001
978.004'973—dc21

                                                    00–059980

The paper in this book meets the guidelines for permanence and durability of the Committee on Production Guidelines for Book Longevity of the Council on Library Resources, Inc. ∞

1  2  3  4  5  6  7  8  9  10

*For Milton and Vivian*

# CONTENTS

# ILLUSTRATIONS

# Maps and Tables

## MAPS

## TABLES

# PREFACE

During the course of researching this book, I came to dislike the term *Cheyenne outbreak,* so often found in the literature of the Northern Cheyennes' great exodus north in 1878–79. Somehow the term seems ethnocentric to me, implying that the Northern Cheyennes were strictly prisoners who had no case for their determination to live in their traditional homelands, even on a reservation. The term likewise is confusingly applied in the literature. Sometimes it is used to label the entire journey north, from Indian Territory to Montana, but more frequently it is applied narrowly to the escape of Dull Knife's people from the barracks at Fort Robinson, Nebraska, on January 9, 1879. I have chosen to use the term (*Northern*) *Cheyenne odyssey* throughout this work to denote the entire fifteen-hundred-mile exodus north to reach their home through Indian Territory, Kansas, Nebraska, South Dakota, and Montana in 1878–79.

Since the great exoduses of the ancient world, other conquered peoples have made journeys, often risking their lives to reach promised lands. The theme is fairly common through cultures around the globe and is no way unique to the history of the American West. Yet the West has had its epic odysseys, usually involving forced displacement of peoples by the Federal government and relocation to less desirable lands outside the boundaries of their historic homelands. The Trail of Tears of the Five Civilized Tribes to Indian Territory during the 1830s and the removal of the Navajos to Bosque Redondo, New Mexico, three decades later are the most familiar examples. Among those people who defied authority and made great journeys for freedom, the Nez Percé have been written about the most. The Nez Percé, of course, in 1877 were actually fleeing their ancestral homelands in the Northwest for a new life in Canada.

No less dramatic, far more successful in the long run, yet strangely less chronicled, was the odyssey of the Northern Cheyennes under the leadership of Little Wolf and Dull Knife in 1878–79. Their goal was to reach their historic homelands in Montana, South Dakota, and northern Nebraska. Their journey occurred between September 9, 1878, when they left Indian Territory, and March 25, 1879, when the last group of Indians under Little Wolf surrendered near Montana's Yellowstone River. With the Northern Cheyennes' perseverance in the face of overwhelming obstacles, their travels attained the stature of an American odyssey. The causes and effects of their remarkable trek encompass a far greater amount of time, extending from 1877 to 1900, and even until today.

The introduction of this study takes the Northern Cheyennes from the end of their participation in the Great Sioux War to their removal to the Darlington Agency in Indian Territory (Oklahoma) in 1877. Chapter 1 recounts the hardships they endured on the southern reservation and their reasons for leaving in an attempt to return home or literally die trying, fighting for freedom against the U.S. Army and white civilians. Chapters 2–8 detail the events of the long journey north, the military campaigns, the difficulties, and the tragedies encountered by the Northern Cheyennes and the non-Indian peoples they met up with along the way. Chapter 9 explains the legal outcome of the violence between Indians and non-Indians in the autumn of 1878 as the Cheyennes passed through settled portions of Kansas. Chapter 10 briefly explores some of the long-range effects of the Northern Cheyennes' odyssey, especially the paradoxical success and simultaneous failure of Little Wolf's and Dull Knife's followers to realize their vision of a permanent home in the North. Although the Indians attained their dream of a reservation in their historic lands as a direct result of their dramatic trek, the vision of their past life on the open plains was unfortunately not the future life imposed upon them on the reservation by the federal government. Indeed, their future was reimagined for them by white reformers, whose goals of transforming the land into ranches and farms made life on the northern reservation much like life had been in 1877 on the southern reservation for some of the veterans of the odyssey.

Yet in another sense, the Northern Cheyennes were, to some degree, successful in the decades of the 1880s and 1890s in actually expanding their lands at a time when many tribes were losing theirs in the wake of the Dawes Severalty Act. The book concludes with a brief overview and recommendations for further reading on the reservation years of the Northern Cheyennes, thus integrating their history beyond the so-called frontier period of the far West into the twentieth century and the broader context of American history, where it rightly belongs.

Although George B. Grinnell, Thomas B. Marquis, George Bent and George Hyde, E. Adamson Hoebel, K. N. Llewellyn, John Stands In Timber with Margot Liberty, Father Peter John Powell, and others[1] have recorded much of the oral tradition of the Cheyenne people, the most familiar account of the Little Wolf–Dull Knife journey flowed from the pen of the renowned "Story Catcher of the Plains," Mari Sandoz, who told the story in her novel, *Cheyenne Autumn*. Sandoz remembered from her childhood in the sand hill country along Nebraska's Niobrara River the stories of many of the old Indians who had hunted with her father, Old Jules, not long after the Indian Wars.

Revealing the human side of the Great Plains people, Sandoz's moving and inspirational tales of pride and suffering have pulled at the hearts of several generations of readers. Her story of the Northern Cheyenne's exodus of 1878–79 is as passionate as it is epic in proportion. Writing during the golden age of the formula Western (depicted both in print and on movie and television screens),

Sandoz, along with a very few courageous historians, boldly chal-
lenged the notion of a triumphant Anglo–American empire in the
West. Mari Sandoz's pathbreaking revisionism was as necessary
as it was bold, and often as not, it polarized reader opinion during
America's paranoid years of the mid-1950s.

Such passion often evokes intense dedication to a specific viewpoint at the dismissal of others, however, and this was the case with
*Cheyenne Autumn*. Sandoz's frequently caricatured portrayals of
bumbling alcoholic soldiers and corrupt white civilians painted
stereotyped pictures of a continuous struggle of race and class, as
defined by the overly simplistic images of "noble savages" being
decimated by unrestrained capitalism, a concept that has significantly influenced the history of the American West. Indeed, emphasis
on race and class in recent decades has perpetuated a myth that
frontier societies were either all good or all bad.

It is surprising that no comprehensive scholarly, nonfiction,
book-length study of the Little Wolf–Dull Knife odyssey has ever
been written. The story, or more appropriately, collection of separate
stories, has been told primarily in fragments focusing on events in
Oklahoma, Kansas, Nebraska, or Montana. For that reason, among
several, I have undertaken this work, an endeavor that has consumed the better part of a decade and a half. Here I have compiled,
for the first time, a comparative analysis of the Cheyenne odyssey,
not only from the established viewpoint of the Ohmeseheso, but
also from the position of the army that resisted their exodus.
Included also are the stories of the settlers of the central plains,
some of whom suffered terribly at the hands of a militant few
warriors against the desire of their leaders, Little Wolf and Dull
Knife.

Given the sheer drama of the Cheyenne odyssey and the numer-
ous resources available in the National Archives, it is a wonder that
only sketchy secondary accounts predominate from the perspective of the military. Most only footnote the event as an indirect
consequence of the Great Sioux War. Using military records from
the National Archives and congressional records, as well as personal

narratives of the soldiers who fought in the engagements, this study
chronicles the Cheyennes' odyssey, in part, from the perspective
of a military campaign. I will highlight not only the engagements
but also the sympathetic efforts of some officers, including Gens.
George Crook and Nelson A. Miles, as well as their junior subor-
dinates, to aid the Northern Cheyennes in their attempt to establish
a reservation in Montana. This book is first and foremost a synthesis of heretofore fragmented sources.

With the exception of the work of Father Peter John Powell, few
Cheyenne sources, including the compilations of original accounts
by Grinnell, delve significantly into the killing by Cheyenne warriors of settlers and livestock in Kansas during the autumn of 1878.
By the time the Ohmeseheso crossed the Kansas border into
Nebraska in early October, they had killed forty-one settlers, raped
twenty-five women (including girls as young as age eight), and had
destroyed an estimated $100,000 worth of property and livestock.[2]

The Cheyennes committed most of the depredations in Rawlins
and Decatur counties along the valleys of Sappa and Beaver creeks,
near the town of Oberlin in the northwest part of the state. In 1911
the people of Decatur County erected a monument in the Oberlin
Cemetery to honor those victims who died in the attacks. Today
the fine Decatur County Museum in Oberlin still commemorates
what western Kansans call "the last Indian raid in Kansas." For the
settlers of northwest Kansas in 1878, perceptions of Little Wolf's
and Dull Knife's journey were quite different from those of whites
living in the East who sympathized over their morning newspapers
with the Northern Cheyennes' struggle to reach their homelands.

More than any other historian, Ramon Powers has studied the
consequences of the Northern Cheyennes' experiences in western
Kansas. In two articles published in 1971, Powers sorts out the
causes and effects as well as many of the details of the Cheyennes'
trek from Darlington Agency through their exit from Kansas.[3]
Along with Powers's work, the research of Barry Johnson and Todd
Epp on the court proceedings against Wild Hog and others accused
of the depredations, and on the civil actions instigated by Kansans

to recover the financial losses of their destroyed property, places the Cheyenne odyssey in a different light than that presented by Sandoz, who barely mentions the raids in *Cheyenne Autumn*.[4]

Certainly from one perspective, the violence in Kansas constitutes a major fulcrum for understanding the complex picture of the Cheyennes' trek north. But only when we view the depredations in context, within the entire scope of the Cheyenne odyssey, can we achieve a meaningful, comprehensive perspective of the significance of this episode in western history. Juxtaposing the Cheyennes' terrible suffering in Indian Territory, the desperate and heroic escape of Dull Knife's hungry people from the barracks at Fort Robinson, Nebraska, and the constant battles with the military alongside the Kansas tragedies, we find a revealing picture that tells us much about the dichotomous and disturbing nature of the Indian wars in American history.

A major purpose of this study is to elucidate the often polarized perspectives of all groups involved in the Cheyenne odyssey: the Cheyennes themselves, agency personnel, settlers, and soldiers. Consequently, whenever original narrative records exist, I have allowed the participants to speak for themselves in my text. To be certain, much of the original Indian oral testimony of this event has been filtered through the senses of white ethnologists and journalists. Some meaning inevitably may have been lost or misinterpreted in original translation, but I assume full responsibility for any errors of fact or interpretation contained herein.[5]

Conforming to the methodological approach I employed in my previous works, I do not judge wide nineteenth-century cultural assumptions, commonly accepted by those peoples, from the perspective of our twentieth-century values and mores. Conceding that to some degree all history is political, I nevertheless contend that such presentist interpretation of widespread societal values precludes meaningful understanding of cause and effect in an often oversimplified and automatically focused search for victims and victimizers. Specific actions, however, that deviate from accepted nineteenth-century norms and assumptions will be examined in depth. I will be demonstrate also that drastic ecological changes to the short-grass prairie environment between 1869 and 1878, principally the destruction of the buffalo and a reenvisioning of the plains by agriculturists, disrupted the Cheyenne worldview and way of life as much as or more than purely societal factors and account, in part, for the actions of some of the warriors during their exodus north. I have used the terms *reenvision* or *reimagine* throughout this work to explain the conflicting visions for the present and future use of the Great Plains lands by Indians and Euro-Americans.

I have undertaken this study from a comprehensive perspective, acknowledging the historical presence and integrity of all peoples in the American West. The Cheyenne odyssey of 1878–79 illuminates the imprecise, conflicting, and unsettling nature of often rapidly reimagined natural and cultural environments in history.

# ACKNOWLEDGMENTS

I owe a great debt of gratitude to others for making this book possible. Over the years, many people have encouraged me, including students and colleagues at Metropolitan State College of Denver. I wish to extend thank, in the metropolican Denver area, Jerome Greene of the National Park Service for his interest and support. The late Eleanor Gehres and her staff in the Western History Department of Denver Public Library have, as always, been vital to my efforts. Thanks also to David Halaas and his colleagues at the Colorado Historical Society and to Ramon Powers's staff at the Kansas State Historical Society, especially Nancy Sherbert. Although I do not know Ramon Powers well personally, I nevertheless owe him a debt of gratitude for his research on the Northern Cheyenne trek through Kansas. Vital documentation of the Kansas segment of the odyssey was already in place because of his efforts. This book should belong partially to him.

My thanks are extended to R. Eli Paul and his former colleagues at the Nebraska State Historical Society, especially Kerrie L. Dvorak and Ann Billesbach, Head of Reference Services. A very special thanks also goes to Deb Lyon of the Archives Division of the Love Library at the University of Nebraska for helping me wade through the ponderous research notes in the Mari Sandoz

Collection. My appreciation is extended to the staffs of Oklahoma State Historical Society, the University of Oklahoma Library, the Montana State Historical Society, Yale Libraries, Brigham Young University Library, Fort Robinson Historic Site, and the Decatur County (Oberlin, Kansas) museum for their valuable assistance. A special thanks goes to DeAnne Blanton of the Old Military and Civil Records Division of the National Archives and Records Administration (NARA) for her help with the voluminous materials and special files of Record Groups 94 and 393 pertaining to the Cheyenne odyssey. I offer a special thanks also to my many Native American students and colleagues over the past fifteen years, who helped me never to lose sight of this important episode in American history.

I owe a tremendous debt of gratitude to my friends, cohorts, and fellow historians John D. McDermott and Margot Liberty, for sharing with me their huge collection, built over many years, of research materials on the Cheyenne odyssey. Originally, "Jack" had planned to write a book on the subject himself, but he kindly selected me as the recipient of those materials. His generosity saved me many gallons of gasoline and a few airline tickets.

I apologize once again to my wife, Linda, and to my son, Darren, for all the time I've taken away from them to complete this project. They have been real troopers-warriors in their own right. Finally, I wish to express my tremendous respect and thanks to my mother-in-law, Vivian Chambers. During the final year of preparing this book, I witnessed her courageously combating the terrifying ravages of old age. I immediately recognized the similarity between her relentless determination, often despite herself, and that of the Northern Cheyennes in 1878–79, as they fought to retain their pride and dignity. Like the people of Little Wolf and Dull Knife, never did Vivian lose her sense of identity. Never did she lose sight of her origins, her affinity for home and place, or the values in which she believed. Long ago, she instilled in her daughter an unyielding sense of right and of humanity that explains our more than twenty-five years of solid marriage. Vivian has inspired me beyond words in my efforts to complete this project. To her and her late husband, Milton Chambers, this book is respectfully dedicated.

# CHRONOLOGY

## 1876

Nov. 26    Dull Knife's winter camp in the Big Horn Mountains is attacked and destroyed by troops, ending the Northern Cheyennes' active participation in the Great Sioux War of 1876–77.

## 1877

Winter     Northern Cheyenne warrior groups surrender to federal authorities following the fighting in the Great Sioux War.

May 28     972 Northern Cheyennes of Little Wolf's and Dull Knife's camps depart Camp Robinson, Nebraska, for the Cheyenne and Arapaho Reservation at Darlington Agency in Indian Territory.

Aug. 5     937 Northern Cheyennes arrive in Indian Territory. Thirty-five escape enroute. The Northern Cheyennes find life in Indian Territory intolerable.

## 1878

| | |
|---|---|
| Sept. 9–10 | About 353 Northern Cheyennes, under Little Wolf's and Dull Knife's leadership, leave Darlington Agency for their northern homelands. Troops of the 4th Cavalry from Fort Reno pursue them. |
| Sept. 13 | The Battle of Turkey Springs in Indian Territory. |
| Sept. 16–17 | The Northern Cheyennes cross into Kansas. |
| Sept. 18 | The Bluff Creek fight in Kansas. |
| Sept. 21–22 | The Sand Creek (Big Sandy) fight in Kansas. |
| Sept. 23 | Northern Cheyennes cross the Arkansas River. |
| Sept. 27 | The Battle of Punished Woman's Fork in Kansas. |
| Sept. 27 | The Northern Cheyennes' pony herd is destroyed by the 4th Cavalry. |
| Sept. 29 (circa) | The Northern Cheyennes cross the Smoky Hill River. |
| Sept. 30 | The Northern Cheyennes cross the Kansas Pacific Railroad. |
| Sept. 30–Oct. 1 | Young Northern Cheyennes kill thirty-one settlers in Decatur and Rawlins Counties in northwest Kansas. |
| Oct. 2–3 | The Northern Cheyennes enter Nebraska's Republican River Valley. |
| Oct. 4 | The Northern Cheyennes cross the South Platte River. They rush to cross the Union Pacific Railroad tracks within one to two days, then cross the North Platte shortly thereafter. They push the march northwesterly toward the Sacred Mountain. |
| Oct. 6 (circa) | The Northern Cheyennes enter the Sand Hills, with troops from the Department of the Platte in pursuit. |
| Oct. (early to mid.) | Little Wolf and Dull Knife part company, each with his own followers. Dull Knife heads toward |

|          | Fort Robinson, Nebraska, and Little Wolf moves north toward the Powder River country of Montana. |
|----------|---|
| Oct. 25  | Dull Knife and 148 of his followers surrender to 3rd Cavalry troops on Chadron Creek, Nebraska, following several days of negotiation. |
| Oct. 26  | Dull Knife's Cheyennes begin their captivity at Fort Robinson, Nebraska. |
| Nov.     | Little Wolf and his followers return to the isolation of the Sand Hills, where they spend the winter hiding from federal troops. |
| Dec. 17  | Capt. Henry Wessells, 3rd Cavalry, assumes temporary command of Fort Robinson. |

## 1879

| | |
|----------|---|
| Jan. 5     | Captain Wessells cuts off food and firewood to Dull Knife's people when they refuse to return to Indian Territory as proscribed by the Indian Bureau. He orders their water cut off on January 9. |
| Jan. 9     | Dull Knife's Cheyennes make their dramatic escape from the barracks at Fort Robinson in a bid for freedom or death. Many are shot down within a mile or so of the fort. |
| Jan. 10–22 | The remaining Northern Cheyennes, hungry and cold, hide in the hills and bluffs near Fort Robinson. Many fight to the death; others surrender to pursuing troops. |
| Feb. 4     | Wild Hog and six other Northern Cheyennes leave Fort Robinson for Kansas to stand trial for depredations in September and October 1878. |
| Feb.       | Fifty-eight survivors of Dull Knife's people are permitted to live on the Pine Ridge Reservation. |

|  | Dull Knife and his immediate family had reached Pine Ridge earlier, in secret, after days of hiding in the bluffs without food. |
| Late Winter | Little Wolf's people reach the Black Hills and then the Yellowstone River country in Montana, pursued by the 2nd and 5th U.S. Cavalry. |
| Mar. 25 | Little Wolf surrenders to Lt. William P. Clark near the Yellowstone River. His people arrive at Ft. Keogh, Montana, on April 1. |
| Apr. | Little Wolf gains the right to remain temporarily near Ft. Keogh, Montana. |
| June 24 | In Dodge City, Kansas, seven Northern Cheyennes, including Wild Hog, begin trial for depredations committed in Kansas the previous year. Charges are dropped against Old Crow, and Hon. Samuel M. Peters grants the remaining six Cheyennes a change of venue to eastern Kansas. |
| Oct. 13 | The trial of the *State of Kansas v. Wild Hog, et al.* begins anew in Lawrence, Kansas, the Hon. N. T. Stephens presiding. The case is dismissed when the prosecution fails to provide witnesses. |
| Nov. | The Indian Bureau permits Dull Knife's followers to move from Pine Ridge to Ft. Keogh. Some move, others remain with Lakota relatives and friends at Pine Ridge. |

## 1881

| Summer | Little Chief, whose band had been sent south to Indian Territory in October 1878, is invited to meet with the Commissioner of Indian Affairs in Washington, D.C., to discuss plans for allowing all Northern Cheyennes who so desire to relocate to agencies in the North. |

Oct. 6              Little Chief's people move from Indian Territory
                   to Pine Ridge.

## 1883

Sept.              360 Northern Cheyennes in Indian Territory
                   resettle at Pine Ridge.
1884–99            The Tongue River reserve near Ft. Keogh, where
                   Little Wolf's people had remained, is formalized
                   by Congress and the Indian Bureau and is
                   gradually enlarged.
1900               The Tongue River reserve is named the Northern
                   Cheyenne Reservation. Some Northern Chey-
                   ennes from Pine Ridge move to the new Mon-
                   tana reservation. Lands of the reservation increase
                   to 460,000 acres, and the Northern Cheyennes
                   begin a new century and a new phase of their
                   history fighting for their rights diplomatically
                   rather than militarily.

*Tell Them We Are Going Home*

# BIG HORN MOUNTAINS

## *The Beginning of the End*

*I am naked. It is very cold. I run for my life. Soldiers
everywhere. . . . Many of my people dead. Others run with
me.*

> —BEAVER HEART, Northern Cheyenne,
> remembering the Dull Knife Battle of November 25, 1876

The events that would lead to the Cheyennes' odyssey began along
the bluffs above the Red Fork of Powder River, near the Big Horn
Mountains (Bighorn, by modern spelling) in Wyoming Territory,
on November 25, 1876. That evening embers from fires set to
destroy the winter lodges of a large band of Northern Cheyennes
under chiefs Little Wolf, Dull Knife, and Wild Hog sputtered in
the cold night. For the Northern Cheyennes this marked an end to
the Great Sioux War and the beginning of what would become a
defining episode in their history. Nearly one hundred Cheyennes
lay dead or wounded on the frozen ground. Early that morning
elements of the 2nd, 3rd, and 5th Cavalry regiments under the
command of Colonel Ranald S. Mackenzie, with several detach-
ments of Indian scouts from various tribes, had attacked the village
and routed the Cheyennes from the valley. One of the first to die

that day was Dull Knife's son. The battle proved to be one of the largest engagements of the Great Sioux War and effectively ended Northern Cheyenne resistance in that conflict. In the Cheyenne village Mackenzie's men found many items that had once belonged to troopers of Lt. Col. George Armstrong Custer's 7th Cavalry, for some of the warriors assembled in this winter camp had participated in the Battle of Little Big Horn five months earlier.[1]

Although Dull Knife's followers, the principal inhabitants of the winter camp, likely knew troops were in the vicinity looking for them, the attack took the Indians off guard. "I rush[ed] from my lodge," Beaver Heart, a nineteen year-old warrior at the time of the battle, remembered in 1934. "I [ran] for my life. Soldiers [were] everywhere. There [was] no time to snatch up even a robe."[2]

Perhaps no other narrative from the last years of Northern Cheyenne independence is so poignant as that of Iron Teeth (Mah-i-ti-wo-nee-ni), wife of the warrior Red Pipe. At age ninety-five she remembered the attack on Dull Knife's village and the death of her husband as if it had happened yesterday. "They killed our men, women, and children," she told Dr. Thomas B. Marquis in 1926, "whichever ones might be hit by their bullets. We who could do so ran away. My husband and my two sons helped in fighting off the soldiers and enemy Indians. My husband was walking, leading his horse, and stopping at times to shoot. Suddenly, I saw him fall. I started to go back to him, but my sons made me go on with my three daughters. The last time I ever saw Red Pipe, he was lying there dead in the snow. From the hilltops we Cheyennes saw our lodges and everything in them burned."[3]

Second Lieutenant Homer Wheeler, G Troop, 5th Cavalry, remembered that the destruction of Dull Knife's village was "no doubt the richest prize that ever fell into our hands. Two hundred and five lodges," he wrote in 1925 of this total war, "mostly of canvas, issued by the Indian Department, and quite a number of buffalo robes and hides were destroyed. . . . Every lodge was fully supplied with food for the winter. There must have been tons of dried buffalo meat, together with deer and elk meat. There were hundreds of bladders and paunches of fat and marrow which had been preserved by the squaws."[4]

The Cheyennes in Dull Knife's band suffered terribly in the days following Mackenzie's "victory," especially the women and children. "We wallowed through the mountain snows for several days," Iron Teeth remembered. "Most of us were afoot. We had no lodges, only a few blankets, and there was only a little dry meat food among us. Men died of wounds, women and children froze to death."[5] Later Lt. Homer Wheeler learned that to survive, the Indians had "killed some of their ponies, removed the entrails and placed their papooses inside the carcasses to keep them from freezing."[6]

Survivors eventually made their way north into Montana and found refuge among Crazy Horse's Oglalas. By April 1877 many had surrendered at Camp Robinson, Nebraska. Authorities decided Dull Knife's people, along with other Northern Cheyennes, would report to Fort Reno and the Darlington Agency in Indian Territory (now Oklahoma) during the summer of 1877. There the northern people, the Omisis or Ohmeseheso, would live among their kinspeople, the Southern Cheyennes.[7] The trip took seventy days. Reluctant, yet somewhat eager to see friends and relatives among the Southern Cheyennes, Dull Knife, known to his followers as Morning Star (his Indian names were Tah-me-la-pash-me and Wohiev), obeyed the government order. So did the esteemed Elk Horn Scraper, Little Wolf, Sweet Medicine Chief of the Cheyennes. Little did the Ohmeseheso realize that the destruction of their lodges that previous winter had only begun their suffering.

Shortly after they arrived in the humid climate of Indian Territory, the Northern Cheyennes began to sicken. Malarial diseases and other infections unknown to them on Montana's high plains began to take a toll. Of the nearly one thousand Northern Cheyennes registered at Darlington Agenc, almost two-thirds became ill within two months of their arrival. Most lodges held at least one sick person.[8] Forty-one died of disease during the winter of 1877–78.[9]

Medical supplies did not arrive until the middle of winter and beef allotments were insufficient to feed adequately the increased population of Darlington Agency. The stringy, poor quality beef was no substitute for the diet of wild buffalo meat the Northern Cheyennes had eaten in Montana, but by 1877 the buffalo had been all but exterminated on the southern plains. Hunger augmented disease that cold winter. By the spring of 1878 many of the Northern Cheyennes found their new lives in Indian Territory intolerable. Sick and dying, they were compelles to request, formally, to be taken back to the high, dry country in Montana, Dakota, and Nebraska—the lands they called home.

Sometime around the Fourth of July, 1878, Little Wolf asked of agent John D. Miles that he be allowed to take his people home, but Miles and the government refused repeated pleas from the Northern Cheyennes to relocate north. So during the early morning hours of September 10, 1878, a group of men, women, and children, including the families of Little Wolf, Dull Knife, and Wild Hog, slipped away from Darlington Agency. Of the 284–353 Cheyennes, depending on the source,[10] who left Darlington Agency that day, only about 60 or 70 were seasoned warriors.[11]

Immediately the army marshaled the technological resources of a modern nation against them. The result was one of the most important episodes in American history and in Cheyenne memory. The fifteen hundred–mile journey from Indian Territory northward during the fall and winter of 1878–79 brought the Cheyennes through Kansas, Nebraska, Dakota, and eventually Montana. The march was equaled in time and hardship only by the more widely publicized exodus of Chief Joseph's Nez Percé the previous year.

Unlike Joseph's 1877 trek through deep, sheltering mountain wilderness, the Cheyennes traversed open plains and partially settled country in recently organized Kansas counties. They had to cross the Santa Fe, Kansas Pacific, and Union Pacific Railroads where converging troops and resources from two federal military departments speedily were amassed against them. When troops caught up with them, the Indians stopped, fought, suffered, then continued their march north.[12]

After crossing the Platte River the band separated. Little Wolf continued north toward Montana where he and his followers were halted by troops under Lt. W. P. Clark near the mouth of Powder River. Dull Knife's group of about 150 headed straight for the site of the old Red Cloud Agency in Nebraska, not knowing that during their time on the southern reservation the Indians at Red Cloud had been relocated to Pine Ridge and the old agency grounds closed. Troops from Fort Robinson cut off Dull Knife's group and captured them. For a time Dull Knife's people had only limited freedom at Fort Robinson, to prevent them from leaving to join Little Wolf to the north. A few of the Indians served as scouts for the army during this time.

In December a roll call revealed that Dull Knife's son, Bull Hump, had left the fort, reportedly to join his wife at the Pine Ridge Agency. For this violation 3rd Cavalry Capt. Henry Wessells, temporary commander at Fort Robinson, insisted thst Dull Knife's people must return south to the Darlington Agency. When they refused, Captain Wessells segregated them by sex and confined them to the post barracks until they agreed to return to Indian Territory. After their continued refusals, Wessells attempted to starve Dull Knife's people into submission by ordering their food and water cut off until they complied. On the bitter cold night of January 9, 1879, the desperate, starving, poorly clothed Cheyennes—men, women, and children—broke out through the barracks windows in an attempt to die as a free people. Poorly armed with old weapons they had kept hidden at the time of their capture, most of the Indians met death during the ensuing days of fighting in the bluff country around Fort Robinson.[13]

After the Cheyennes'plight was brought to public attention through the regional press and the *New York Times*, the so-called outbreak from the Fort Robinson barracks was featured on the front page of the February 15, 1879 edition of *Leslie's Illustrated News*. Public opinion in the East favored the cause of the Northern Cheyennes. Eventually the federal government allowed the Northern

Cheyennes, with the exception for a short while of Wild Hog and a few others accused of committing depredations against civilians in Kansas, to return officially to their homelands and subsequently to settle at Pine Ridge, then a newer reserve near Fort Keogh, Montana.

CHAPTER ONE

# THE NORTH

## Exile

*All get ready to move. The Soldiers are going to take us from here tomorrow.*

—STANDING ELK,
May 27, 1877

Col. Ranald Mackenzie's destruction of Dull Knife's winter village in the Big Horn Mountains in November 1876 was one of several defining moments for the Ohmeseheso, or Northern Cheyennes. That terrible winter marked the beginning of the end of independent lifeways in their northern homelands. The survivors of the attack who were not too badly wounded eventually tried to take refuge with Crazy Horse's Oglalas on Beaver Creek, but the resources of that overcrowded winter village were meager, and many of the Cheyennes felt stressed and unwanted among their Lakota allies.[1] The soldiers evacuated those of Dull Knife's band who were too sick or wounded to escape to Fort Fetterman on the North Platte River.[2] By early 1877 many of the already fractionalized Northern Cheyennes began to surrender, presaging the final acts of the Great Sioux War. Although smaller groups surrendered to Col. Nelson A. Miles on the Tongue River in Montana,[3] Little Wolf, Sweet Medicine Chief, brought the largest group into the

Red Cloud (White River) Lakota Agency, guarded by Camp Robinson, Nebraska. They came through deep snows in the Powder
River Valley and arrived in late February. Later that spring more
people would come in, including a sizable group led by Dull Knife,
whose progress had been impeded by the sick and wounded in his
charge. By May 15 about 370 Northern Cheyennes were registered
at Camp Robinson.[4]

Among Little Wolf's party were a number of the more able-
bodied wounded, although some suffered from frostbite and malnutrition. They had no tepees. Most had only old skins for protection from the biting northern plains winter. Little Wolf was middle
aged when he brought his people into the Red Cloud Agency that
year. He had a long record of fighting the Vehoe (spiders), as the
Cheyenne named their white enemies. The renowned Lakota physician, Charles Eastman (Ohiyesa), knew the Cheyenne leader well
in his later years. In his memoirs Eastman told of Little Wolf's
lifelong sense of compassion, the foundation for the other qualities
for which he became chief. One of Eastman's stories tells how Little
Wolf, during meager times when he was only a small boy, was
promised a piece of meat by his mother in return for his good
behavior. A dog ran off with the meat, but when his mother tried
to punish the dog, Little Wolf intervened. "Don't hurt him mother,"
Little Wolf cried, "he took the meat because he was hungrier than
I am."[5] As a young warrior, Little Wolf saved the life of another
man when their hunting party was caught in a fierce blizzard.
Little Wolf gave the man his buffalo robe, and he "took the other's
thin blanket."[6]

Little Wolf rose to become a headman, or little chief, of the Elk
Horn Scraper military society. After the northern bands had established themselves in the comparative isolation of the Powder and
Tongue River valleys, by the time of the Red Cloud War, Little Wolf's
people were strongly allied with the Lakotas in the struggle to
resist white encroachment, corresponding with the opening of the
Bozeman Trail, of their homelands. Little Wolf led the Cheyennes
in the Red Cloud War; he participated in the Fetterman fight in

1866 and the eventual burning of Fort Phil Kearny following its
abandonment. During this time Little Wolf was chosen one of the
four "Old Man" chiefs among the traditional Council of Forty-four,
a high honor.[7]

Because of his ability as an organizer and his apparent self-
discipline, Little Wolf, even before the Fetterman fight in about 1864,
was chosen Sweet Medicine Chief, bearer of the Chief's Bundle. The
Chief's Bundle contained the spiritual incarnation of Sweet Medicine, the culture hero of the Cheyennes, who long ago had taught
them their way of life on the Great Plains. As Sweet Medicine Chief,
Little Wolf was expected to be above anger, to think only of his
people and not of himself, as Sweet Medicine had taught from the
instructions of Maheo, the creator. Now Little Wolf sat at the head
of the Council of Forty-four in their deliberations, the seat of highest
honor and esteem among all Cheyennes. "Only danger that threatens
my people can anger me now," Little Wolf pledged as he took the
oath. "If a dog lifts its leg to my lodge I will not see it."[8]

At first Little Wolf had opposed the great war with the whites
that came in 1876, but in the spring he and a small band of followers moved to join their Lakota brethren in the unceded Montana
lands. Although Little Wolf did not participate in the Battle of Little
Big Horn, some members of his party were discovered by soldiers
of the 7th Cavalry who were looking for lost quartermaster supplies
on June 25, 1876. This was the event that persuaded Lt. Col. George
Armstrong Custer to attack the great village on the Greasy Grass
River (Little Big Horn River) on June 25, 1876, rather than to strike
at dawn on the 26th, a fateful, catastrophic decision for the 7th
Cavalry. Some Cheyennes criticized Little Wolf for not reaching
the fighting in time. Lame White Man instead led the Elk Horn
Scrapers in the battle and was killed in action.[9]

Little Wolf tried never again to fail the Cheyennes. He was in
the winter village in November 1876 when Mackenzie's troops
attacked. Suffering several wounds, Little Wolf still successfully
directed the withdrawal of the women and children from the
beleaguered village.[10] With Little Wolf at the time of his surrender

were many of the important chiefs and headmen: Wild Hog (Hog), who greatly admired the Sweet Medicine chief, American Horse, and Turkey Leg, all hardened veterans in the wars with the whites. Also with Little Wolf's entourage was Esevone, the Sacred Buffalo Hat through which Maheo pours life into Cheyenne women and makes them fruitful.

Esevone, brought to the Cheyennes by the Suhtai culture hero, Erect Horns, had long resided with the northern people rather than with the Southern Cheyennes, but around 1872 Esevone was desecrated in a fit of anger by Standing Woman, the wife of Calfskin Shirt, a minor headman who was the temporary custodian of the Sacred Hat. Many of the Cheyennes, both northerners and southerners, believed it was that calamity that led to their current hardship.[11]

Little Wolf presented his rifle to Brig. Gen. George Crook, commander of the military Department of the Platte, who from the Battle of the Rosebud the previous spring through the Slim Buttes fight had pursued the Lakotas and the Cheyennes relentlessly in a war of attrition for the Indians. Now Crook, as administrator of military affairs at Red Cloud Agency, used some of Little Wolf's warriors to his own advantage to further splinter the old alliance. Many of these men, including Little Wolf and Wild Hog, were angry at Crazy Horse for his lack of hospitality in winter camp and enlisted, along with some of the Lakota agency chiefs such as Young Man Afraid of His Horses, in Lt. W. P. "Philo" Clark's company of Indian Scouts. Some of their friends on the Tongue River, White Bull and Two Moon (Two Moons), the headman of the northern Kit Foxes, and a veteran of Little Big Horn, would also serve as scouts in the North against Chief Joseph and the Nez Percé. Now their duty was to fight Crazy Horse. Some Cheyennes fought the Lakotas in the Lame Deer fight in the spring of 1877, and Cheyennes are credited with killing the Lakota chief Lame Deer in that battle. Less than three months after Little Wolf laid down arms, Crazy Horse surrendered.[12]

For many Cheyennes, hope died when Little Wolf surrendered in February of 1877. When Dull Knife's party arrived on April 21, although other bands were still scattered, the process of defeat was finalized. The thirteen-year history of resisting the whites, which started in the wake of the Sand Creek Massacre of the southern people in 1864 and ended with Mackenzie's destruction of the Northern Cheyenne village in the Big Horns, had for many seemed a lifetime. Now they found themselves divided over what their future should be. For some, life on the Cheyenne and Arapaho Reservation at Darlington Agency in Indian Territory, among their southern relatives, seemed the best among bad alternatives. Others, like Little Wolf wished to remain in the North if possible, near the beloved Powder River and Tongue River country.

Once, before the whites contested the Great Plains, the Cheyennes had been a unified people. Originally they had migrated onto the plains from the north and east in the land of the Great Lakes, pushed west by Chippewa enemies, disease, and diminishing resources.[13] They had called themselves Tsis tsis tas, meaning "people alike" or simply "the people." On the plains the much larger Lakota nation gave this Algonquian linguistic group the name *Shaiena*, or "people speaking a strange tongue." Not long after, whites corrupted the name in English to "Cheyenne."

As invaders on the Great Plains, the Cheyennes fought many wars before settling in the lands east of the Rockies on the northern plains. The center of their universe was Noahvose, the Sacred Mountain, known today as Bear Butte near the modern town of Sturgis, South Dakota. It was here that Maheo bestowed upon the Cheyennes Maahotse, the Sacred Arrows, through which he poured his divine life into the people. In the early years they cultivated corn and other crops, but bison was a resource that drastically transformed the Cheyennes' way of life. Within a generation or so they became exclusively buffalo hunters. After acquiring the horse from neighboring peoples, the Cheyennes' formed powerful alliances with more populous nations such as the Lakota. Now they followed the herds over the plains, expanding their territory into the traditional transition or neutral zones shared and contested with other tribes.

Around 1780 the Cheyennes numbered close to thirty-five hundred. By the dawn of the nineteenth century, they had attained great affluence on the Great Plains as burgeoning middlemen in a system of trade that drew guns from the east and north and horses from the southwest. As trade facilitators they became even more reliant on horses. During the 1830s and 1840s the American fur trade disrupted the Cheyennes. They began dividing into two distinct geographical regions. One group, even before the Peace of 1840 with some of the southern plains tribes, was attracted to the trade around Bent's Fort on the Arkansas River, in what is today Colorado. Others preferred to remain in the North, near the Tongue and Powder River valleys, the Black Hills, and the sacred Noahvose. Traditional bands and even the warrior societies were, to various degrees, fractured by this economic realignment.[14]

By this time the Cheyennes were beginning to overuse their resources. Their vast pony herds overgrazed the prairies, especially after a cycle of drought on the plains during the 1840s. Intertribal warfare, along with disease, took quite a toll, an even greater toll than the later wars with the whites. By trading with whites, even as centrally located facilitators, the Cheyennes by 1850 had changed their future by locking themselves into an economic dependency from which they could not escape. Essentially, historian Elliott West writes, "the Cheyennes were caught up in an old theme of gain and cost. As they broadened their command over valuable resources, they became absolutely reliant on the essentials they were helping to destroy."[15]

The split between northern and southern people became further accentuated following the Sand Creek Massacre of Black Kettle's Southern Cheyenne followers in 1864. The Pike's Peak gold rush in Colorado, the subsequent Treaty of Fort Wise in 1861, and the expansion of the agricultural frontier in Kansas less than a decade later were perhaps the most catastrophic in a series of events in Southern Cheyenne history. White settlement thus drove a wedge between the northern and southern groups. Warfare in the 1860s raged between the lands of the northern and southern people along a central corridor within the ancestral neutral grounds between the Platte and Arkansas Rivers. But the Cheyennes had always considered themselves one people and journeys to see friends and relatives between Northern Cheyennes and Southern Cheyennes were still frequent well into the 1870s when much of the central corridor had been organized into counties and settled by white agrarians.[16]

In addition to the difficulties thrust upon them through the intrusive worldview of the whites, other calamities had, in the early 1830s, forecast the trouble the Cheyennes would have during the 1860s and 1870s. About 1830 or 1833, Pawnees captured Maahotse, the sacred arrows, from which flowed the energy of Maheo to the Cheyennes in their everyday lives. In the years that followed, the Cheyennes suffered as never before. Cholera swept the overland trails, and the war with the whites following Sand Creek left the southern people displaced from their former lands. The Treaty of Medicine Lodge (1872), following the defeat of the once influential Dog Soldiers at Summit Springs in 1869, forced most Southern Cheyennes onto a reservation in Indian Territory (now Oklahoma). The northern people meanwhile retreated even farther into the mountains following the Red Cloud War.

By about 1872 the Cheyennes came to believe that the desecration of Esevone was affecting northern and southern people alike, since the Sacred Buffalo Hat was especially sacred to the Suhtai, once a group completely separate from the Cheyennes but whose people now lived in both northern and southern camps. Soon afterward the Southern Cheyennes witnessed the trespass onto their reserved lands of mercenary buffalo hunters, determined to rid the plains of the Indians' main resource. The subsequent Red River War would bring an end to the independence of the Southern Cheyennes. For the Ohmeseheso, likewise, Esevone's desecration would manifest itself in the Great Sioux War of 1876 and 1877 and an end to independent life in their beloved north country.[17]

When Dull Knife's pitiful band reached Camp Robinson on April 21, 1877, many military analysts thought the Cheyennes could never again mount an effective fighting force in the field. Brig. Gen. George Crook accepted Dull Knife's surrender. Colonel Mackenzie was also present at Camp Robinson, as was Maj. George A. "Sandy" Forsyth, who had fought the renowned Northern Cheyenne Crooked Lance warrior, Roman Nose, at the Battle of Beecher Island in Colorado Territory in 1868. Forsyth had recently been on an inspection tour of the Little Big Horn Battlefield.[18]

Although Dull Knife's people were wearing rags and many were sick or suffering from wounds, they rode proudly into Camp Robinson. They sang as they came in and some of the men fired their guns into the air, as was customary when entering a friendly village. The warrior societies formed into companies, recalled Capt. John G. Bourke, Crook's adjutant, who followed the general as a dog follows its master. The Indians maneuvered their ponies in the manner of soldiers on the parade ground. A white flag snapped in the breeze at the head of the first company, led by the Old Man Chief, Dull Knife, and Standing Elk, and other important men rode nearby.[19] From Camp Robinson troops escorted the Indians to Red Cloud (White River) Agency where Crook and his entourage awaited them. There Dull Knife's people laid down their arms.[20] In May the remnant bands of Ohmeseheso, the principal one led by Last Bull came into Camp Robinson.[21] They numbered about thirty individuals, including the warrior Wooden Leg, who later recorded his remembrances of the Great Sioux War.

Like Little Wolf, Dull Knife had a long history of resisting the whites. Dull Knife, or Morning Star, was in his sixties when he surrendered on April 21, 1877. He was born circa 1810 on the Rosebud River. Sometime in his early adulthood, a brother-in-law nicknamed him "Dull Knife" because he never seemed to have a sharp knife. The name would follow him throughout his life and through history. At one time in his youth, Dull Knife was a renowned Dog Soldier. His skills as a negotiator led him to be chosen a member of the Council of Forty-four, and in the 1870s he became one of the four "Old Man" chiefs. He represented, as Little Wolf had, one of the mystical four Sacred Persons who dwelt at the cardinal points of the universe, where they guarded all of creation.[22]

According to Charles Eastman, Dull Knife was a chief of the "old school," in which caliber was measured by courage, unselfishness, intelligence, and proven worth. In his youth Dull Knife's self-reliance became well known among the Cheyennes. Eastman tells of an a early exploit in battle that endeared Dull Knife to his people and demonstrated his capacity to become a chief. One day in the midst of an intertribal engagement, "his brother-in-law was severely wounded and left lying where no one on either side dared to approach him. As soon as Dull Knife heard of it he got on a fresh horse, and made so daring a charge that others joined him; thus under the cover of their fire he rescued his brother-in-law, and in so doing was wounded twice."[23]

As a teenager during a raid on a Pawnee village, Dull Knife captured Little Woman, a girl near his own age. He saved her life by making her a member of his own family, to replace a loved one lost earlier to the Pawnees. When Dull Knife became a chief, he married Little Woman, making her his second wife. She bore him four daughters. Dull Knife's two other wives were Goes to Get a Drink, who bore him two daughters, and her sister, Pawnee Woman, with whom he had four sons and a daughter.[24]

With Dull Knife's people when he surrendered were many women and children who cared for the sick and wounded on the journey from the North. Among them was the grieving widow Iron Teeth, who had lost her husband, Red Pipe, in the evacuation of Dull Knife's village in the Big Horns when Mackenzie attacked in November 1876. Although she was forty-three at the time, Iron Teeth had a young daughter who would now grow up not knowing her father. Iron Teeth kept the youngster lashed to her breast in times of danger and during long periods of travel. She had four other children, two sons and three daughters in all. They ranged in age from the toddler she carried to her eldest son, Gathering His Medicine (Mon-see-yo-mon), age twenty-two, now charged with

This is the best known photograph of Little Wolf (standing) and Dull Knife taken about the time of the Northern Cheyennes' odyssey, circa 1877. Courtesy Nebraska State Historical Society.

the responsibility of protecting his mother and his brothers and sisters.

Like the other Indians, Iron Teeth's family had traveled through the snows of the Powder River country with all members severely weakened by the journey. They were grateful for the provisions ordered for them by General Crook. Iron Teeth carried her worldly possessions in a small parfleche strapped to her back. In her hands she clutched a buffalo hide scraper made from an elk antler and decorated by her husband, Red Pipe, as a wedding gift. "He cut off the small prongs," she remembered years later, "and polished [the] main shaft."[25] Since the birth of her children, Iron Teeth had carefully notched five rows on the scraper with a single notch for each year of life for each child. She had been clutching the precious gift at the moment of her husband's death and would carry it throughout the difficult times to come. For the rest of her life, she kept it within reach, a remembrance of her lost husband, a symbol of good times in former days on the plains and in the mountains and a reminder of their shattered hopes and dreams.[26]

Almost immediately after Dull Knife's surrender, the federal government took action to remove the Northern Cheyennes to Indian Territory (Oklahoma). Although the bands of Little Chief and others were still at the cantonment on Tongue River, the Indian Bureau and the military insisted that the main body of Northern Cheyennes, under Little Wolf and Dull Knife, leave at once for the Darlington Agency to live among the Southern Cheyennes. Indeed, Little Wolf learned that the government had made the decision the previous September as a backlash against Little Big Horn.[27] Among the government officials confusion over the disposition of the Northern Cheyennes had existed for decades. Much of the ensuing trouble stemmed from the refusal of Congress and the Indian Bureau beginning with the original Fort Laramie Treaty of 1851, to recognize the division of the tribe into northern and southern branches.

In the final negotiations over the Treaty of 1868, the so-called Blue Ribbon Peace Commission, which the federal government

sent onto the plains to help restore relations with the Indians following the Sand Creek Massacre, gave the Northern Cheyennes
three choices. Within one year they could choose to attach themselves to the newly created Lakota agency on the Missouri River
near Fort Randolf, or to the Crow Agency to be established on Otter
Creek, or to the agency to be created for the Southern Cheyennes
and Southern Arapahos in Indian Territory. The treaty stipulated
that "it is hereby expressly understood that one portion of said
Indians may attach themselves to one of the aforementioned reservations, and another portion to another of said reservations, as each
part or portion of said Indians may elect."[28] The treaty's ambiguity
was further confused when the government allowed the Cheyennes
to roam over ceded lands for the purpose of hunting buffalo.[29]

By 1874 the Indian Bureau began to force the issue. In that year
they "invited" the Northern Cheyennes to join the Southern Cheyennes in Indian Territory. The Indians respectfully declined. Consequently, Congress cut off the delivery of annuities and supplies
until the Indians complied. The prohibition was extended in the
appropriations bill of 1875.[30]

With the Black Hills gold rush, however, the Northern Cheyennes moved into the Black Hills area, which they considered theirs
by right of the Treaties of 1851 and 1868. At this time the Ohmeseheso
forged an even greater bond with the Lakotas, which would intensify with the Great Sioux War. By now, individual Cheyennes had
formed families among the Lakotas and lived in Lakota camps
both on and off the agency lands. They were included with the
Lakotas in the decree of the government in December 1875 that
precipitated the Great Sioux War. The order stipulated that all
roving Indians must report to their agencies by January 31, 1876,
or face compulsory removal by the U.S. Army, a strange order
considering the Northern Cheyennes had no agency.[31] By the spring
of 1877, both the government and the military determined that the
Northern Cheyennes, especially the people of Little Wolf and Dull
Knife, should be removed once and for all as punishment for their
participation, albeit limited, in the Great Sioux War.

In their deliberations with Crook and Mackenzie, Little Wolf and Dull Knife and possibly most of their people believed that the two officers were offering to allow them to remain in the North with the Indian scouts whose families were on Tongue River, or even at the Red Cloud Agency at Camp Robinson. Later the officers changed their minds, telling the Indians they must go south.

In essence both the military and the government took advantage of the increasing divisions within the Northern Cheyennes brought about by the Great Sioux War. During 1876 and 1877 various bands, separated by distance and the common enemy, began to act independently of one another, without knowledge of one another's actions. On September 26, 1876, Living Bear, Spotted Elk, Black Bear, Turkey Leg, and Calfskin Shirt signed a treaty with the government negotiated by the so-called Sioux Commission. These chiefs had originally asked in the deliberations that their people be incorporated into the Lakota nation. During the negotiations one of the commissioners, George Manypenny, asserted that the spirit of the wording in the old Treaty of 1868 gave the Northern Cheyennes and Northern Arapahos the right to a home on the Lakota reservation.[32]

Ethnohistorian George Hyde argues, however, that some unnamed commission members "argued among themselves on a new wildcat scheme" to remove the Lakotas as well as the Northern Cheyennes and Northern Arapahos to Indian Territory. Lakota leaders ultimately rejected the idea, but some of the minor Cheyenne chiefs, among them Calfskin Shirt and Spotted Elk, did not.[33] These chiefs had visited the southern reservation in summer 1876 and had given a favorable report to their people, also convincing Standing Elk and Turkey Leg that the move south was the appropriate thing to do.[34] These chiefs, with the exception of Standing Elk, effectively agreed to removal when they put their marks to the treaty in September 1876.[35]

Thus, Crook and Mackenzie may have been confused themselves when they parleyed with the Cheyenne chiefs in April and May 1877. In April, prior to Dull Knife's and Crazy Horse's surrenders, they had been ready to offer the Cheyennes their choice of a home based on the spirit of the language in the Treaty of 1876; the Indians could go south to Darlington Agency in Indian Territory, to the Shoshoni agency at Fort Washakie, Wyoming, or stay at Red Cloud (White River) Agency near Camp Robinson, Nebraska, for one year while the government decided their final disposition. Crook's offer had changed however, by May, when he and Mackenzie again met with Little Wolf, Dull Knife, Wild Hog, Standing Bear, and Calfskin Shirt, in a council that united these chiefs for the first time in a long while.

Crook had received a telegram on May 25 or May 26 from the adjutant general's office informing him that the Indian Bureau had approved the removal of the Northern Cheyennes to Indian Territory and that almost two hundred Indians from various bands were already settled there awaiting the arrival of the rest.[36]

Crook informed the delegation of chiefs that they would have to move their people south in light of the provisions of the new 1876 treaty. Little Wolf and Dull Knife, who were at the time of the treaty still fighting the whites and consequently had never signed, did not feel bound by the removal order. Most of their followers wished to remain in the North, but at this juncture the chiefs failed to present a united front. This antipathy, between Little Wolf, Dull Knife, and Wild Hog on the one side and minor chiefs like Calfskin Shirt on the other, weakened the Cheyennes' position with Crook. Wild Hog later testified that Calfskin Shirt betrayed all the Ohmeseheso by promising Mackenzie secretly that the tribe would move to Indian Territory willingly. Wild Hog claimed that Calfskin Shirt bore a grudge against Little Wolf and some others because he had come into great disfavor with the Old Man Chiefs after his wife, Standing Woman, desecrated Esevone.[37]

Others, too, blamed Calfskin Shirt for softening the Indians' position. But most remembered Standing Elk, who had been with Dull Knife through the recent conflict, as the one who committed the ultimate betrayal. Coming under the influence of Calfskin Shirt, Turkey Leg, and Spotted Elk, Standing Elk gained the ear of Gen. George Crook. Standing Elk told the people it would be better if they went south. "I think there were not as many as ten Cheyennes in our whole tribe who agreed with him," the warrior Wooden Leg remembered years later. "There was a feeling that he was talking this way only to make himself a big Indian among the white people. The white men chiefs would not talk much to any Cheyenne chief but him. They gave him extra presents and treated him as if he were the only chief in our tribe."[38]

Even the widow Iron Teeth, fifty years later, remembered Standing Elk as a key figure in the Northern Cheyennes' exile. "None of us wanted to go there [Indian Territory]," she told Thomas Marquis. "But one of our chiefs . . . Standing Elk, made friends with the white men soldier chiefs by lying to them and telling them we were willing to go."[39] Although the chiefs' council at Red Cloud Agency decided against the move, to Little Wolf's complete surprise, Standing Elk told General Crook, in a parley probably held the following day, that the Ohmeseheso would move willingly to Darlington Agency in Indian Territory to live among their southern friends and relatives.[40]

Little in the written record suggests how Crook, Mackenzie or others finally persuaded Little Wolf, Dull Knife, Wild Hog and others to accept removal. However, a letter written to the Indian Bureau one and a half years later by John D. Miles, agent for the Cheyennes and Arapahos at Darlington Agency suggests an age-old tactic. "No one ot the chiefs [Little Wolf, Dull Knife, Wild Hog, etc.] signed the treaty of September 26, 1876," Miles wrote, "and on more than one occasion one of the chiefs who left [in 1878] informed me in substance that they had never made a treaty, and had only come south *on trial* [emphasis mine] and under great pressure, and had continually talked of returning, and threatened to return when matters did not go to suit them."[41] Wild Hog later testified that both Crook and Mackenzie had made it clear, through an interpreter named William Rowland, that if the Ohmeseheso should go to Indian Territory and not like it, they could move back north after a year. Crook and Mackenzie denied the allegation, suggesting that a misunderstanding might have occurred through the interpreter.[42] As it turned out, however, this "misunderstanding" proved ultimately critical in bringing about the Cheyenne odyssey of 1878–79.

By the end of May 1877 Little Wolf, Sweet Medicine Chief of the Cheyennes, along with his people knew they had no choice but to leave their beloved north country for the Indian Territory. Shortly before the move Standing Elk walked through the Cheyenne camp, which was composed mostly of canvas army tents Crook had issued to the people, for they no longer had many tepees. "All get ready to move," Standing Elk shouted. "The soldiers are going to take us from here tomorrow."[43]

"Lots of Cheyennes were angry," Wooden Leg recalled,[44] but most, like Little Wolf, became resigned to the move, at least for the moment. "My two sons . . . said it was the only thing our family could do," Iron Teeth remembered. "I suppose all of the other Cheyennes felt the same way. So all of us were taken to the lands of the South."[45]

Lt. Henry Ware Lawton was the officer Crook selected to escort the Ohmeseheso to Darlington Agency in Indian Territory. The Indians called him "Tall White Man" out of respect. "He was a good man," Wooden Leg remembered, "always kind to the Indians."[46] A handsome, hulking officer, Lawton had served in the 4th Cavalry since 1871. Although volatile and a heavy drinker, Lawton always held the respect of his commanding officers as a man who could get the job done while showing compassion to his defeated enemies.[47] Although he already had fought in the Civil War, Lawton was just beginning an illustrious military career in 1877.[48] He assembled the Cheyennes for departure on May 28, 1877. With him were about ninety troopers of the 4th Cavalry and William Rowland, who came along as an interpreter. Crook returned the Indian ponies he had seized at the Indians' surrender and provided mounts for those without horses. Several ambulance wagons accompanied the expedition for the benefit the old and the sick. Little Wolf and the other chiefs assembled at the head of their people in descending order of importance, followed by the headmen of the warrior societies. With them at the front of the entourage was Esevone, the Sacred Buffalo Hat.[49] Following the chiefs were the warriors and their families. Wooden Leg was there as was the widow Iron Teeth, clutching her precious buffalo hide scraper.

Lawton reported that 972 Cheyennes began the journey, which followed the old, established routes the people had always used to visit relatives in the South. They rode through the once great buffalo range, now depleted by market hunters and reimagined by farmers, who had drained the energy-giving grasses of the plains that for so long had nurtured the Cheyennes' horse herds. In Kansas small settlements had appeared to the east, near the travel route through land that once served as a neutral interaction zone for peoples of the northern and southern tribes.[50] After some initial hesitation, Lawton, at the conclusion of the trip, allowed some of the Indians to keep their guns for hunting.[51] The seventy-day journey was largely uneventful, and the Ohmeseheso arrived at Fort Reno and the Darlington Agency in Indian Territory on August 5, 1877.[52]

Officially, 937 Northern Cheyennes were enrolled at Darlington that August.[53] There were approximately 235 men, 312 women, 386 children, 3 Arapaho men, and 1 Arapaho woman. En route some 35 Cheyennes had disappeared, presumably returning to friends and relatives among the Lakotas or among the camps of White Bull, Two Moon, and the Cheyenne army scouts around Tongue River.[54] The others, including Little Wolf, Dull Knife, and Wild Hog, remained. They felt assured that if they did not like their new lives in Indian Territory, they could go home to the North. At the very least, they believed, they could return to Red Cloud Agency, and perhaps even to the Powder and Tongue River country, or even to the Black Hills, the land of Noahavose, the Sacred Mountain from which Sweet Medicine had taught them how to become a great people.

## CHAPTER TWO

# INDIAN TERRITORY

## *Exodus*

*Listen now to what I say to you. I am going to leave here; I am going north to my own country.*

—LITTLE WOLF,
September 9, 1878

In August 1877 a German immigrant stood on the bank of the East River in New York supervising his half-finished $15 million marvel, a suspension bridge that would link Brooklyn to New York City. The Brooklyn Bridge, a titan of steel girders and cables, when completed in 1883, would cost twenty lives including that of its chief designer, the German immigrant, John Roebling. In another part of the city, fashionable couples strolled on Sunday afternoons in the year-old Central Park. John D. Rockefeller presided over Standard Oil of Ohio, and Americans caught on to Alexander Graham Bell's revolutionary invention of the previous year, the telephone. By summer's end, the Boston Nationals (Braves) had won the championship of the three-year-old National League, led by Jim O'Rourke, who compiled a batting average of .278 with one home run and twenty-nine RBI through the sixty-game season. A golden age of urban economics had dawned for America as the financial panic that had gripped the nation since 1873 finally was becoming a memory, even if the federal government had not quite realized it. Among those who did not share the dream for the future that summer, ordained by the new urban society of Rutherford B. Hayes, were the Northern Cheyennes, newly arrived in Indian Territory and far from the clamor of the industrializing Northeast.

During the early days following their arrival in August, some of the Indians thought their lives actually would improve. The agent for the Cheyennes and Southern Arapahos at Darlington, John D. Miles, who had superintended the final settlement of the Southern Cheyennes during the Red River War three years earlier, issued cattle, and Little Wolf's people feasted. Families and old friends were reunited. One of the Southern Cheyenne chiefs, Old Whirlwind, who had counseled his own people on peace and assimilation during the Red River War, was especially hospitable to the Ohmeseheso. "Brothers," he told them, "we are very happy that you have come down and joined us . . . to live with us as one people. Now we want you to join us in whatever we have already begun to do; to learn how to farm, as we have done [and] to give your children up to the schools as we have done."[1]

But it was not long before trouble brewed at Darlington Agency. Essentially, three calamities overtook the Northern Cheyennes during the next year, hitting the close followers of Little Wolf and Dull Knife especially hard. Disputes with the Southern Cheyennes, inadequate food, and epidemics devastated the newcomers until they could no longer tolerate life in Indian Territory.

Although the Cheyennes had always thought of themselves as one tribe, about thirteen years had passed since the northern and southern people had gathered in ceremony together to renew the Sacred Arrows, to share the Sun Dance, and to confirm the knowledge that all of them were truly Maheo's chosen, called-out people.[2] By 1878 many of the northerners had married into the Lakota culture while many southerners had formed kinship ties with other southern peoples such as the Kiowas, Comanches, and Arapahos. Although Standing Elk and the other northern chiefs who had

The Cheyenne and Arapaho Indian Reservation, Darlington Agency, shortly after the Northern Cheyennes left on their journey north. The commissary building where the Indians drew their allotments and provisions is in the foreground. Archives and Manuscripts Division of the Oklahoma Historical Society, negative #6731, Thoburn Collection.

wanted to come south in the first place easily gained acceptance among the Southern Cheyennes, those who followed Little Wolf and Dull Knife, who had always wished to remain in the North, were not readily welcomed. They began to camp far apart from the southerners on the reservation and soon trouble developed.

Many southerners began to resent the newcomers who were not members of their families. Essentially, the limited resources and inadequate government allotments were now divided even more thinly, causing the southerners to view their kinspeople as usurpers. They felt the northerners had no right to take the land, food, and clothing issued to the southern people. They called them "fools" and "Sioux" since many of the Northern Cheyennes had families among the Lakotas. One southern chief, Little Robe, was particularly antagonistic toward the newcomers. "What are you

Sioux doing here?" he asked Wild Hog one day.[3] When horses of the northern people were stolen, Little Wolf's followers often blamed the Southern Cheyennes.[4]

It seems clear that Little Wolf's and Dull Knife's people openly resisted unification with the Southern Cheyennes. Perhaps this was a kind of wish fulfillment; they remembered the promise they believed Crook and Mackenzie had made to them the previous year, that they could go back north if they did not like Indian Territory. According to John W. Seeger, superintendent of the Darlington Agency School, the followers of Little Wolf and Dull Knife refused to cooperate from the start. "Instead of falling in with the agent's ideas of farming and raising corn," he remembered, "they began to give dances and sing war songs and tell of their exploits and battles, and soon had their southern brethren unsettled and dissatisfied."[5]

By winter, agent Miles reported that about three hundred of the almost nine hundred Ohmeseheso who had come south in the summer, principally the immediate followers of Little Wolf and Dull Knife, still resisted their new surroundings.[6] Miles reported to his superiors that Little Wolf's people had become a drawback to the advancement of the other Indians in his care.[7]

Soon the Northern Cheyennes in Little Wolf's isolated camp retaliated against the hostilities of their southern kinspeople. They ridiculed the parents of southerners who sent their children to the agency school. "Will you let the white wolves whip your boys?" they chided. They called the southern children names for following the requirement of wearing their hair short "like the Negro."[8]

What had emerged was a schism between the southerners, those Northern Cheyennes who, like the followers of Standing Elk, readily accepted the changes forced upon them, and the followers of Little Wolf and Dull Knife, who had never willingly come south. This last group was determined from the outset not to cooperate with the agent's program of assimilation or with the so-called agency chiefs who had accommodated it. Through their recalcitrance they hoped to be returned home to the lands near Noahavose or to the Powder River-Tongue River country at the conclusion of a year.

These Cheyennes were particularly antipathetic toward the white values of industry and thrift taught in the school and the agricultural program of the agency, principles the agency tried to "inculcate into the Indians," in agent Miles's words, for their own benefit.[9] As for the evangelical effort, Miles stated that "although we see but little fruit just now, I have faith to believe that 'bait' is now being scattered that will eventually attract many souls to the 'Gospel net.'"[10] By resisting these cultural visions of Christianity and agriculture-based capitalism, the followers of Little Wolf nullified the entire scope and purpose of the Indian Bureau, the Darlington Agency specifically, and the reservation system in general.[11]

Throughout the 1870s, it seems, the federal government blundered with its concentration policy of bringing together kindred peoples who traditionally, prior to final conquest, had lived apart. This narrow vision stemming from a misunderstanding of Indian kinship relationships would taint the results of federal Indian policy from the Apache lands of the Southwest to the Great Plains. When such hardships as limited food allotments and insufficient agricultural equipment and other resources were added to cultural frictions, conservative fiscal policy from the halls of the Capitol in Washington translated into disaster on Indian reservations, including Darlington Agency.[12]

From the outset of the Northern Cheyennes' experience in Indian Territory, food was in short supply. Throughout the 1870s, as Congress pressured the Indian Bureau to maintain budgets, Indians suffered, as reservations swelled with conquered tribesmen. Estimated annual appropriations never kept pace with actual population increases. At Darlington Agency during 1877 and 1878, agent John D. Miles worsened the situation by withholding certain food allotments (flour, sugar, coffee) selectively as a negative incentive to break up tribal customs and force speedy assimilation of the Northern Cheyennes. As it turned out, his shortsighted, desperate methods proved, perhaps unintentionally, inhumane and led directly to the exodus of Little Wolf's and Dull Knife's followers from the reservation in 1878. Miles's failure was fully revealed in 1879 during a Senate hearing called in the wake of the Cheyenne odyssey, but the Indian Bureau in Washington took most of the blame.

During the first month of the Northern Cheyennes' stay at Darlington, food was issued to them in bulk through the chiefs, who allowed the military societies, according to tribal custom, to distribute it directly to the people. Miles asserted that this practice was not equitable. He thought the chiefs and headmen of the military societies were keeping an unequal share of the beef. Consequently, he began requiring the head of each kinship band or extended household to come in on allotment day to receive individual portions from agency personnel.[13]

According to the Treaty of 1876, which outlined the provisions of the Northern Cheyennes' relocation to Indian Territory, every Indian would receive a ration of one-and-a-half pounds of beef, one-half pound of flour, and one-half pound of corn, or the equivalent, daily.[14]

Either due to delays and other red tape in shipping the food allotments or to Miles's non-issuance orders to recalcitrant Indians, the stipulated amount of food was never provided in 1877–78. Also, since the food was issued weekly, the Cheyennes would consume all of their beef rations in three or four days and subsist on flour, coffee, and sugar for the remaining three days.[15] "They gave us corn meal ground with the cob such as a man feeds his mules," Wild Hog remembered, "some salt and one beef for forty-six persons to last for seven days. We ate it in three and starve[d] in four days."[16] In all likelihood, the pound and one-half daily ration, even if it had been regularly issued, probably equaled only about half the amount of meat consumed by the Cheyennes when they had hunted on the open plains in former days of independence.[17] In 1878, Miles held back flour, coffee, and sugar under the authority of Interior Department circulars of April 15 and May 1, 1878, in order to force speedy compliance with mandated agricultural training. Later, however, he abandoned the practice when he saw it brought even more dissatisfaction among the Northern Cheyennes.[18]

Old Whirlwind, the Southern Cheyenne chief, concerned for the plight of the northerners, remembered that "There was seldom a time but something or other was missing from the rations; they were out of flour part of the time, and part of the time they were out of bacon; they were always out of something that ought to have been issued."[19] "We were *always* hungry, Wild Hog later testified, "we *never* had enough."[20] Old Whirlwind's remarks demonstrate that these shortages were felt most severely among the northerners, rather than the southerners, exposing the degree of selectivity agent Miles imposed on his already inequitable food distribution methods. Indeed, little evidence addresses the Southern Cheyennes' want of food. Old Whirlwind did complain, however, about inadequate supplies of farming equipment and clothing for the southern people.[21]

In one instance, the Indians themselves made their own situation worse. Most of the people preferred to receive beef rations on the hoof so that the animals' skins could be used for moccasins, clothing, or sold for money. In complying with their desire, however, the Indian Bureau arbitrarily decided that three pounds of beef on the hoof was equivalent to one-and-a-half pounds butchered. Unfortunately, most of the marginal-quality steers that contractors singled out for sale to the reservations in Indian Territory were emaciated. They were scrawny animals that could not be sold elsewhere. When butchered, the individual meat allotments equalled less than one and one-half pounds per person. William Leeds, head clerk of the Indian bureau, later testified that he personally had seen steers delivered to Indian Territory reservations "which did not have enough beef . . . to be worth trying to get it off."[22]

The shortages became so severe that military authorities at Fort Reno investigated the matter. Post commander Maj. J. K. Mizner was shocked by what he found. Having dispatched Lt. Henry W. Lawton to ascertain the extent of the rumored shortage, Mizner discovered that the quantity of food issued was about two thirds the amount had been stipulated in the 1876 treaty. In addition, Lawton discovered that the live beef was not weighed prior to distribution but rather delivered one beef to a band of fewer than forty-six persons, and two beefs to groups of forty-six or more. Thus, a band of twenty might receive a sufficient steer to meet their needs while a group of forty-five might go hungry with the same steer. The result was that individual allotments were grossly unequal. Agent Miles later testified that these inequities continued through 1878, even though the appropriations for 1878–79 were increased by Congress.[23]

Later, during the proceedings of the Senate investigating committee, the Commissioner of Indian Affairs, E. P. Hayt, accused Major Mizner of falsifying his findings, but Hayt's own clerk, William Leeds testified that it was Hayt himself who ordered the records of ration issues to the Northern Cheyennes altered.[24] In addition, the weight of *live* beef, in excess of the legal allotment, was calculated in lieu of other foodstuffs, as allowed by the treaty. Leeds explained how beef issued on the hoof could deceive the Indians as well as the U.S. Congress. "The *excess* [emphasis mine] of beef charged over against the other rations at three pounds instead of one and one half pounds," Leeds stated, "instead of being *food* [emphasis mine] consisted of hides, horns, and refuse, so that there really is a deficit instead of a surplus as appears by the Commissioner's statement."[25]

Apparently, agent Miles was likewise concerned by the allotment shortages, especially in 1877, but never did he claim that he purposefully withheld beef rations as punishment. Coffee, sugar, flour, and farm implements were the items he stated he used as leverage with the Cheyennes. Money also could also be given for compliance with agricultural training, but Miles awarded no vouchers. He felt that none of the Indians had shown enough interest in farming to deserve a monetary incentive. Both Mizner and Lawton felt the situation of insufficient allotments was beyond Miles's personal control. In 1877, even before the arrival of the

TABLE 2.1

*Food Shortages at Darlington Agency*

| ITEM | REQUISITIONED (LBS.) | ISSUED (LBS.) | SHORTAGE (LBS.) |
|------|---------------------:|--------------:|----------------:|
| Beef | 4,320,000 | 3,000,000 | 1,320,000 |
| Flour | 20,145 | 260,000 | 460,145 |
| Coffee | 57,611 | 21,936 | 35,645 |
| Sugar | 115,222 | 44,019 | 71,203 |
| Bacon | 143,929 | 45,657 | 98,272 |

SOURCE: "The Revolt of Little Wolf's Northern Cheyennes," 54; Powers, "Why the Northern Cheyenne Left Indian Territory," 78.

Northern Cheyennes in Indian Territory, Miles drafted a report estimating the food shortages at Darlington Agency. It can only be assumed that these deficiencies became more severe immediately following the arrival of the Ohmeseheso. Table 2.1 illustrates Miles's findings.

Considering that Miles indeed withheld some of these supplies as punishment for various acts of noncompliance, and that some of these items were not regularly delivered to begin with, it seems he is not without blame for the Northern Cheyennes' lack of adequate food.

In prior years the Indians' beef allotments had been augmented by an annual buffalo hunt on land adjacent to the reservations, as stipulated by treaty provisions. The 1878 hunt, however, was a disaster. Led by Wild Hog, the hunting party found no buffalo, nearly froze, and were forced to kill and eat their own horses to survive. The lack of hides that winter also meant that winter blankets and new moccasins were in short supply, and the clothing allotments, like the food, were slow in arriving and insufficient in quantity. In addition, revenues garnered by the tribe for hides that year (Longhorn cattle hides) only totaled a few hundred dollars, scarcely enough to purchase additional necessities.[26]

John D. Miles, agent for the Cheyennes and Arapahos at Darlington Agency. In 1878, despite a shortage of food and other provisions, Miles waged a war of wills with Little Wolf and Dull Knife that led to the Northern Cheyennes' exodus north in September. Archives and Manuscripts Division of the Oklahoma Historical Society, negative #5961.

The systematic buffalo hunting in the mid-1870s on the southern and central plains had impoverished the Indians, taking from them their chief natural resource with which they formerly had sustained their independence. In Indian Territory by 1878 the buffalo had been all but exterminated, fulfilling a policy aimed at forced assimilation, a plan wholeheartedly endorsed by the federal government and Darlington Agency chief, John D. Miles. "In the future," he wrote "the Indian must rely on tilling the ground as the principal means of support."[27]

Yet agricultural supplies were also in short supply. The Cheyennes had arrived too late in 1877 to plant crops. Most of them resented the notion of agriculture anyhow, and by 1878 only a few women, including Iron Teeth, planted small plots as their ancestors had when the people lived near Noahavose. Some adopted a pragmatic approach that indicated how disillusioned they had become. If they could not hunt the buffalo because the buffalo were gone, they would exist at the subsistence level provided by the government. Still, they starved. "When we were not sick we were hungry," the widow Iron Teeth remembered. "Much of the time we had not any food. Our men asked for their guns . . . so they could kill game. . . . Sometimes a few of them would take their bows and arrows and slip away to get . . . meat. . . . The bows and arrows were used at times for killing cattle belonging to white men. Any time it happened, the whole tribe was punished. The punishment would be the giving of less food to us, and we were kept still closer to the agency. We had a great many deaths from both the fever sickness and starvation."[28]

Agent Miles did issue farming equipment to Standing Elk and others who more readily complied with his assimilation program, but such equipment was not issued to most of Little Wolf's followers, who showed their open disdain for tilling the soil. Even the so-called agency chiefs such as Standing Elk and his followers could not escape the hunger caused by the inequitable system of beef allotment and distribution.[29]

When malnutrition was augmented by disease, life at the Darlington Agency became intolerable for many of the Ohmeseheso. Infectious disease, especially measles among the children and malaria among the general population, took a big toll in 1877–78. On August 18, 1877, agent Miles reported that measles in epidemic proportion had struck the Indians the previous April. Seventy-four of the 113 school children were sick with measles at one time and the school was converted into a hospital. The agency kept such poor records that at any given time Miles could only estimate the number of deaths. "The Arapahoes," he wrote, "say they lost 136 children and the Cheyennes 83 during the epidemic."[30] Since Miles's report was written less than 2 weeks after the arrival of Little Wolf's and Dull Knife's bands, presumably many of these 83 deaths were among Southern Cheyenne children.

Indeed, disease, unlike inequitable food distribution, did not discriminate. Charles H. Searing, agent for the Pawnees in Indian Territory in 1877, reported that "conditions among the Pawnee Indians was much the same as for all. . . ."[31] Tribes that traditionally lived farther north frequently suffered from malaria and other diseases common to the warm and humid climate when they were removed to Indian Territory.

Agent Miles admitted that the Cheyennes and Arapahos, both northern and southern, suffered terribly from the heat-borne diseases during the summer of 1878. He estimated the number of sick people to be 2,000 of a total population of 5,004.[32] It is impossible to ascertain how many of this number were Northern Cheyennes. Given their recent arrival and consequent lack of immunity to the new diseases in comparison with the southern people, some of whom had been in Indian Territory since 1868, the totals may have been disproportionate. In his interviews with Little Wolf and others, ethnologist George B. Grinnell calculated that about 41 of Little Wolf's band lost their lives to disease during the winter of 1877–78, more than had been killed in battle during the Great Sioux War.[33] Wild Hog claimed before a U.S. Senate Select Committee that over 50 Northern Cheyenne children died during the first winter at Darlington Agency, while Cheyenne historian Peter John Powell estimated 58 deaths of children from among the various camps.[34]

Disease that summer ravaged even tribes that had long inhabited the southern plains. Dr. J. W. Smith, agency physician for the Kiowas and Comanches, reported that disease was widespread among those tribes in 1878, although he did not reveal numbers.[35] Exact numbers and proportions of deaths among the Ohmeseheso in comparison to other peoples is impossible to ascertain. Their suffering was intensified by their lack of physiological immunity and was augmented in some instances by lack of nourishment. Their self-imposed isolation on the reservation and their reluctance to comply with agency policies explain why many did not receive medical treatment.[36]

What made matters worse was the grossly insufficient supply of medicines, especially quinine, available to physician L. A. E. Hodge at Darlington Agency. Medical supplies requisitioned on May 12 did not arrive until January 17, 1879, four months after Little Wolf's and Dull Knife's people had left Darlington Agency. When the supplies were exhausted, Dr. Hodge out of necessity refused the Indians treatment, leading to further misunderstanding between the races.[37] Here was a new form of death the Northern Cheyennes had never experienced in the dry climate of their homelands near the Rocky Mountains. They did not know how to combat the germ as they had their enemies in council or on the battlefield. "To us it was a new kind of sickness," Wooden Leg remembered. "Chills and fever and aching of the bones dragged down most of us to thin and weak bodies."[38]

Spotted Elk was the first of the northern chiefs to die in the south. Iron Teeth was still ill when she and her children decided to make the trek north with Little Wolf and Dull Knife.[39] "Our people died, died, died, [and] kept following one another out of this world," Wooden Leg surmised of this terrible time of misery.[40] Even agent Miles would finally admit of that year, "They have lived and that is about all."[41]

It was understandable, therefore, that by the summer of 1878, many of the Northern Cheyennes had become homesick for the northern plains and pine-covered mountains where hunger and disease had been rare. Wild Hog's nostalgic recollections were eloquent: "We could not forget our native country where we grew up from childhood, and knew all the hills and valleys and creeks and places we hunted over; where the climate was cooler, the air purer and healthier, the water sweeter and better. . . ." In the South, "everything was so much worse, we became homesick for our own country again."[42]

"We talked among ourselves," Iron Teeth remembered of that summer, "about the good climate and plentiful game food in our old northern country hunting lands."[43] John Stands In Timber told a tale from oral tradition about a feeble old woman near death that year. "Up north," she said almost with her dying breath, "the pines make a rustling sound in the wind, and the trees smell sweet."[44]

Although a few of the Ohmeseheso, such as Old Man Chief, Old Bear, and the warrior Black Horse, tried to escape Darlington Agency in small groups, it was Little Wolf who in the summer of 1878 resolved to take his people home. Among those who knew the old chiefs of the Cheyennes, Dull Knife has emerged through history as the greater spokesman for his people, while Little Wolf has been endowed with the reputation of superb military strategist. By all accounts, however, Little Wolf, as Sweet Medicine Chief, in 1878 took the lead as spokesman in a war of wills with agent John D. Miles. He was determined to return the Ohmeseheso to the north country. "Finally, Chief Little Wolf declared that he for one was going to move back North [sic]," Wooden Leg emphasized, "whether the white people consented or not. Others said they would follow him. . . . Dull Knife said he too would go."[45]

Little Wolf's version of the resulting confrontation between himself and Miles and others was faithfully documented by George B. Grinnell, through an interpreter, in an interview with Little Wolf on October 9, 1897. Grinnell later transcribed the substantive dialogue from his field notes into *The Fighting Cheyennes*. Despite criticism due to the military's alleged "surprise" at the Cheyennes leaving the agency on October 9, the Grinnell work remains the best Cheyenne source on these confrontations which led directly to the Northern Cheyennes' exodus from the reservation.[46]

When Little Wolf became resolved to take his people home, sometime between July 4 and early September, 1878,[47] he went to see agent Miles about the matter.[48] He told Miles: "These people were raised far up in the north among the pines and the mountains. In that country we were always healthy. There was no sickness and very few of us died. Now, since we have been in this country, we are dying every day. This is not a good country for us, and we wish to return to our home in the mountains. If you have not the power to give us permission to go back there, let some of us go on to Washington and get permission for us to go back north."[49]

Miles's answer was no, the Ohmeseheso would have to stay another year; then he would consider it. Miles's answer, in the view of Little Wolf and his chiefs, was a violation of the promise they believed Crook and Mackenzie had made to them before they agreed to move south. "No," Little Wolf told Miles, "we cannot stay another year; we want to go now. Before another year has passed, we may all be dead and there will be none of us left to travel north."[50] Miles then accused Little Wolf of allowing several of his people to escape north, but Little Wolf had no knowledge of such an event. After about an hour, Little Wolf and the other chiefs went back to camp to discuss whether to remain at Darlington Agency for another year as Miles demanded.

Not long after the Cheyennes returned to their camp, a group of agency police entered the village and informed Little Wolf they had come to see if all of the Indians in Little Wolf's band were going to leave. "You go back," Little Wolf told them, "and tell the agent that we intend to move a little way up the river [North Canadian River] to camp there, and that then we will come and see him again."[51]

On September 5 a group of Southern Cheyennes informed Miles that they had located some horses, which recently had been been stolen from them on the Cimarron River. They told Miles the horses were being guarded by a number of Dull Knife's warriors. They likewise told Miles that indeed three of Little Wolf's warriors had escaped the agency to return home in the North.[52] Accordingly, Miles informed Major Mizner at Fort Reno, who dispatched Capt. Joseph Rendelbrock, 4th Cavalry, with two companies of troops to camp within four miles of Little Wolf's new camp, about twenty miles above the agency. The soldiers may have brought with them a Howitzer as a show of force. About September 6 or 7, Miles sent word that the Cheyennes should return to the agency to be counted. Few, if any, of Little Wolf's and Dull Knife's people reported back to the agency.[53]

On September 9, 1878, mixed-blood Edmond Guerrier, interpreter for the army with the Cheyennes since the 1860s, rode into Little Wolf's camp and informed the Sweet Medicine chief that agent Miles wished to see him again. Little Wolf took with him Wild Hog and Old Crow (Crow). According to George Bent, Dull Knife was also present. "What do you want with me," Little Wolf demanded upon entering Miles's office, "why did you send for me?" "Three of your young men have run off," Miles replied, "and now I want you to give me ten of your young men, to hold here as prisoners until I get back the three that have gone off. The soldiers will go after these three, and when they have brought them back, I will give the ten men their liberty."

Standing up and shaking hands with Miles and Major Mizner, the Sweet Medicine Chief asserted his position. "I will not do what you ask," he said. "If you follow those three men, you cannot find them. Three men who are traveling over the country can hide so that they cannot be found. You never could get back these three, and you never would set my men free. You would keep them always."

"If you do not give me these ten men," Miles retorted, "I will give you no rations. I will give you nothing to eat until I get them. You shall starve until they are given to me. So you must give me those men at once."

Clearly, by this point Little Wolf and agent Miles were engaged in a strong test of wills. "I cannot give you the ten men you wish, to be held for the three who have gone," Little Wolf said. "I will not give them. I am a friend to the white people, and have been so for a long time. I went to see my Great Father in Washington, and he told me that he did not wish any more blood spilled; that we ought to be friends and fight no more."[54]

Miles insisted on the hostages. "You and I have always been friends," Little Wolf said, "but today I cannot do for you what you ask. I do not want any trouble, nor do I wish to have blood shed at this agency, but I cannot do what you ask."

Still Miles insisted on the hostages. Finally Little Wolf had had enough. He stood up and shook hands with Miles again and with several soldiers present, and possibly with Major Mizner. His next words, substantially reconstructed by Grinnell, have been widely quoted. "My friends," he informed them with finality, "I am now going to my camp. I do not wish the ground about this agency to be made bloody, but now listen to what I say to you. I am going to leave here; I am going north to my own country. I do not wish to see blood spilt about this agency. If you are going to send your soldiers after me, I wish that you would first let me get a little distance away from this agency. Then if you want to fight, I will fight you, and we can make the ground bloody at that place."[55]

Edmond Guerrier, the interpreter, became alarmed during this meeting. He later told his brother-in-law, George Bent, that he had tried to persuade the Northern Cheyennes not to leave, offering them presents out of desperation. George Bent, who by all accounts was not present, later stated that Major Mizner was the cause of the break, rather than Miles. "Mizner talked very rough to them," Bent wrote.[56]

By then, however, Little Wolf was determined to leave Darlington at once. He and his chiefs rode back to their camp to make preparations. "We are sickly and dying here," some of his young men reportedly sang, "and no one will speak our names when we are dead. We will go north at all hazards, and if we die in battle our names will be remembered and cherished by our people."[57]

The Indian Bureau only had themselves to blame for the exodus of Little Wolf's and Dull Knife's Northern Cheyennes from Darlington Agency. Their demands that the Indians learn agriculture and send their children to the agency school for subservient labor roles within white society were too precipitate to be effective. To expect peoples, who in 1877 had been at war with the United States, under the stress factors of inadequate food and epidemic, to become assimilated into their enemy's culture within one year, was not only unwise policy, but was also an ethnocentric, paternalistic, and arrogant assumption.

The Ohmeseheso followers of Little Wolf and Dull Knife left the agency in the late hours of September 9, 1878. Officially there were 353, only about one-third of those who had come south in 1877. Their numbers included 92 men, 120 women, 69 boys, and 72 girls. Only 60 or 70 were seasoned warriors.[58] They left their lodges standing and their fires burning to deceive agency authorities and troops from Fort Reno, but they were going home.

## CHAPTER THREE

# INDIAN TERRITORY

## The Battle of Turkey Springs

*Go back and tell them we are going home.*

—CURLY HEAD (Twin),
September 13, 1878

For Capt. Joseph Rendlebrock of the 4th Cavalry, the undetected exodus of Little Wolf's and Dull Knife's people became an embarrassment that, combined with the events immediately following, ended his career in the U.S. Army. On the night of September 9, 1878, the Cheyenne women had stripped the tepees of cloth and hide, leaving the poles standing. The pony herd had been driven in quietly and the fires left ablaze. The entire encampment was vacated, and the Ohmeseheso gained a head start of about five hours before their absence was reported to agent Miles by the Northern Cheyenne American Horse, one of the forty-four council chiefs, and agency (Southern Cheyenne and Arapaho) police, at around 3:00 A.M. on September 10.

Immediately Maj. A. K. Mizner ordered Rendlebrock with Companies G and H of the 4th Cavalry and Indian scouts from Fort Reno to pursue and overtake the fleeing Northern Cheyennes. Mizner hoped Rendlebrock could at least back the Indians up against the Arkansas River, reportedly in flood stage from recent rain, and prevent their crossing. This would stop their line of flight north and keep them away from the fringes of the Kansas settlements. Rendlebrock, however, intended to engage the Cheyennes before they vacated the open spaces of Indian Territory. The command consisted of eighty-one enlisted men, several Indian scouts, and four officers. Besides Rendlebrock the officers were Capt. Sebastian Gunther and Lts. Abram E. Wood, David M. McDonald, and Wilber Wilder. The command left the vicinity of the agency about 8:00 A.M., their pack animals loaded with ten days' rations.[1]

Rendlebrock, a Prussian immigrant, was nearing retirement when he set out in pursuit of the fleeing Northern Cheyennes. He had risen through the ranks between 1851 and 1862 as a member of the old U.S. Mounted Rifles, which later became the 1st Cavalry. During the Civil War he was promoted to 2d Lt. in the 4th Cavalry. He won brevets to the rank of Major for actions at Franklin and McMinnville, Tennessee, and Selma, Alabama. In 1867 he was promoted to the rank of Captain in the regular army. Despite his good service record, the possibility was very real indeed that he might shoulder much of the blame in the twilight of his career for failure to engage and capture Little Wolf's "stampeders," as the press would call them.[2]

About noon Indian scouts picked up the Cheyennes' trail just north of Raven Springs, now called Left Hand Springs in Blaine County, Oklahoma, about four miles east of the modern town of Greenfield, Oklahoma, and twenty miles northwest of Darlington Agency.[3] Rendlebrock ordered a quick pursuit until dark, when the battalion halted for supper. The march resumed about 10:00 P.M. at which time Rendlebrock ordered camp to be made sixty miles from Darlington. He dispatched couriers northwest to Camp Supply to alert them of the Indians' apparent line of flight. It appeared to Rendlebrock that the Cheyennes were following the general route of the Western Cattle Trail, which came up from Texas and traveled across Indian Territory to Dodge City, Kansas, where it met the Santa Fe Railroad.[4]

Meanwhile at Fort Reno, Major Mizner wired Gen. John Pope, commander of the Department of the Missouri at Fort Leavenworth, Kansas, about the exodus of the Northern Cheyennes. Pope contacted Divisional Commander General Philip Sheridan, and soon the technological resources of the United States were marshaled to halt the northward advance of the desperate Cheyenne refugees trying to return home. Only a decade earlier, during the Indian War of 1867–69, when the Cheyennes and their allies were defending the buffalo ranges from the advancing railroads and settlers moving into the newly organized counties on the central plains in Kansas, troops stationed in frontier outposts routinely encounted huge war parties of hundreds of Indians. Isolated by lack of communication, the troops could little hope to successfully push such large war parties, intact, into converging troops.

By the mid-1870s, following the Treaties of Medicine Lodge and the completion of the railroads and telegraph lines across the plains, the balance of military power shifted to the U.S. Army. The vast spaces of the Great Plains seemed to shrink dramatically in the wake of technological advancement, thus diminishing any strategic advantage the fleeing Cheyennes might have had otherwise. Now military authorities could amass converging troops from all directions to any vicinity in a matter of hours, as they had in the Red River War of 1874–75, by transporting soldiers and horses by rail to intercept parties of Indians moving off the agencies.[5]

The strategy to halt the Ohmeseheso was extensive and elaborate, rivaling strategy employed during the Nez Percé War the previous year and, at least in theory, holding a better chance for success. Once across the Arkansas River, Little Wolf's people would have to cross three major east-west railroads, the Santa Fe in southern Kansas, the Kansas Pacific across the old Smoky Hill Route in central Kansas, and finally the Union Pacific in southern Nebraska. They faced only the expansive plains; no sheltering mountains, forests, or vast canyons offered them the concealment the Nez Percé had enjoyed in 1877. Indeed, through Kansas and into Nebraska, the Indians would collide with the burgeoning ranching frontier. In northern Kansas they likely would have to run the western edge of expanding farm communities. They would be spotted easily by citizens along the way on the open prairie, a useful strategic situation the army was soon to recognize and take advantage of in their pursuit of the fleeing Indians.

Within hours on September 10, General Sheridan alerted the military departments of the Missouri under Gen. John Pope, the Platte under Gen. George Crook, and Dakota under Gen. A. H. Terry of the exodus of the Northern Cheyennes. Sheridan's plan was to spread out a network of troops on an east-to-west perimeter to intercept the Indians along the Kansas Pacific, with backup points along the Union Pacific to the north.[6]

Accordingly, General Pope dispatched from Fort Leavenworth one hundred mounted men of the 23rd Infantry. They moved toward Fort Hays to intercept the Cheyennes should they be encountered east of Hays. Three companies of the 3rd Infantry moved west from Fort Hays, connecting with two companies of the 16th Infantry from Fort Wallace to block the route between these posts. The garrison at Fort Lyon, Colorado, would patrol west of that post as well as eastward toward Wallace. Meanwhile a company of the 19th Infantry from Fort Dodge, Kansas, would be joined by a company of 4th Cavalry from Camp Supply in Indian Territory along the Arkansas in an attempt to intercept the Cheyennes early, as Rendlebrock's two companies of 4th Cavalry from Fort Reno drove them north. Failing this, Rendlebrock would join these forces on the Arkansas where Lt. Col. William H. Lewis, commander of the 19th Infantry at Fort Dodge, would take command of the pursuit northward to the interception net along the Kansas Pacific Railroad.

In all about 250 soldiers had been put in the field by the Department of the Missouri by September 12. By the end of the Cheyenne odyssey, that figure would escalate to over 1,000. Within the next few days, Pope dispatched reinforcements of 4th Cavalry from Fort Sill to Fort Reno, as Rendlebrock's two companies, now in pursuit of the Cheyennes, were no longer available to guard against

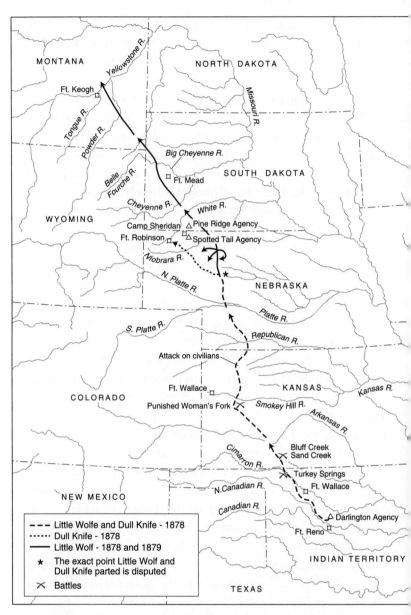

The Northern Cheyennes' travel route, from Indian Territory to Montana.

further trouble at Darlington Agency. Additional reinforcements of the 4th Cavalry under Capt. Clarence Mauck came up from Fort Richardson, Texas, to Fort Dodge in the optimistic plan to halt the Indians early on the Arkansas.

Meanwhile the Department of the Platte took measures to establish a second line in the unlikely event the Cheyennes made it all the way north to Nebraska. Troops of the 4th, 9th, and 14th Infantry Regiments, under Maj. T. T. Thornburg, who would in the next year be killed in the Ute War in Colorado, were rushed from Omaha by General Crook over the Union Pacific to Sydney, Nebraska. There a special train kept up a head of steam night and day to move these troops either east or west as needed once it was determined the Indians had broken across the Kansas Pacific. The War Department had directed its might against sixty or seventy able warriors of Little Wolf's and Dull Knife's desperate people. Sheridan's orders to the troops were to attack the Indians wherever found unless they surrendered and agreed to be dismounted and disarmed.[7]

Rendlebrock's scouts were correct in their assumption that Little Wolf had led his people northwest from Darlington. When the Indians left the agency, they crossed the North Canadian River twice and rode onto the open plains toward the Cimarron, which they crossed probably on September 12, after three days of hard, almost continuous flight. They then came back on the trail a ways and made camp north of the river behind some sheltering bluffs; Little Wolf feared pursuit by troops and decided that spot would be a good area to defend. Along with shelter for the women and children, there were bluffs and some long, sandy ravines useful for establishing a defensive position in front, and water was available from a spring. The whites called this place Turkey Springs.[8]

Many of the Indians were familiar with the route they would take back north. Since the formation of the southern agency in 1869, southerners and northerners often had risked their lives moving across Kansas between the northern agencies and the Cheyenne and Arapaho Agency at Darlington to visit friends and relatives or to escape conflict with the whites. Occasionally they made raids in this central escape corridor. During the Red River War, Stone Fore-head (also called Rock Forehead and Medicine Arrows), then the Sacred Arrows keeper, had risked his life bringing Maahotse north to safety through these lands. During that same time, a group of southern people led by Little Bull, who had sought refuge among the Ohmeseheso at the conclusion of that war, were almost anni-hilated by a battalion of the 6th Cavalry under 2d Lt. Austin Henley on Sappa Creek in Decatur County, an act that called for revenge according to Cheyenne custom.

The women and children especially among Little Wolf's and Dull Knife's people were hungry and exhausted from the long flight. To expedite speedy travel the Indians took only what they could carry on their backs in bundles or packs, and there was little food for either children or adults. Iron Teeth, widow of Red Pipe, still suffering from dysentery, had come with all of her children as members of Dull Knife's immediate band. "My two sons joined the band determined to leave there [Indian Territory]," she remem-bered. "I and my three daughters followed them. . . . my older son [Gathering His Medicine] kept saying we should go on toward the North unless we were killed, that it was better to be killed than to go back and die slowly."[9]

Iron Teeth had with her a small pack with her few remaining possessions, including her prized elk antler hide scraper, made by her slain husband as a wedding gift. Because of the limitations on what reasonably could be carried, the Ohmeseheso who made the odyssey north were instantly bereft of most worldly possessions. Keeping families together and staying alive were the important things now. "Chills and fever kept me sick along the way," Iron Teeth reminisced. "We had not any lodges. At night when we could make any kind of camp, my daughters helped me at making willow branch shelters. Day after day, through more than a month, I kept my youngest daughter strapped to my body, in front of me, on my horse. I led another horse carrying the next-youngest daughter. The oldest daughter managed on her own mount. The two sons stayed always behind, to help in watching for soldiers."[10]

Gone were the Northern Cheyennes' days of fighting glory, of extensive war paint and dress, of counting coup to gain status as a warrior by touching an enemy with a quirt and letting him live, and boasting their exploits around the fire. The warriors no longer resembled the splendidly arrayed fighting men described by so many of the army officers who had fought them in the late 1860s. Now these were simply a sick, hungry, destitute people trying to go home; their only advantage was their ability to travel swiftly, though they were exhausted, over familiar ground. Some of those who had fought the Vehoe when there was still some illusion of hope were with the Sweet Medicine chief for this last, desperate act of self-determination.

Besides Little Wolf, Dull Knife and Wild Hog, the aged council chief Black Crane was present, wishing to die as a free man. Chiefs Old Crow and American Horse apparently accompanied the group, but American Horse was ambivalent about the trek north and probably either returned to Darlington shortly after September 9, telling Agent Miles of the escape, or may never have left the agency in the first place.[11]

Little Wolf's own Elk Horn Scraper society was well represented, including Wild Hog and his family, Broken Jaw, Wolf Medicine, Little Shield, all Elk headmen. Other Elks on the journey included Little Hawk, Yellow Eagle, Crooked Nose, and White Bird, as well as Strong Left Hand and Calf of the Crazy Dogs. Little Wolf's sons, Wooden Thigh and Pawnee, were with their father as were Little Wolf's two wives. Dull Knife's eldest son, Bull Hump, rode with a few remnant Dog Soldiers who had chosen life in the North, the most important being Tangle Hair, a half-Lakota, half-Cheyenne headman. Blacksmith and Noisy Walker (Noisy Walking), too, were probably among the Dog Soldiers.

Other fighting men heading north included Bridge, Howling Wolf the Northerner, White Antelope the Northerner, a warrior named Curly Head (Twin), Starving Elk, Fire Wolf, High Walking, and Bullet Proof, who had led Cheyennes against the Buffalo Soldiers of the 10th Cavalry during the war of 1867–69. Also traveling were

Brown Bird; Little Bear; Painted War Club; Gathering His Medicine (Iron Teeth's eldest son); Limpy, a hero of the Battle of the Rosebud; Red Cherries, who was an aged warrior now; Great Eyes; Old Sitting Man; and Porcupine, who had at age nineteen helped derail and burn a Union Pacific train in Nebraska, near Plum Creek Station, in 1867. All these men were hardened veterans of the wars with the Vehoe.

A warrior named Little Finger Nail was the leader of a small faction of younger men, not veterans of the old wars. These young men probably felt anxious to make their names in battle against the whites, as their elders had, but with that attitude, they posed a threat to Little Wolf's and Dull Knife's hopes of making it north without much fighting. Among these young warriors were Roached Hair, Roman Nose[12], Charging Bear, Pug, and Black Beaver. Little Finger Nail carried with him a ledger book containing drawings of the exploits of his people.[13]

Still only about one third of those who had come south with Little Wolf in 1877 now decided to follow him back home. Besides American Horse, Brave Bear, and Yellow Nose, other brave warriors and veterans of the Great Sioux War decided to remain in Indian Territory. Wooden Leg also chose to remain in the south. "My father and I considered joining Little Wolf," he remembered. "But we managed in one way or another to keep our family from starving, and we believed that after a while the food would be more plentiful. . . . none of us had yet come near death. We sympathized fully with our deceived and suffering people, and both of us had a high admiration for Little Wolf. But we settled our minds to stay here and keep out of trouble." Wooden Leg would marry a Southern Cheyenne girl who as a child had survived the Battle of the Washita in 1868.[14]

Absent, too, was Coal Bear, the keeper of Esevone. The Sacred Buffalo Hat had long resided with the northern people, but now the Ohmeseheso, in perhaps their most important hour of trial, would have to make their way north against all odds without their two most sacred covenants, Esevone and Maahotse (the latter had always resided with the Southern Cheyennes, and their present keeper was Black Hairy Dog). Only Little Wolf's medicine bundle, the incarnation of the prophet Sweet Medicine, accompanied the people as inspiration. Fortunately, its safety was vested in Little Wolf, one of the greatest warriors the people had ever known.[15]

On the morning of September 13, 1878, Cheyenne wolves (scouts) reported seeing a dust cloud rising from an approaching column of troops to the south.[16] Immediately Little Wolf took charge. "Do not any of you shoot until the troops have fired," he commanded his warriors. "Let them shoot first. But do you all get your arms and horses, and I will go out and meet the troops, and try to talk with them. If they kill any of us, I will be the first man killed. Then you can fight."[17]

The column of soldiers rode in close to the Cheyenne camp and Little Wolf went out to meet them. An unidentified trooper of Company G or H of the 4th Cavalry, probably an officer, recalled what happened next.

> The cavalry column advanced to within 400 yards of them, and as they had a splendid position, Capt. Rendlebrock dismounted the command and formed in five yard distances skirmish order. The Indians were now moving north and south and performing various feats of horsemanship, but their chief, Dull Knife [this was actually Little Wolf] stood square in our front, not moving with the rest. It was now 9 o'clock and Capt. Rendlebrock sent one of the Arapahoes to have a parley which lasted about three minutes; [Little Wolf] saying he did not wish to fight, but would before he would be taken back to the hated Southern agency.[18]

Rendlebrock sent the Arapaho scout Chalk (Ghost Man) to request the Cheyennes' surrender. When he approached the Cheyennes' position, Chalk called out the names of Little Wolf, Dull Knife, Wild Hog, and Tangle Hair. "The white men want you to go back," Chalk told Little Wolf. "If you will surrender and return, they will give you your rations and will treat you well."

"Tell them that we do not want to fight," Little Wolf replied, "[but] we will not go back. We are leaving this country. I have had no quarrel with anyone. I hold up my right hand that I do not wish to fight with the whites; but we are going to our old home and stay there."

Again Chalk pleaded for Little Wolf to surrender. "No," Little Wolf told him. "We are going back to the country where we were born and brought up."[19] A warrior named Curly Head (Twin) called out, "Go back and tell them we are going home. We don't want any fighting. If the army wants to fight us they can. We are not going back."[20]

During the parley, Captain Rendlebrock noticed warriors moving through the ravines to his right and left. When Chalk returned to the soldiers' lines, Rendlebrock obeyed his instructions from high command and ordered his dismounted troopers to fire on the Indians, with G Company opening the volley. By 10:00 A.M. the fighting was general, and the troops dug rifle pits in the sand for protection. Captains Rendlebrock and Sebastian Gunther held the middle of the line with Lts. Abram E. Wood, David M. McDonald, and Wilber Wilder on the right and left flanks respectively.[21]

"Fighting now became general," the anonymous trooper recalled. "A knoll towards the east, held mostly by men of H Company, was twice assaulted by the Indians and twice repulsed, the defenders losing one man, Private Slater of H Company was [wounded] and the Arapaho scout Chalk, wounded. One horse was killed and two wounded at the same place. The horses were then placed in a deep ravine and remained there all day. At the base of the hill facing Turkey Springs, Corporal Lynch of G Company was killed and Privates Burrows and Leonard of the same company wounded."[22]

"Had we lost our position," Capt. Sebastian Gunther, recalled, "we would have been lost. Lieut. Wood held the right from me and Lieut. Wilder the rear [left] of me, and neither suffered any loss. A knoll was held by [Captain] Rendlebrock, and they [the Indians] charged to within 75 yards and came near taking it."[23]

During the night, Little Wolf's warriors set fire to the prairie grass around the 4th Cavalry position and fired volleys into the camp. Shortly after dark a group of skirmishers advanced to obtain water but the Cheyennes beat them back. "There was no medical attendance in the command," the anonymous trooper remembered, "and the wounded suffered terribly. At night the troops lay around the ravine . . . but no one slept. At dawn a reconnaisence [sic] was ordered, when it was discovered the Indians were secreted all around us. We were now 24 hours without water and Capt. Rendlebrock saw that in holding his own another day, he would run out of ammunition as each man had but 100 rounds apiece when leaving [Fort] Reno and as he had no water, all were suffering for the want of it; some having drank the urine of horses during the night, so great was their thirst."[24]

On the morning of September 14, Rendlebrock consequently ordered a general retreat seven miles back to the water source, the Cimarron River. Lieutenant Wilder's company feinted to the front to create a diversion while selected troopers brought the horses up from the ravine, one mounted man leading four additional horses for his concealed comrades. Quickly Little Wolf detected the maneuver and sent his warriors to the rear of Rendlebrock's troops to cut off their retreat; a running fight ensued. "The Indians soon lined the hills," Captain Gunther recalled, "and then we all mounted . . . but as the horses were such a mark and as the Indians closed in around us we dismounted. We fought for six miles."[25]

"The command then moved to the right in the direction of the Cimarron River," the anonymous trooper recalled, "when the Indians, yelling demonically, appeared in our front. At this juncture, a small piece of woods was espied in a valley. The pack animals were driven towards it and the troops charged the Indians thrice, driving them in all directions. . . . Water was reached at 9 o'clock [A.M.], for which a rush was made, some of the men being unable to articulate for the want of it."[26] Shot twice, overrun and killed during the running fight on September 14, at a spot called Red Hill, was Pvt. George Sand. Officially Rendlebrock lost Sand,

Cpl. Patrick Lynch, Pvt. Francis Burton, and Arapaho scout Chalk (Ghost Man) who was listed as killed, but survived his severe wounds, and official reports list one man wounded. In all likelihood, however, two or three troopers suffered wounds along with the scout, Chalk, from the fighting on September 13. On September 15 an escort set out with the wounded for Camp Supply as Rendlebrock rallied to continue pursuing the Indians.[27] The Northern Cheyennes counted no dead but five badly wounded including a little girl hit in the heel by a stray bullet. Thereafter the Cheyennes called this child "Lame Girl."[28]

Thus ended the Battle of Turkey Springs, the last known encounter between Indians and the U.S. Army in Oklahoma. When the news of Rendlebrock's failure to defeat and capture the Ohmeseheso was released, the regional "penny press" predictably misconstrued the events and marginalized the Cheyennes. "The officer in command before the fight twice demanded their surrender," stated one newspaper, "but the savages replied that they had come back to have a fight and they were hungry for it."[29]

Captains Rendlebrock and Gunther, although they would retain their commands for a few more weeks in pursuit of the Indians through Kansas, were eventually scapegoated for the disastrous events that befell the army at the Battle of Turkey Springs. These officers were returned to Fort Reno in October, where an investigation resulted in their arrests in February 1879 and courts-martial in March. Gunther was charged with cowardice in the face of the enemy; he was acquitted of one charge and returned to duty as a company commander at Fort Reno on April 11, 1879. Rendlebrock was charged with misbehavior in the face of the enemy, disobedience of orders, neglect of duty, and drunkenness on duty. He was found guilty and sentenced to dismissal from the service. President Rutherford B. Hayes commuted the sentence because of Rendlebrock's long, credible service record and because his defense counsel demonstrated that his age and physical condition made him unfit for the duties of an active campaign. He was allowed to retire from the army, and he left Fort Reno on August 2, 1879, for Hoboken, New Jersey—and obscurity.[30]

In reality Rendlebrock probably did the best he could under difficult circumstances. Immediately he found himself at severe tactical disadvantage at Turkey Springs. Sensing his presence, Little Wolf had doubled back on his line of flight to secure familiar, defensible ground of his own choosing upon which to fight. Little Wolf commanded the water, cutting the soldiers off from that vital resource. Slightly outnumbered, Little Wolf nevertheless controlled the field; he outmaneuvered and outfought a battalion of the 4th Cavalry, forced them to abandon their position due to lack of water, gained their rear guard and harassed their line of retreat, and ultimately inflicted an embarrassing defeat upon them. As with the the scrutiny following Little Big Horn, the condemnation of Rendlebrock and Gunther assumed white commanders must have failed in their duties, for no group of Indians could achieve decisive victory over the U.S. Army on its own merits. At Turkey Springs the U.S. Army lost simply because the Cheyennes won, not by sheer numbers but by virtue of superior tactical leadership.

Certainly Rendlebrock's failure to defeat and capture the Ohmeseheso while they were still in Indian Territory caused a furor among the citizens of southwest Kansas, who now found themselves in the line of flight of the Indians. Their fears were not unfounded. Around the time of the Turkey Springs fight, a scouting party of young Northern Cheyenne warriors killed two civilians, Rueben Bristow and Fred Clark, cowboys in the employ of the Charles Colcord Jug Ranch, which was located about twenty-five miles southeast of modern Coldwater, Kansas, near the Salt Fork of the Arkansas. The two young men were a nephew and an employee of Charles Colcord. The Indians left the men's wagon but rode off with their team of mules.[31] The only question is, when exactly did the killings occur? Grinnell and later popular writers like Mari Sandoz have asserted the killings took place only after the Indians were fired upon by Rendlebrock's troops at Turkey

Springs. A report to the assistant adjutant general, however, gives the date as September 12, the day before the Battle of Turkey Springs. Some modern historians, Peter John Powell among them, accept the AGO report of the event while also accepting Grinnell's estimated timeframe.[32]

Several days later Charles Colcord found the bodies of his nephew and his employee near the salt beds of the Cimarron River, north of Turkey Springs and near the Kansas border with Indian Territory. "I pulled four arrows out of Bristow's heart, shot in from the right side," Colcord remembered years later, "and drew three or four out of Fred's body."[33] Colcord buried the bodies on a high divide between the Salt Fork and Cimarron Rivers, northwest of Turkey Springs, and left a crudely carved stone to mark the spot. Many years later the gravesite was enclosed with a pipe fence and a marker was erected proclaiming the spot "Cowboy Cemetery." The site has been recognizable well into recent times.[34] Considering that the Cheyenne scouts were out ahead of the main band at the time of the fight, it is likely that they did not know Little Wolf had engaged the soldiers. Hence whether the killings of Bristow and Clark occurred on September 12, before the fight, or following the battle is a moot point since the Indian scouts probably were unaware of the fight anyhow. Thus the incident likely was not an act of revenge by the Cheyennes for Turkey Springs.

Nevertheless such disputed points of fact have long shadowed the interpretation of the Cheyenne odyssey; the killing of civilians somehow diminished the heroic, justifiable efforts of Little Wolf and Dull Knife to take their sick and hungry people home. Many of the so-called depredations inflicted on civilians during the flight north have remained shrouded in mystery, for the Cheyennes have purposefully and understandably not talked much of these events since 1879.

The question remains, however, that if the Cheyennes shot at civilians, was it because civilians at the same time were shooting at them? From the Battle of Turkey Springs until the Indians reached northern Nebraska, they ran the gauntlet of the burgeoning open-range ranching frontier on the Great Plains. Little Wolf knew that the success of his march north would depend on a continuous supply of fresh horses for his people. Feeding over three hundred people every day on the long journey was also a significant logistical problem, especially considering the ecological changes occuring on the central plains at that time. The buffalo ranges in western Kansas had been disastrously depleted by 1875 to free the ranges for the longhorn cattle brought into replace them. Consequently, the Ohmeseheso depended on foraging for horses, mules, and domestic cattle among the civilian population in order to survive long enough to reach their homelands. It was the young outriders, foraging for provisions, who encountered civilians.

Grinnell and others have repeatedly pointed out that both Little Wolf and Dull Knife instructed their young warriors to avoid killing civilians whenever possible, emphasizing that the fight was with the U.S. Army.[35] Cattlemen, however, by nature of life on the open range were skilled in defending their herds and territorial claims, occasionally aggressively. It is unreasonable to assume that cattlemen like Bristow and Clark would have remained passive when the Indians approached, intent on stealing their livestock, especially if they encountered only a few warriors.

Throughout the pursuit north, the army relied extensively on local cattlemen to keep them informed of the Northern Cheyennes' direction at any given time. Occasionally posses of cowboys voluntarily formed and rode with the troops to engage the Indians. When the Northern Cheyennes embarrassed the U.S. Army by actually reaching Nebraska, General Sheridan authorized departmental commanders to recruit and pay civilian cattlemen for their assistance. General Crook issued a notice claiming that "liberal compensation would be paid for reliable information concerning the Cheyennes."[36] Since Little Wolf's hope for success depended on keeping his people out of sight as much as possible, so that his whereabouts at any given moment might not be known, it is absurd to think the Indians, with the approval of their chiefs, would have gone looking willingly for trouble among the cattlemen.[37]

A distinction should be made at this point, too, regarding the classes of civilians encountered by the Northern Cheyennes on the odyssey. When the Indians arrived in northwest Kansas, they encountered some of the early wave of farmer-homesteaders in Decatur and Rawlins Counties, in the southern portion of the Republican River country. This was important contested land. Once prime buffalo range, it was a blending or neutral zone for northern and southern tribes. By 1878 the old ecological balances of these lands were starting to be reimagined drastically in the form of dry land agriculture. So too were these valleys the sites of unavenged conflicts with the whites. Some of the Cheyennes with Little Wolf and Dull Knife unfortunately would kill homesteaders here, citizens who had even stronger claims than the cattlemen of being innocent victims since they had experienced fewer violent encounters with Indians. It was these killings that would for so long darken the world's view of the Cheyennes' odyssey.

After tending to the wounded, Little Wolf ordered his people northward again on September 15, 1878. They scattered into small groups and traveled at night whenever possible to avoid detection. Outriders were sent to forage for horses, cattle, and other food.[38] They crossed the Kansas state line late on September 16 or early on September 17. With Rendlebrock's troops sure to pursue them from the rear, with reinforcements of the 4th Cavalry under Capt. Clarence Mauck moving up from Fort Richardson, and with the network of Texas troops waiting for them on the Arkansas and along the Kansas Pacific Railroad, Little Wolf and Dull Knife would face stiff resistance in Kansas, unlike the flimsy resistance they had encountered in Indian Territory.

## CHAPTER FOUR

# KANSAS

## The Battle of Punished Woman's Fork

*Little Wolf did not seem like a human being; he seemed like
an animal—a bear. He seemed without fear.*

—TANGLE HAIR,
Dog Soldier

On September 18, the day after the Ohmeseheso crossed the Kansas
border, federal troops caught up with them north of the Cimarron
River. The subsequent chase, as the press labeled it in 1878, became
a prolonged series of scouting expeditions covering a large area of
open plains and ravines. This task was monotonous work for the
troops involved, and historians have found reconstructing their
exact movements to be an equally tedious job. Following their
defeat at Turkey Springs, Capt. Joseph Rendlebrock's command
retired to Camp Supply, fifty miles away, where they arrived on
September 16. The next morning Rendlebrock dispatched forty
men under Lts. Abram Wood and W. E. Wilder across the Kansas
state line, in advance of a second column, under his own immediate command. Wood's orders were to link up with Company I of
the 4th Cavalry under Capt. William C. Hemphill in the Sand Creek
(Big Sandy Creek) area of southwestern Kansas, in modern Clark
County southeast of Dodge City.

Hemphill was patrolling the region north of the Red Hills in response to Rendlebrock's dispatch to Camp Supply for aid on September 12. Fortunately for Little Wolf, Captain Hemphill found the Northern Cheyennes on September 18, before Lieutenant Wood could provide reinforcement troops. Once again Cheyenne wolves saw the soldiers advancing, and consequently the Indians commanded a defensive position of their choosing along a shallow ravine.

Hemphill ordered his men to dismount and advance on foot in skirmish order, with every fourth trooper remaining in the rear and holding his own plus three other mounts. With only thirty-two effectives, Hemphill attempted to draw the Cheyenne fighting men from the ravine, but again Little Wolf and Dull Knife with their sixty warriors held off an element of the 4th Cavalry. The fighting lasted for one hour, after which Hemphill ordered a retreat to the safety of Bluff Creek and then Fort Dodge, where he arrived at 3:00 A.M. on September 19.[1] One trooper was wounded in the so-called Bluff Creek skirmish, and there were no Cheyenne casualties.[2]

On the morning of September 19, Hemphill's I Company and Capt. Charles E. Morse's A Company, 16th Infantry, departed Fort Dodge. They were accompanied by a party of about twenty civilian cattlemen under the leadership of a rancher named Day. All had offered their services in chasing the Indians from what they liberally considered to be their "range rights" in southwest Kansas.[3] The combined force of more than one hundred men rushed westward on the Santa Fe Railroad to Cimarron, Kansas, then on to Pierceville in Finney County, near modern Garden City, where they disembarked and were met by a small force of 19th Infantry under Col. Charles E. Smith. Smith had no idea of the Cheyennes' whereabouts, so Hemphill and Morse traveled back to within seven miles of Cimarron Station, disembarking at that point about 3:00 A.M. on September 20. By sunrise the command crossed the Arkansas River with the cavalry in advance and flankers out. The troops marched southwest until noon when they zigzagged back to the southeast looking for an Indian trail. They reached Crooked Creek, some-where in modern Gray County, at 6:15 P.M., where they bivouacked for the night.[4]

On the morning of September 21 Hemphill and Morse moved out in the direction of Sand Creek. About noon Rendlebrock's rear column caught up with them and as senior captain, Rendlebrock took command. The troops made camp at 4:30 P.M. on Sand Creek while the cattlemen rode out to scout for the Indians. Thirty minutes later they found them. After hearing shots, the cattlemen's first engagement with the Indians, Lieutenant Wood and his G Com-pany moved out, with Hemphill and Lieutenant Gunther's men from Rendlebrock's column close behind. Rendlebrock himself remained in camp. When they caught up with the cattlemen, Hemphill's men moved up in skirmish order, supported by Wood's company. The long-range shooting only lasted until dusk, when the troops and cattlemen pulled back to camp. There were no casualties on either side.[5] Charles Colcord, whose nephew had been killed by the Cheyenne outriders on September 12 or 13 was with the cattlemen on September 21. "We had a long range fight with the Indians that evening," he remembered years later. "We were quite a long distance from them, and everybody had short range guns. . . ."[6]

That night Lieutenant Morse put out pickets of eighteen men at a distance of about four hundred yards apart to prevent a surprise attack on the camp.[7] During the night Rendlebrock dispatched a courier to Fort Dodge for more ammunition, and later in the evening the command was reinforced by about forty more volunteer cattle-men from the Dodge City area, who were fired on mistakenly by the nervous pickets. About 6:00 A.M. the next morning, September 22, 1878, the entire command, under Rendlebrock, moved out to attack the Northern Cheyennes after burying a cattleman they had found near camp. They presumed he had been killed by Cheyenne outriders a couple of days before.[8]

Meanwhile Little Wolf's and Dull Knife's men built a crude stone fortification, about forty feet long and four feet high, above some ravines and hills and dug rifle pits as a second line of defense behind this fortification to protect their women and children. They occupied their stone breastwork and awaited the morning attack that was sure to come. W. E. Iliff, one of the cattlemen present in the command, remembered that: "the Indians had taken their stand in a short, deep canyon that led back a few hundred yards into the open prairie. They had piled up stone breastworks all around the rim of this little canyon."[9] "Our entire command attacked the Indians in their [stone fortification and] rifle pits," Rendlebrock later told a reporter from the *New York Herald*, "and fought them until five o'clock in the evening."[10]

Troopers moved the supply wagons into position below the Cheyenne breastwork, and Rendlebrock ordered his men to dismount and advance on foot. Squads of ten cavalrymen and ten infantrymen advanced on the right and left flanks and to the rear respectively. Somewhere in the attack were the civilian cattlemen, probably advancing with the center rear column. Skirmishing began as the assault wings closed in on the Cheyenne's defenses and concentrated their fire on the center of the stone breastwork.[11] Little Wolf steadied his fighting men. "Let no man fire a shot, and do not get excited. They have plenty of ammunition; we have very little. Lie and wait."[12] When the troopers closed within range, Little Wolf gave the command to open fire.

But the soldiers and cattlemen were too many. Soon they drove the Cheyennes back from this fortification to their second line of defense while the troopers occupied the front breastwork. From there the whites and Cheyennes kept up the firing until about 4:30 P.M.[13] "The Indians fought like devils," Rendlebrock remembered, "and with as much system as if they had been drilled."[14]

Toward the end of the day Rendlebrock ordered Lt. Nance Wilder with ten troopers and forty of the cattlemen to get below the Indian position and encircle them. But Little Wolf had positioned Tangle Hair and a group of warriors, possibly including Dull Knife, on a hill above Wilder. These men charged down on the troopers while Little Wolf led another group of warriors to meet Wilder's advance head on. The Indians drove Wilder's men back to the supply train. Then they routed the wagons, recovering a much-needed box of ammunition that had fallen from one of the wagon beds.[15] Wilder later downplayed this almost disastrous incident. "Nothing in particular was accomplished," he testified before a Senate Select Committee. "I . . . went around their position, examined it, went back and made a report regarding it."[16]

Shortly thereafter Rendlebrock ordered a general retreat. Following the withdrawal of the supply train, the troopers in the skirmish line occupying the Cheyenne breastwork moved to the rear, followed by the right flank. Captain Morse's infantry covered the retreat from the left flank. The command moved to a new location near water and went into camp.[17] Although some sources disagree, no casualties officially were reported on either side.[18] Later some of the civilian cattlemen with the command criticized Rendlebrock for losing his nerve at the end of the so-called Sand Creek fight. "We advanced within 300 or 400 yards of them, and fired around them all day," J. W. Berryman remembered years later. "Everybody was anxious to charge into them, and endeavor to capture them, except the ranking captain. . . ."[19] Charles F. Colcord later remembered that

our crowd wanted to close in on the Indians and clean them up that night, but that Captain [Rendlebrock] the German Army officer insisted on talking [sic] charge and waiting until morning. . . . all our crowd told the soldiers that the Indians would be gone before daylight, but this German officer said that he would keep them surrounded and attack them in the morning. We told him that those Indians could ride farther in one day than his horses could in two. Nelson [a cattleman] protested vigorously; in fact, so vehemently that we cowmen all rode off and went into camp. Next morning, just as Nelson told him, those Indians were forty or fifty miles away.[20]

Rancher J. W. McNeal remembered that he and his party "returned to Barber County, thoroughly disgusted with the management of the campaign."[21]

Again, as at Turkey Springs and Bluff Creek, Little Wolf's and Dull Knife's men had commanded a favorable defensive position. Their sixty warriors held that position, without loss against a much larger force of two-hundred Vehoe including elements of Companies F, G, H, and I, 4th Cavalry, Company A, 16th Infantry, and about sixty civilian cattlemen.[22] But Little Wolf and Dull Knife were not about to linger, since converging troops might reinforce Rendlebrock at any moment. That night the Sweet Medicine Chief said to his people, "My friends, there are too many troops here for us to fight. We must run away. We must move out this night and try to get away from here." Later that evening the Ohmeseheso pressed their northward march forward unchallenged.[23] After the Sand Creek skirmish the ill-fated Capt. Joseph Rendlebrock achieved the undesirable reputation of superb master of retreat.[24]

The Northern Cheyennes crossed the Arkansas River on September 23, 1878. Little Wolf pushed the people relentlessly, forcing night travel to avoid their detection in the open country northwest of Dodge City. The Sweet Medicine chief related to Grinnell years later that the Indians came upon a party of white buffalo hunters shortly after the crossing. The warriors "rushed in on them," Grinnell paraphrased Little Wolf, "and took eighteen buffalo cows they had killed." The Indians took the hunters' guns and ammunition, too, but did not harm the hunters, who had given up. Soon, according to Little Wolf, "plentiful" buffalo were sighted and some of the warriors went hunting while the women dried the meat.[25]

No other Cheyenne testimonies collaborate this incident. Indeed, Iron Teeth, who would have been among the women jerking pemmican (drying strips of meat), remembered only one buffalo calf being taken for food on the entire trek north, and remembered the Indians' provisions consisting primarily of cattle stolen from ranches in the country.[26] Given the extensive devastation of the south-central buffalo herds by 1875, through both professional and provisional hunting, as well as the alteration of buffalo habitat and breeding and migration patterns, the Northern Cheyennes would have been fortunate indeed to have encountered such a serendipitous windfall as Grinnell described.

Meanwhile, Rendlebrock's command received rations and ammunition from Fort Dodge on September 24. By 4:00 P.M. of that day Lt. Col. William H. Lewis, commander at Fort Dodge, disgusted with Rendlebrock's lack of success, arrived in the field to take command of the pursuit. Several supply wagons had been damaged in the Sand Creek fight, so Capt. Charles E. Morse's company hauled the wagons back to Fort Dodge. Lewis now had five companies in the field, B, F, G, H, and I of the 4th Cavalry, including those reinforcements up from Fort Elliot, Texas, under Capt. Clarence Mauck, as well as smaller elements of Companies D, F, and G of the 19th Infantry under Capt. James H. Bradford. With over 200 men Col. Lewis began the chase anew.[27] On September 26 Lewis moved forty miles over easy ground following a broad trail, determined to stop the Cheyennes before they crossed the Smoky Hill River east of Fort Wallace.[28]

Lewis was forty-nine years old when he took command of the campaign to stop the Cheyennes. Born into a slave-holding family in Alabama, Lewis had graduated fifteenth in his class at West Point in 1849. Since 1856 he had been an Indian fighter, having taken part in the Seminole War of that year. He served on the Navajo Expedition of 1860–61 as First Lieutenant in the 5th Infantry. Although he was a southerner, he remained a loyal Unionist during the Civil War, serving in the West. He won a brevet of Major for gallant and meritorious service at the Battle of Apache Canyon, New Mexico, on March 28, 1862, and one month later, was breveted Lieutenant Colonel for bravery in action at the Battle of Peralta, New Mexico, April 15, 1862.

Following the Civil War he retained the rank of Major in the regular army and served as post commander of Fort Fred Steele, Wyoming in 1869 and 1870, and as Special Inspector for the Department of Dakota from 1871 to 1874. He was promoted to Lieutenant

Fort Dodge, Kansas, at the time of the Cheyenne odyssey, circa 1880.
Courtesy Kansas State Historical Society.

Colonel of the 19th Infantry on December 10, 1873, and was reassigned to Fort Dodge, Kansas by 1877. In that year Lewis led a company of troops in a "siege" of Dodge City, which was a successful attempt to gain fair treatment for soldiers who had run afoul of the law with the town's civil authorities. Lewis became post commander of Fort Dodge on March 29, 1878. Most of his military career had been spent in the West.[29]

Perhaps knowing that Lewis's large force was closing fast to their rear, Little Wolf and Dull Knife pushed the people harder. Traveling at night northwest from the Arkansas, the Cheyennes moved toward the country broken by ravines, north of White Woman Basin in modern Scott County. Here was the last defensible terrain between the Arkansas River and the settlements and scattered croplands of northwest Kansas. If Little Wolf and Dull Knife could inflict enough punishment on the soldiers here, perhaps the Ohmeseheso could make it all the way through Nebraska to Lakota agency lands before encountering fresh troops from Gen. George

Crook's Department of the Platte. Consequently Little Wolf decided to risk drawing Lewis' command into a carefully laid trap.

The chiefs decided to make their stand near the breaks of Punished Woman's Fork, which the Cheyennes called Running Creek.[30] Here were familiar lands along the route between the northern and southern peoples' territories. Bluff country broken by small canyons and ravines, the land here presented natural obstacles to pursuing troops. In front of one of these small canyons the Ohmeseheso built stone breastworks with rifle pits excavated from sandstone as a second line of defense toward the rear. Behind these defenses was a cavelike depression in the rocks that could serve as shelter for the women and children. The ponies could also be sheltered inside an adjacent ravine. In front of the canyon, a bluff rose close to the creek bed. Here Tangle Hair and some warriors were situated to draw fire from advancing troops, luring them into the narrow stream canyon where the bulk of the fighting men would be waiting for them. Tangle Hair's men would sweep down from the bluff and cut off their retreat.[31] On the afternoon of September 27, Cheyennes on the bluffs spotted a column of dust raised by Lewis' troops in the distance. Quickly the ponies were brought in and the warriors prepared to lure the soldiers into the canyon, along the Indians' well-marked trail and spring the trap.

Lewis's command found the Indian trail easy to follow as Little Wolf and Dull Knife had intended. The scouts serving under Lewis included Chief of Scouts Amos Chatman, Ben Jackson, Bill Combs, Levi Ritchison, Ed Cooley, a man known as "Kokomo" Sullivan, and George W. Brown, a resident of Ford County, Kansas.[32] Somewhat self-glorifying in his recollections, Brown later wrote how the command followed the trail into the ambush set for them by the Northern Cheyennes. The battle began about 4:00 or 5:00 P.M. on September 27, following a march of fifty miles in two days, burdened with supply wagons. Brown remembered:

This creek [Punished Woman's Fork] runs northwest and the Indian trail went down the west side. The command followed down the creek after them, the scouts about two or three hundred yards in advance. We had gone about a mile and Amos Chatman said, "Brown, you go back and show the wagons how to get around that big canyon." I started back and found Colonel Lewis riding at the head of his command. I rode up to him and said, "Have you got any flankers out?" he said he had not. "Colonel, I believe those Indians are right in here close."[33]

As Brown continued toward the wagon train, he heard shooting in front of him. "The Indians, strongly entrenched," Brown recalled, "waited for Colonel Lewis and his troops to ride into this trap. But the ambush was prevented when one impatient Indian fired on one of the [advance] scouts and the fight was on. The Indians had . . . fortified themselves in this ravine the approaches to which were very hilly and rocky. The constructed rifle pits were concealed by stones, earth and grass, on the side of the hill. The women and their children were hidden in the cave that later attained the name of 'Squaw's Den.'"[34]

Fortunately for the 4th Cavalry, that impatient warrior who fired prematurely, before the troops were drawn into the canyon, may have prevented a decisive victory for the Cheyennes. After this alarm Capt. Sebastian Gunther noted that "the Indians appeared about eight hundred yards from us on bluffs in numbers and fired on us. We were then in a narrow valley or ravine. The left-hand side was protected by high bluffs and the right-hand side by a very boggy creek."[35] "It was a complete surprise," Lt. W. E. Wilder recalled.[36] "For some minutes great confusion existed," an unidentified officer remembered, "but Colonel Lewis quickly got the troops on the hills in their front and the infantry to the right and partial rear."[37]

"The [dismounted] command by common consent rushed the bluffs," Lieutenant Wilder remembered. "On reaching the bluffs a skirmish line was soon formed and the Indians were soon driven back rapidly. We then found that the Indians had prepared a fortification; rifle pits, and such means of defense as the natural features of the country afforded."[38] The "red devils expected to make another Custer business of it," Capt. Joseph Rendlebrock told a *New York Herald* reporter a few weeks after the battle, "but they didn't know Colonel Lewis. He rallied his men and held the ground, and drove the Indians back to their fortifications on the edge of the canyon."[39]

Little Wolf knew that allowing the troops to advance too far into the canyon could bring fire down upon the women and children hiding in the Squaw's Den, from which they could not escape, if the Cheyenne defenses broke down. As he watched the progress of the fighting from the bluffs, his concentration became apparently intense, as if he were willing the soldiers' destruction. As the skirmish line spread out through the small canyon, Little Wolf directed his warriors as he sat on a rock smoking a pipe. "Do not get excited," he encouraged his men, "keep cool, and mind what I say to you. . . . get ready, but let every shot you fire count for a man."[40] According to Tangle Hair, who was fighting nearby: "Little Wolf did not seem like a human being; he seemed like an animal— a bear. He seemed without fear."[41]

The Cheyennes, from their stone fortification and from their positions on the bluffs to the side, rained lead into the little canyon, slowing the soldiers' progress. "Colonel Lewis then rode in front of his [largely dismounted] skirmish line and urged his men on," Capt. Joseph Rendlebrock recalled. Lewis himself relentlessly pressed the advance, but as he approached

within one hundred and fifty yards of the Indian fortification . . . his horse was shot in the [flank], and two old soldiers of Company B almost dragged him from it and begged him not to expose himself unnecessarily. He jumped to his feet, grabbed a carbine and fell into line with the skirmishers. The skirmishers rushed forward, Lewis with them, and when 100 yards from the enemy he, of all the rest, was struck by a ball. It severed the femoral artery of the left leg and felled him to the ground. He examined it as coolly [sic] as any man could and said to Lieutenant Martin of Company B, who was with him, "I guess it's all over with me." Then he took the buckskin strap from his revolver, and with his own hands tied his wound . . . using his revolver to tighten it. He was picked up, carried back and put in an ambulance and carried to the rear.[42]

With Lewis out of the action, the assault lost momentum even though the second officer in command, Capt. Clarence Mauck, 4th Cavalry, tried to press the troops forward. Once again the Cheyennes held, this time against the largest force they had faced since leaving Darlington Agency. As the evening darkness descended into the canyon of Punished Woman's Fork, the soldiers withdrew to the perimeter of the wagon train. Besides Col. William H. Lewis, one man from G Company and one man from F Company, 4th Cavalry, also suffered wounds. Although official reports list no Cheyenne casualties,[43] all of the officers later writing accounts of the battle describe either one or two Cheyennes killed. Scout George Brown asserted that he found the body of one dead Cheyenne on the field the morning after the battle, following the Indians' departure north.[44] According to one source, somewhere on the plains about this time, perhaps in the melee of the Battle of Punished Woman's Fork, Dull Knife's wife Little Woman was killed by a horse stampeding through the Cheyennes' camp.[45]

Despite their ostensibly successful defense, the Cheyennes for the first time on the trek north had paid a high price at the Battle of Punished Woman's Fork. Not only did the impetuousness of one warrior in firing too soon result in the Indian's failure to engulf the soldiers in the canyon and inflict serious punishment on them, but during the height of the fighting they lost between sixty and eighty-five of their best ponies. Many of the animals were saddled with packs and parfleches full of vital supplies, including dried meat and the few worldly possessions their owners had left.

Scout George Brown gave to history the best account of this important incident. "While the fight was going on," he remembered, "I saw Ben Jackson, one of the scouts. He motioned to me to come to where he was [on the bluffs]: I went and he said, 'look over that little hill there.' I went and peeped over. I saw a little creek valley and it was full of Indian ponies with their packs on and I did not see an Indian."[46]

Cut off from these ponies, the Northern Cheyennes left during the night without the precious mounts. The next morning about 9:00 A.M., Capt. Clarence Mauck ordered the ponies and all the provisions destroyed. "The scouts, each one," Brown recalled, "roped a pony . . . I got my rope on [one] and . . . cut the pack off the pony's back . . . and found all kinds of Indian trinkets in it. I found a pair of buckskin gloves worth about three dollars. . . . There were about 60 ponies. [They] were rounded up in a close bunch and were all shot down and killed."[47] More succinctly, Capt. Sebastian Gunther reported that "a great many horses had been killed in the canyon . . . and a great many packs had been left there. The property was immediately destroyed."[48] "We captured a great deal of their food," Lt. W. E. Wilder remembered, "dried meat; also many of their pack saddles."[49]

The next day, September 28, 1878, Capt. Clarence Mauck ordered 2d Lt. Cornelius Gardner, 19th infantry, and twenty-five men to escort the ambulance with Colonel Lewis and the two wounded enlisted men to Fort Wallace, Kansas. George Brown guided the party as scout. "We followed the [old Smoky Hill wood] road until we crossed the Smoky Hill River," Brown remembered. "Here we watered our horses and rested a short time. The lieutenant said, 'How far is it now to Fort Wallace?' I said it was about fifteen miles. This was about ten o'clock at night. We took up the march again to Fort Wallace and a soldier came up from the rear guard and said, 'Lieutenant, the colonel has just died.'"[50]

From Fort Wallace Col. William H. Lewis's remains were sent by train to Fort Leavenworth, and thence on to the family home in rural Alabama. The funeral, held on October 6, 1878, was attended by reporters from the East. "The casket was laid in the parlor of his mother's residence," wrote one, "where crowds of his friends went to take a last look at his manly form. He was dressed in full [dress] uniform and appeared as though he was enjoying tranquil repose. . . . The beautiful church [where the services were held] was crowded with friends and acquaintances of the deceased, thus showing the esteem in which he was held by the townspeople."[51] Lewis had never married, and according to scout Brown, "had an old Negro attendant at Fort Dodge, a former slave of the Lewis family. Before his death the colonel gave instructions to send the old man back to the Lewis family."[52]

Although casualties on both sides at Punished Woman's Fork were minimal, the loss of the Cheyenne pony herd and pack supplies would, in the next few days, be paid for in the high price of human life. Because the Northern Cheyennes could only succeed in their quest with frequently renewed supplies of horses, food supplies, and ammunition, the loss at Punished Woman's Fork made their needs even more acute. Following their first violent encounters with civilian cattlemen around the time of the Battle of Turkey Springs, the Indians had realized these whites would not give up their livestock and other property without a fight. Consequently, the Cheyenne foragers, moving swiftly in small parties through southwest Kansas cattle country, became ever more wary of these men. Prior to Punished Woman's Fork, foraging warriors had ranged over a wide area in this region looking for horses and livestock. The outriders scoured the prairie about twenty miles east and west of the main body of warriors, women, and children.

Besides the earlier killing of Rueben Bristow and Fred Clark, by the time the Northern Cheyennes reached Punished Woman's Fork, they had inflicted further damage in the ranch lands. According to historian Ramon Powers, the losses sustained by the ranchers in southwest Kansas included 10 persons killed, 5 wounded, and 640 head of livestock stolen or destroyed, including 400 sheep, 126 horses, and 144 cattle.[53]

According to rancher Charles Colcord, "the first person killed was Tom Murray," then "the Payne family, all of whom they shot but all of whom later got well. Then they went off northwest and killed a cook and a horse wrangler."[54] The cook Colcord mentions probably was an African American man named George Simmons, who was shot in Ford County after a long chase when he tried to rescue a brace of mules the Indians had taken from his chuck wagon.[55]

Frank T. Dow and John Evans, two wranglers in the employ of Colonel Sheeter in Comanche County, were gunned down in their cow camp on the evening of September 17 by a group of Cheyenne outriders who had been refused food and tobacco by the cattlemen.[56] Cheyennes stopped Washington O'Conner's wagon in Meade County and slit his throat from ear to ear, then drove away his mules while another party of frightened settlers watched from a distant hillside.[57] On the Salt Fork of the Cimarron, the Indians hit the Wiley Payne ranch where they shot Payne in the neck, his wife in the thigh, and their infant child in the chest.[58]

Reports in regional newspapers fostered panic among the local white population. "Settlers left everything they had in their homes and pulled out of the country, never to return," stated one reporter. "One in particular, a Canadian, was not notified [of danger from the Cheyennes] until . . . the family was sitting down to breakfast. Not even waiting to eat the meal already cooked, they bundled into the wagon, started for the railroad and took the first train east."[59] Other local newspapers, fearful that hysteria over the possibility of Indian attack might hurt the local economy, pronounced the raids a hoax.[60]

As with the great Dog Soldier raids in western Kansas during the late 1860s, civil authorities requested additional aid from the military and additional arms for citizens. Kansas governor George T. Anthony sent panicked pleas to the commander of the Department of the Missouri at Fort Leavenworth, Gen. John A. Pope. Eventually 600 carbines and 20,000 rounds of ammunition were sent to Dodge City, less than 10 percent of the quantity citizens had requested.[61] Indeed, the Cheyennes had reason to fear the possibility of encountering armed civilians.

Some of the cattlemen now confronting the Northern Cheyennes had in previous times known and traded with them, either along the familiar routes of travel north and south, through Kansas and

Nebraska, or at the Darlington Agency in Indian Territory. Ranchman John Bratt, for example, remembered extending hospitality
and dinner to Dull Knife and some of his warriors at a cow camp
on the Dry Fork of the Cheyenne River in about 1872.[62] Charles
Colcord, who lost a nephew to the Cheyennes near Turkey Springs
and who later engaged the Cheyennes at the Sand Creek fight on
September 21, had only a few months earlier at Darlington Agency
given Wild Hog three dollars as payment for, in his words, "the
prettiest pair of leggins [sic] I ever saw, made of Elk hide and orna-
mented with Elk teeth."[63]

When the Ohmeseheso departed from Punished Woman's Fork,
they successfully eluded the 4th Cavalry for the next week. Captain
Clarence Mauck, now in command of the pursuit following Lewis's
death, moved north and crossed the Smoky Hill River at Russell
Springs on about September 29; then turned east and crossed the
Kansas Pacific Railroad, after a day's march. Never again did
forces from the Department of the Missouri engage the Northern
Cheyennes.[64]

Little Wolf's and Dull Knife's people miraculously had made
their way through two-thirds of western Kansas in less than three
weeks following their departure from Darlington Agency. During
this time their camps were never taken by surprise by the pursuing
troops. They fought four pitched battles with the U.S. Army and
armed civilians, engaging them from fortified defensive positions
of tactical advantage and repelling mostly dismounted troops skirmishing in textbook formations. Indeed, the military engagements
of the Cheyenne odyssey in Indian Territory and in Kansas during
September 1878 were anomalies in the record of army-Indian
warfare on the plains. Not only did these engagements vastly
diverge from the surprise offensive tactics against Indian villages
executed by the army from the 1850s through the 1870s, but the
familiar style of individualized warfare practiced by the Cheyennes
also seems to have given way in some measure, for the collective
survival of the group, to the organized and disciplined leadership
of Little Wolf.

In southwest Kansas during September, the Cheyennes inflicted a larger number of casualties on soldiers and civilians than had been inflicted upon them. By early October 1878, military authorities around the country justifiably began to criticize severely the largely fruitless operations against Little Wolf's and Dull Knife's determined warriors conducted by troops from the Department of the Missouri.

It was the Cheyennes' lack of horses, food, and other supplies, in the long run, that proved to be their downfall. If the army had one success in the Kansas engagements, it was the destruction of most of the Indians' extra stock of horses and food reserves at the Battle of Punished Woman's Fork. It was an important turning point in the Cheyenne odyssey, yet ironically, this coup, in the days ahead, would result in more deaths among the civilian population than might have been inflicted had the ponies and supply packs survived the battle. Up until that point, the Cheyennes' needs had resulted in hit-and-run raids by small parties of warriors on the civilian population, reminiscent of the Indian Wars in Kansas during the 1860s. With the destruction of so many of their extra horses and their reserve food on September 28, 1868, these raids would intensify, temporarily turning public opinion against the Indians despite their legitimate grievances. Now as the Northern Cheyennes moved north from the Smoky Hill country, their need to forage from among the ostensibly more defenseless farming population of northwest Kansas took on a desperate urgency.

## CHAPTER FIVE

# KANSAS

## Trouble in the Settlements

*Our house was a wreck. Nothing of value was left. . . . We went to Oberlin which was crowded with fugitives from the Sappa Creek district, and found the place panic-stricken.*

—MRS. EMMETT (STREET) MARTIN,
1935

On the evening of September 29, 1878, three wranglers herding cattle up the Texas Trail to Kearney, Nebraska, stopped on a knoll overlooking the divide between Prairie Dog Creek and the South Fork of the Sappa in the northeast corner of modern Thomas County, Kansas. Below, in the valley to the north, they witnessed a sight they would never forget. "We looked down on . . . as nice a scene as I ever saw," A. N. Keith remembered in 1924 from his ranch in Midwest, Wyoming. "The stream [Prairie Dog Creek] was skirted with timber with a fine string of farms along [it]. That part of it was sure fine, but there was more to it. Something seemed out of place. There were bands of horses scattered here and there with camps along the creek, with the camp fires sending up long columns of smoke." The cattlemen had run headlong into Little Wolf's and Dull Knife's Northern Cheyennes. The Indians spotted the white men and soon drove them away, as Keith's party had only six revolvers among them. "By this time it was nearly sun-down," Keith reminisced, "and we could hear the crack of rifles down toward [our] camp and knew that the Indians would have plenty of beef for supper. [Later] we found about eighty of [our] steers they had killed that night."[1]

The killing of the cattle sent a few nearby settlers fleeing from their houses that evening. The next morning small groups of Chey-enne foragers left camp and rode along the border between Rawlins and Decatur counties and the tiny new hamlet of Oberlin, only about twelve miles from the Nebraska border. By the time the Ohmeseheso crossed out of Kansas on about October 2 or 3, 1878, approximately forty-one settlers had been killed. Officially, ten had already been reported killed in the cattle country south of Dodge City. Five whites were wounded and about 640 head of cattle were driven off in southwestern Kansas. By early October, according to a Kansas State Senate resolution compiled the next year, thirty-one more people lost their lives in the embryonic farm settlements along Prairie Dog and Beaver Creeks and the forks of the Sappa. In addition, twenty-five women and children, ages eight and older were raped, a figure that seems inflated given existing evidence. One hundred thousand dollars in property was destroyed in Decatur and Rawlins Counties.[2]

Following the bloody work of September 30, panic and hatred spread through the isolated settlements of northwest Kansas, as the local jingoistic press sensationalized the news with warnings and a call for revenge, long after the Northern Cheyennes had left the state. One editor wrote: "It is about time that the border states and territories took a contract for missionary work, in which a few companies of frontiersmen should civilize or exterminate the Government pets."

Revealing the paranoia typical of westerners living in fear of Indians, the editor predictably summarized his thoughts by casti-gating the eastern reformers, whose lives were no longer threat-ened by Indians whom they had long displaced from their states. Describing the supposed "brutal lust" of the Cheyennes in Kansas, he charged that "every day or two we read accounts of how some philanthropic . . . ass in Boston or New York dishes up a lot of slush concerning the nobility of the savages."[3] "This harsh western mindset, so offensive to eastern reformers," wrote western Kansas historian Craig Miner, "was created step by step as grisly news reached the local press and fear was transformed into aggression."[4] Indeed, the haunting details of individual incidents fueled the climate of fear and anger that erupted in western Kansas in the fall of 1878. Settlers did not know how far to the east or west the Indians would range. They did not know whether or not their own families might be the next visited by the people whom many referred to biblically as Lo the Poor Indian. Panic-stricken farmers knew little about the specific tribe or band they considered a horde of savage terrorists loose in their land.

Decatur County, created in 1873 and organized in 1879, experienced some of the worst violence that day. Neighboring Rawlins County, just to the west, created by the legislature in 1873 but yet to be organized, suffered almost as much at the hands of Little Wolf's and Dull Knife's foragers. In 1878, Decatur County, one of the last areas to be settled in northwest Kansas by white agriculturists, had a population of about one thousand, mostly farmers from other parts of Kansas, Missouri, and Iowa. There were also a small number of recent German and Swedish immigrants. Decatur County's principal community was Oberlin, just northeast of the confluence of the forks of Sappa Creek. The village had only been laid out in 1878, and that September it consisted of one sod and one frame store, a log hotel, and a log blacksmith shop. Two houses were under construction. Most settlers worked small farms in the flood plains of the Sappa forks, where they built dugouts into the bluffs near the creek banks. In between the watersheds, much of the land was still open range where cattle grazed. The region was in transition from open cattle range to farm country but only ten years earlier had been prime buffalo habitat for the Plains Indians. After September 30, 1878, farmers and cattlemen would set aside any differences they might have had to assist those families who suffered at the hands of the Northern Cheyenne foragers. Few if any of these newly arrived settlers in northwest Kansas, some recent European immigrants, had ever encountered Indians.[5]

Undoubtedly the family in Decatur County that suffered the most was William Laing's. Originally from Canada the Laings had only recently filed for land near Oberlin. The father and three sons were killed by a party of a dozen Cheyennes, while Laing's wife and two of his daughters, ages twelve and nine, were gang-raped by what may have been the same group of warriors later in the day. Early on the morning of September 30, William Laing and his son Freeman, age fifteen, had left their homestead at a place called Mud Draw in the Sappa Valley for the federal land office in Kirwin, Kansas, where they intended to prove their claim. With them in their wagon were two neighbor girls, Eve and Louise Van Cleave. About eight miles from their home, a party of twelve Cheyennes rode up to Laing's wagon in a friendly manner. Two of the Indians shook hands with Laing and his son while two others fired shots into the backs of their heads, killing both instantly. The father fell into the lap of one of the Van Cleave sisters while the son sank to his knees in the wagon bed. The girls were told to hold the horses while the warriors ransacked provisions from the wagon. The Van Cleave girls were then taken to a nearby creek bed and raped by as many as all twelve of the Cheyennes. Afterward they were released naked on the prairie and told to go to a nearby homestead, that of Jacob Keifer, about a half-mile away. At first the girls were too terrified to move, fearful of being shot if they turned their backs. Finally they left amidst the general laughter of the warriors. The bodies of William Laing and his son were left in the wagon unscalped and unmutilated.[6]

About sunset that evening, eight miles away at the Laing home-stead, the two eldest sons, William Jr., and John, returning home in a wagon from their cornfield, came upon a dozen Cheyennes. The boys had mistaken the Indians for wranglers trying to round up wild horses, animals that still existed in small numbers spread across northwest Kansas. With the boys were their three sisters,

Mary, age twelve, Elizabeth, age nine, and Julia, age seven. The girls had come out to ride back for supper with their brothers. Again the Cheyennes acted friendly and were offered an invitation to dinner. But after a short distance, one of the warriors said in English, "Look there." As the boys turned their heads, the Indians shot both of them, killing them instantly. One of the boys fell completely from the wagon. The Indians ordered the three girls to the house, making threatening gestures to insure they would obey.

The Laing homestead was a dugout with sod walls but well furnished inside. Entering the home, the warriors took things of value, including several hundred dollars in cash. Five of the men then ravished the terrified mother, four raped the oldest girl Mary, and four raped Elizabeth. Seven-year-old Julia was left unharmed. According to Mrs. Laing's brother-in-law, who first revealed her story, the Cheyennes then "placed the three little girls between the feather ticks of the bed, kindled fire in different parts of the room . . . and began to take the bed cord from the bed to tie the poor little ones between the ticks. The mother almost despairing stood by wringing her hands and entreating for the lives of her little ones."[7]

As the Cheyennes rode off, Mrs. Laing and her daughters escaped the burning dugout and made their way eight miles to the Keifer homestead, arriving there about 2:00 A.M. Mrs. Laing received the news about her husband and other son, Freeman. In one day Mrs. Laing had lost all the men in her family. A neighbor, Billy O'Toole, later surmised that the reason the Cheyennes attempted to burn the women may have been because the Laings had salvaged "hundreds of teepee poles, earlier abandoned by the Indians in the vicinity of the Laing homestead . . . and were using them for firewood."[8]

Whether or not the Indians thought these poles might have been from the Southern Cheyenne camp of Little Bull, whose band was massacred by H Company, 6th Cavalry, in the Sappa Valley in April 1875, is speculative. Some more modern writers, especially Mari Sandoz, have contended that the violence committed by the Northern Cheyennes in the Sappa Valley in 1878 was revenge for the massacre of Little Bull's camp three years earlier, when allegedly soldiers had tossed a live Cheyenne child into the flames of the burning camp. In any event, according to Billy O'Toole, Mrs. Laing, despite her lucky escape and that of her three daughters, "later became demented by her grief and loss."[9]

Wise Wiggins was eight years old when he saw his father killed near their dugout. "Papa's gone," Wiggins's mother cried. "There is nothing we can do. Papa's gone. I dread telling about it even now," Wiggins, the oldest surviving resident of Oberlin who remembered the Northern Cheyennes, told a reporter from the *Kansas City Star* in 1962. "I never could keep from crying—the shock of what it meant to me never dimmed."[10]

Like the Laings, Ferdinand Westfall thought a small party of Cheyennes who entered his house was friendly, and he offered them food. The warriors killed him and his son in the yard and chased down Mrs. Westfall and shot her in the back, wounding but not killing her.[11]

James G. Smith and his son, Watson, were making hay in their field on September 30 when a party of warriors rode up and fired at them. "I saw my father fall," Watson remembered. "[I] saw him after he was dead. He was shot by both bullets and arrows—twice I believe with bullets and 3 or 4 arrows." Watson and a neighbor escaped to a nearby ravine.[12] The Cheyennes killed a man named Lull and John Irwin on Billy O'Toole's property and then bashed in their heads with an ax. Edward Miskelley and John Wright were killed near the Charley Miller homestead, and Dory Stradman was shot through the arm. As the Indians rode up to finish Stradman off, they saw, or so Stradman claimed, that he had a wooden leg, and they rode away. Stradman survived.[13]

An immigrant named Hanock Janousheck and his son, Paul, were on their way to Logan County with a wagonload of flour when they were ambushed and slain, their team of horses stolen.[14] On the South Sappa, John Hudson and James Smith were putting up hay in the stream bottom when Cheyennes discovered them. Hudson was killed instantly, but Smith escaped down the streambed with severe wounds. He died the next day. Moses Abernathy and Marcellus Felt were shot off their horses and killed. George Walters, returning home with a load of lime, was killed alone. His body was found three weeks later.[15]

Events were equally tragic in neighboring Rawlins County where the killing continued through October 1, 1878. George Harrison was shot as he brought in horses from his field. A party of Indians who spotted another team of horses owned by Anton Stenner went to his house. "Nice team," one of them said, then shot him in the head and heart. I "saw them shoot Pa," Louise Stenner remembered in 1879. "The Indian [who killed him] had a light gray shirt. He had something on his head—it glittered."[16] Stenner's wife and children escaped and hid for three days in a nearby draw, where they had nothing to eat or drink, until they were discovered by a soldier who gave them a crust of hard bread. Rev. George Fenburgh was told of shots coming from the Stenner farm by a neighbor, Mrs. Blume. When he went to investigate, a warrior shot and killed him as he crossed the threshold of the house.[17]

Fred Hamper and Patrick Rathburn were out looking for stray horses when they passed a party of twenty-five Cheyennes. The Indians seemed friendly, but as the men rode on, Rathburn looked back and saw rifles leveled at them. Rathburn shouted out, but it was too late. A bullet struck and killed Hamper before he could get off of his horse. Another bullet passed between Rathburn's arm and his body, missing him. He found shelter in an old buffalo wallow where he held off the Cheyennes for several hours, killing some of their ponies, and wounding several warriors.[18] During the stand Rathburn recalled, "the grass all around me seemed alive with bullets."[19]

A cattleman named Alex Foster was killed on October 1, as was young Chris Abbott who fended off the Indians from his sod house, wounding one, before he died of his own wounds. The boy was buried in his front yard. A party of Northern Cheyenne outriders descended on a small community of Eastern European immigrants on Beaver Creek. On the Frank Spivacek farm, Frank Sochar,

Spivacek's father-in-law, met the Indians. Thinking the visitors were friendly, Sochar gave them a loaf of bread whereupon the Indians shot him and drove a hatchet into his skull. Then they told the women to leave the house, after which the warriors cooked some food on the Spivacek's stove. After destroying property on several other homesteads, the Indians killed a settler named Cubitz and then moved on to the farm of Paul Janousek Sr. While Paul was in Crete, Nebraska, on business, his family was decimated.[20]

Undoubtedly the Janousek family suffered the most among the settlers along Beaver Creek. Honock Janousek and his son were killed enroute to Logan County. Two other relatives, Peter and Egnac, were killed as Egnac held his infant son, Charlie, in his arms. Mrs. Paul Janousek was raped by some of the Cheyennes and driven from her home, forced to leave her baby behind. As they had done at other homesteads, the Indians drove off the horses and what cows they needed for food and slaughtered the remaining livestock.[21]

For other settlers there were narrow escapes, desperate and brave actions to defend their property, and finally, acts of retribution. Henry Steffen, one of the first white children born in Decatur County, was only four years old that September when his mother drove him in a farm wagon to a willow thicket where they remained for three days, frightened and without food. "I have no actual memory of it," Steffen told a reporter in 1962, "but I can find that thicket to this day. Sometimes I go there and reflect on the changes that have occurred in my lifetime."[22]

Mrs. Jacob Keifer, who took in the Van Cleave girls and the Laing survivors, likewise spent the early morning of September 30, 1878, fending off the Cheyennes while her husband was away on business. Mrs. Keifer was in her house with her six-year-old son, Henry Anthony, his brother, Harry, age thirteen, and a visiting cattleman named Lynch when Cheyenne foragers came calling. Mrs. Keifer and Lynch barricaded the door and loaded the only weapons they had, a Winchester with four rounds of ammunition and a .22 caliber revolver. Lynch took the revolver and Harry took the rifle. "One Indian crawled onto the roof of the house and pulled out our stovepipe," Henry recalled years later. "Then he sat down on the hole in the roof evidently intending to smoke us out of the house. Finding that wouldn't work, the Indian came down off the house . . . [and] started up to the window. Then Lynch shot him. It was a dead center shot, having gone through near his heart." Cheyennes recovered the body of the dead warrior and departed without molesting the Keifers again. Soon thereafter Mrs. Keifer received the Van Cleave refugees.[23] A neighbor, Wilson Saunders, claimed a few days later that Lynch told him the warrior who was killed was wearing an apron probably belonging to one of the Van Cleave sisters.[24]

Billy O'Toole and several neighbors found concealment in a wild grape thicket, where they had a harrowing close call. "We were hiding about an hour," O'Toole remembered, "when the band of warriors made a charge on [my] house, filling the valley with their unearthly war whoops. They passed along the creek bank within 20 feet of where we were hiding. Three of them rode down a cow path so close we could have reached out and touched them." O'Toole watched as the Indians ransacked his house and slaughtered his livestock. "Cows were shot full of arrows and pigs and chickens were killed," he recalled. "After destroying everything in sight, the Indians moved on, taking with them a team of horses. We remained concealed until after dark."[25]

H. D. Colvin, the first Superintendent of Schools for Decatur County possibly escaped harm because of an accident. Colvin and his wife were in their front yard when they saw riders approaching rapidly. "Probably they are cowboys coming for eatables," Colvin said. "'No sir,'" exclaimed Mrs. Colvin, 'those are Indians.' I told my wife to go to the house and get out the gun and ammunition. The guns were all old fashioned cap and ball [a] Colt's Navy revolver and a muzzle loading double barrel shotgun. . . . One Indian rode around and got between [the house] and the stable. My wife attempted to get that old [shot]gun up to the loophole I had made on that side but in some manner the gun was discharged into the ground. On hearing the report of the gun the Indians at once left the house and kept out of gunshot distance for some time."[26]

A party of Cheyennes surprised E. P. Humphrey and his son John while they were cutting hay. The father was killed instantly but John, badly wounded, escaped and walked to the home of George B. Street, warning the family of the danger. George Street, his wife, daughter, and infant son along with his brother, Richard Street, and the wounded Humphrey made it to a hiding place in a cave below a limestone cliff. Richard Street stayed close to John Humphrey, but the boy became delirious and later died of his wounds.

"I can remember lying awfully close [to the mouth of the cave] when we heard the Indians yell," Street's daughter remembered years later when she went by her married name, Mrs. Emmett Martin. "It was a bright day, and the shadows of the Indians could be seen as they rode on the banks above. My brother Sam was six months old and wanted to play. Mother had to hold her hand over his mouth to keep him from laughing for fear he would be heard." The Streets remained in the cave for three days and then made their way into Oberlin where other refugees were gathering for protection.[27]

After the initial shock of the raids, a number of angry settlers in Decatur and Rawlins Counties organized impromptu posses to drive off the Cheyennes. But they spent most of their time burying the dead and helping their grief-stricken neighbors. Some, especially local cattlemen, engaged the Indians in isolated long-range shooting skirmishes. In a few cases the citizens committed isolated incidents of retribution that equaled individual acts of brutality committed by the Cheyenne foragers.

Gus Cook and C. C. Pierson ran cattle along Prairie Dog Creek. While herding steers toward the Holstine and McCoy Ranch on Beaver Creek on the morning of September 30, the two men ran right into the shooting at the Keifer homestead. They took flight, but the Cheyennes pursued them in a running fight. "They were shooting at us from behind and from either side," Cook remembered. "I was thoroughly scared. My hair stood up straight. . . . I promised that if I got back on Dog Creek again that I would do better and would attend church regularly." The men made it back to their herd and set up a defense. "They then tried to stampede us and get our chuck wagon," Cook said, "but we held them off."[28]

In other times the presence of cattlemen in the advancing farm country might have produced friction. But between September 30 and October 2, 1878, Cook and Pierson visited several beleaguered farms in Decatur and Rawlins Counties to lend assistance to the stricken families. On the South Sappa, Cook spotted a tent near the creek. "And when I got near," he remembered, "[I] saw a woman go in, and going up to the door [I] saw her sitting back in there with two revolvers . . . and she looked very independent."[29]

They visited the Keifers in Decatur County and recovered the bodies of Anton Stenner and Reverend Fenburgh on the Beaver. The Stenner house, Cook remembered, "has ever since been known as *dead man's ranch*." At another claim on Beaver Creek, Cook encountered an unidentified woman by the side of the road trying to dig a grave. Nearby lay a man's corpse. "I took the spade from her," Cook wrote, "and tried my hand at digging, but the ground was hard and dry and we did not have time to give him a decent burial, so we concluded to roll the poor fellow up in our saddle blankets for the present." When the woman saw that the men were preparing to take the corpse away, she came up, pulled off the overalls from the deceased victim, and quietly walked away. At another dugout Cook found the corpse of a man inside the home, "and outside the door was the wife and children. The eldest girl [who was otherwise naked] had a bed quilt around her for a dress."[30]

Some settlers, forming posses, scoured the countryside for days after the Ohmeseheso had left the state, looking for stragglers. H. D. Colvin, who along with his wife had fended off a party of the Indians at his house with an old shotgun and a small revolver, joined the chase with a cattleman named Sol Reese. Near the

Decatur and Rawlins County line, about a week after the raids, Henry Tyrell and several other members of the posse went to a well to get a drink. Shots were fired at them from a willow thicket. Colvin and Tyrell soon discovered the gunfire came from an old Cheyenne man, a Cheyenne woman, and a young boy. They wounded the old man, but he rode off on a mule captured from one of the farms. The woman and boy escaped in a different direction. A man named Willis Gorman fired a shot at the old man.

"When the boys rounded him up by [an] old cottonwood tree," Colvin remembered years later, "there was blood on the saddle, leaving us to believe the bullet from Gorman's rifle had pierced him." The old warrior tried to shoot at the men even after he had fallen from his mule. A "Mr. Jennings pulled his gun down on him," Colvin recalled, "and said: 'You would try to shoot me!'" Jennings shot the old Cheyenne at point-blank range. "Sol Reese scalped the Indian," Colvin remembered, "and the scalp hung in the Pioneer Drug Store at Oberlin for many years."[31]

A. N. Keith, one of the first to spot the Northern Cheyennes on Prairie Dog Creek on September 29, claimed that a group of cattlemen killed a party of eight or nine Cheyennes on the divide north of Beaver Creek, just south of the Nebraska line, but no other reliable sources account for such casualties in this region. In the same area of Rawlins County, "we found an old man who had been left behind," Keith remembered in 1924. "He was old and almost blind and toothless, [and] must have been a hundred years old. They had been carrying him in a travois and it had broken down and he had been left to die. The boys were discussing what to do with him when some one said to remember young [Chris] Abbott and then some one grabbed the end of the travois pole and the old warrior drew the blanket over his face and the cowboy hit him with the club and killed him."[32]

Later Keith's party discovered a dead horse with strips of flesh cut from its body. Searching some nearby timber, they found a Cheyenne warrior with a broken hip. Chris Abbott's cousin, Arthur, claimed Chris had shot this Indian before he died but that the warrior had gotten away. "So some one shot and scalped [the Cheyenne]," Keith remembered. "He had a long braid of coal black hair as thick as one's wrist and three feet long. I do not know what became of it. . . . "[33]

In another account, which may have been about the same incident, Keith tells of the warrior with the broken hip. Arthur Abbott and a friend named Harney were herding cattle near Beaver Creek some time after the raid when they discovered a Cheyenne boy pointing a gun at them from a draw in the grass. One of the whites rode around the draw, and when the boy raised his head, the drover sent a bullet crashing through his skull from the rear. Investigating further, Abbott and Harney discovered the youth had a shattered leg, explaining why he had been left behind. Near the body were some rabbits he had been able to trap for food with a snare, along with some dried beef. His "gun" turned out to be a dark wooden stick. Years later C. E. Perkins, president of the Burlington and Ohio Railroad, erected a monument on the exact spot in memory of the Indian lad. In part it read: "An Indian boy about 19 years old was wounded and left behind and after living six weeks on the meat of the cattle which had been killed by the Indians on what has since been known as 100 head draw, near where this stone stands he was killed on this spot about Nov. 16, 1878 by Abbott and Harney who were herding cattle here. The body was never recovered except by the coyotes."[34] The following spring a patrol of the 16th Infantry discovered the shriveled body of a Cheyenne that might have been this boy standing upright in a ravine (although the location near Smoky Hill Station would place it as a separate incident). Someone had stuck the feet down a prairie dog hole, and because of the stench, the soldiers did not bother to bury it.[35]

From the time the Ohmeseheso left Indian Territory until their exit from Kansas and their eventual capture, the fighting men, to the consternation of their chiefs, Little Wolf and Dull Knife, had killed far more civilians than soldiers. None of the dead were women, although Mrs. Wiley Payne and Mrs. Ferdinand Westfall, were wounded. However, the trauma of the sexual assaults was indeed just as catastrophic as death to the women and children of northwest Kansas who were victims. Ironically, although the assaults were horrible, there are no reliable records of ritual scalping or mutilation, committed by the Indians, though white citizens took at least two Indian scalps.

In at least one isolated incident in northwest Kansas, the Northern Cheyennes showed compassion to white children. About October 1 two teenagers, Eddie Race and Elwin Judkins, were riding horses to a neighbor's house when they mistook a party of Cheyennes for cowboys. Before they realized their mistake, the warriors were upon them, jerking at their reins. The Indians took the boys into their main camp and turned them over to the women. Some of the women threatened them by brandishing knives about their heads as if to simulate a scalping. Finally, an older chief, whom Billy O'Toole later claimed to be Dull Knife, took the boys by the hand, led them down a stream about fifty yards, and told them in English to "go east." They made their way to the Keifer home and finally to Oberlin without their horses.[36]

While doing research for her 1953 novel *Cheyenne Autumn*, Mari Sandoz transcribed a short note she had obtained from a Mrs. Grantham. This woman told Sandoz that when she was a small child, during the time of the Cheyenne odyssey, she and some neighbor children were hiding in a hay baler on the farm of the Heron family when a band of Cheyennes entered the Heron house. Soon the Indians emerged with a barrel of cheese and some crackers that they proceeded to eat on the front porch. After they went away, one of the girls hid the cheese. The Indians came back a while later looking for the cheese, surprising the children. One of the girls showed the warriors where the crock of cheese was hidden "and the Indians laughed." Soon they rode away without harming any of them.[37]

Twentieth century-historians have speculated about the motivation for the violence committed by the Northern Cheyenne foragers in northwest Kansas on September 30 and October 1, 1878. Logically, these warriors should have realized that this violence ultimately would be detrimental to their cause of living in the North, and the advice of the chiefs should have been further deterrence to unnecessary violence. As Little Wolf later stated, "We tried to avoid the settlements as much as possible. . . . I often harangued my young men, telling them not to kill citizens, but to leave them alone. . . . I know they killed some citizens, but I think not many. They did not tell me much of what they did, because they knew I would not like it."[38]

The most commonly accepted reason given since the early 1900s for the violence of September 30 and October 1 has been revenge for the killing of the band of Southern Cheyennes under Little Bull by H Company, 6th Cavalry, on April 23, 1875. The troops involved on that day were under the command of 2d Lt. Austin Henely. Little Bull's people were escaping violence that had erupted at Darlington Agency at the conclusion of the Red River War. They, like Little Wolf's and Dull Knife's people, were seeking refuge in the North. There were intimations of a massacre by Henley's troops, horrifyingly detailed in stories of soldiers burning live Cheyenne wounded, including an infant, when they set fire to the camp after the fight.[39]

The earliest reputable historical account linking the 1878 violence to the Sappa Creek fight in 1875 was written by a member of the Street family in 1908. William D. Street homesteaded for a time near the now defunct town of Achilles, Kansas, close to the site of the battle. He often visited the location of the fight that was known as Cheyenne Hole. Later, he became one of the earliest residents of Oberlin. He married one of the Van Cleave sisters, who had survived the killing of the Laing family in Decatur County. In 1897 he became Speaker of the Kansas State House of Representatives. His early years spent near the Sappa Creek battleground and his marriage into the Van Cleave family inspired in Street a special interest in both events. In an article on the Sappa Creek fight of 1875 for the Kansas State Historical Society, Street wrote, "The massacre of the [Southern] Cheyennes by Lieutenant Henely, and the massacre of the white settlers by Dull Knife's band of [Northern]

Cheyennes, always appeared to me to be closely connected in the annals of border warfare, now a closed book forever."[40]

William D. Street was in the field during the Cheyenne odyssey in 1878. Following the violence on September 30 and October 1, Street had been employed by the 4th Cavalry as a courier to carry military dispatches. For a time he even joined one of the posses searching for Cheyenne stragglers and engaged some of the Indians in a skirmish. Street later wrote of his experiences in the Cheyenne campaign. He made no mention in this work of any connection between the Little Wolf–Dull Knife trek of 1878–79 and the Sappa Creek fight of 1875. Although undated, the unpublished manuscript was surely written *before* his published article on the Sappa Creek battle or he likely would have made mention of the connection between the two events in the earlier manuscript.[41]

Another early resident of the region, F. M. Lockard, published a similar article in 1909 about the 1875 Sappa Creek fight. Although filled with errors, Lockard's account picked up on Street's theme and also attributed the 1878 Northern Cheyenne raids in Decatur and Rawlins Counties to revenge for the 1875 Sappa Creek affair.[42] Like Street, F. M. Lockard had written earlier of the Cheyenne odyssey, relating mostly the reminiscences of Gus Cook in attempting to aid beleaguered settlers after the raids of October 1. Nowhere in this narrative, published in 1894, did Lockard mention a connection between the Northern Cheyenne raiders and the Sappa Creek fight.[43] Most likely he was simply influenced by William D. Street in ascribing revenge as a motive for the 1878 raids in his later article.

The strongest proponent of the "revenge factor" theory was Mari Sandoz, whose novel *Cheyenne Autumn* exhaustively casts the 1875 Sappa Creek fight as an atrocity equal in magnitude to the infamous Sand Creek Massacre, thus lending justification to the Northern Cheyenne revenge raids in the same vicinity in 1878, though she makes little specific mention of the latter. Most assuredly, Sandoz had access to the same accounts of the 1878 violence as later historians. Her research notes at the University of Nebraska are filled with the same source material, but it is important to note that there are *no* unique revelations among her materials linking the two events. Sandoz's sole source for the 1875 Sappa Creek fight and the assertion that the 1878 raids were revenge for that event was the 1908 article by William D. Street. A letter from one H. D. Wimer of Stratton, Nebraska, dated February 11, 1949, referred Sandoz to Street's work, and thus she became aware of both the Sappa Creek fight of 1875 and the so-called revenge factor theory in relation to the Northern Cheyenne raids of 1878. "Checked with version on my files from Kans Hist Soc, col[lections] Vol X," Sandoz wrote in a note to herself. "He [Street] goes on to say that three years later, 1878, Dull Knife raid turned aside to wreak vengeance on the innocent settlers on Sappa and Beaver in Rawlins and Decatur county, in revenge for their people killed in 1875 here."[44] There is virtually no evidence that William D. Street ever knew any Cheyennes personally. The source of his conception of the revenge motive for the 1878 raids remains a mystery, but the theory has had a significant effect on historical interpretation through the years.

The only early Cheyenne account linking the 1875 Sappa Creek fight to the 1878 raids comes from the correspondence between ethnologist George Hyde and mixed-blood Southern Cheyenne George Bent, recorded in Hyde's book *Life of George Bent*. Hyde recounts the events of the Sappa Creek fight of 1875 and lists the names of Cheyenne casualties. In summary, he writes that "Dull Knife's band avenged their deaths when they swung through this part of Kansas in 1878."[45]

Undiscovered until 1968, *Life of George Bent* was unknown to William D. Street and Mari Sandoz. But was this claim made by legitimate Cheyenne informants of George Bent's or was it an editorial insertion of George Hyde's? Were either or both men familiar with Street's article? Perhaps the claim was Hyde's since George B. Grinnell, one of whose primary informants was George Bent, makes no mention of the revenge factor in his works on the Cheyennes.

In any event, the motive of revenge for the 1875 Sappa Creek fight has been widely accepted in the late twentieth century as an explanation for the violence in Decatur and Rawlins Counties in 1878. Cheyenne historian Father Peter John Powell even links this revenge not only to the Sappa Creek fight but to the earlier 1864 Sand Creek Massacre as well;[46] however, Powell found no viable Indian sources to support Street's claim. Understandably, the Northern Cheyennes have been silent on the 1878 raids and reluctant to claim the raids as revenge for the 1875 Sappa Creek fight. "The author was unable to find any detailed account of the Sappa raiding [of 1878]," Powell wrote in *People of the Sacred Mountain*, "from any warrior who had taken part in it. However, the Old Ones living in the early 1950s to the early 1970s spoke of it to him, saying [simply] that the men who took part in the killings spoke rarely about them afterward."[47]

As mentioned earlier, it seems illogical that the Ohmeseheso would have made time to revenge past grievances given the urgency to escape the open country of the Kansas settlements and make their way into the more sheltered north country in the fall of 1878. Also, given the recent discord at Darlington Agency between the Northern Cheyennes of Little Wolf and Dull Knife and the Southern Cheyennes including their competition for inadequate resources and influence on the reservation, the idea that the Northern Cheyennes were avenging the deaths of Southern Cheyennes, as a motivation for these raids, seems unlikely, even though the people historically and culturally always had regarded themselves as one tribe.

Yet the cultural *necessity* to avenge past wrongs was a powerful honor-bound duty among the Cheyennes. That Powell and others have ascribed the killings to "wilder young men" must not be taken lightly. Wild Hog later told a Senate investigating committee that a number of *young* men would often ride away and return with provisions obtained from whites, despite being told not to do so by the chiefs. Wild Hog told the investigators that these young men refused to discuss their raids.[48] Often, young fighting men, having grown up hearing the tales of their elders' exploits and the fabled stories of the tribe's culture heroes, were eager to build their own reputations as warriors. Yet in Kansas in 1878 the absence of scalping, counting coup, and other war rituals may contradict even this explanation. If young warriors seeking a reputation had taken the time to kill and rape without concern for consequences to the remainder of their people or chastisement from their chiefs, why did they not take a scalp or count coup?

The historian who has studied the Kansas raids of 1878 most carefully is Ramon Powers. In a 1972 article, Powers advances the argument that cultural conflict rather than revenge for a specific incident motivated the killings. "In truth the plunder of the countryside in Indian Territory and Kansas to the extent of claims for property loss of $101,766.83," Powers writes, "and the killing of around forty settlers and herders, was the result of cultural shock with random reprisals against any and all manifestations of white culture."[49] The stress of the flight north, the constant fear, the visible destruction of once familiar environments newly reenvisioned by whites as farming or cattle country, the control of vital natural resources by the settlers, and the recognition that their way of life was coming swiftly to an end, certainly had a significant psychological impact on the Ohemeseheso. The very need to live in their traditional homelands, in any modified fashion, became so intense that by January 1879 many were willing to die instantly in the bloody escape from Fort Robinson rather than return to Darlington Agency.

In essence Powers's explanation is, although logical, a bit generalized. Perhaps in Indian Territory and Southern Kansas some of the killings may have resulted from surprise encounters with whites and the Indians' feelings of vulnerability. But given the accounts of neighbors, living sometimes within sight of each other, and the extent of the death and destruction in Decatur and Rawlins Counties on September 30 and October 1, 1878, although the raids were not sanctioned by the chiefs, they hardly seem to be surprise encounters as Powers claims. Rather, they seem to be the work of young warriors for varieties of reasons.

Certainly both Street and Powers make their points adequately. Yet based on historical evidence, the most we can conclude given the nature of individuality codes among Cheyenne warriors is that *some* of the killings in northwest Kansas *may* have been revenge motivated on the part of individual warriors. Other killings *may* have resulted from cumulative anger and stress resulting from the physical and psychological demands, and the constant threat of attack and capture, of the trek north over the previous two weeks.

What modern observers seem to have overlooked, however, was readily recognized by the overwhelming majority of eyewitnesses to the Cheyenne odyssey who have left their accounts to history. After the destruction of much of their reserve pony herd and most of their pack supplies at the Battle of Punished Woman's Fork three days earlier, the Northern Cheyennes were suddenly put in a position of desperate and immediate need. Unless horses and food could be systematically replenished in large quantities quickly, the continuation of their flight north would be in grave jeopardy. Success depended on a constant supply of fresh mounts to keep the Indians ahead of the 4th Cavalry. To obtain horses from the comparatively sedentary settlers of northwest Kansas was the most expedient course. Lieutenant Wilder told a Senate investigating committee that between September 30 and October 1 the Cheyennes captured between 200 and 250 horses in Decatur and Rawlins Counties.[50] Settlers' claims filed with the state bear Wilder out.

Since the initial Battle of Turkey Springs in Indian Territory, despite the hopes of the chiefs, the Northern Cheyennes had discovered that the civilians in their path were almost as dangerous as the soldiers trying to halt their northward advance. Certainly the farmers of northwest Kansas were more vulnerable and less well armed than the cattlemen of southwest Kansas. When they could, however, these settlers, like the cattlemen, defended their property and shot at Indians. The Cheyennes had multiple incentives for shooting settlers: the need to obtain quickly the necessary horses and other provisions, to do it in open country, and to accomplish this before the 4th Cavalry caught up with them. On balance they were successful. Certainly the destruction inflicted among the civilian population in northwest Kansas had the effect of slowing up the military pursuit as the soldiers stopped to assist the beleaguered settlers. Capt. Clarence Mauck and elements of the 4th Cavalry began arriving at the site of the devastation on October 2, 1878, about the same time Little Wolf's and Dull Knife's people slipped into the Republican Valley in southern Nebraska. Soon other troops were also on the scene.

Among the first to arrive were Col. Richard Irving Dodge and an Infantry detachment. In 1882 Dodge published some of his memoirs, and in writing about the Battle of Punished Woman's Fork and the Northern Cheyennes' odyssey, he offered one of the earliest explanations for the killings in northwest Kansas. His theory, though, has since fallen into obscurity, overshadowed by the ideas of persons who were not actual eyewitnesses. "What remained [of the Cheyenne Ramada after Punished Woman's Fork]," Dodge wrote, "were sufficient for a few days' march, but not for such a race as they now realized they had to run; so, deviating from their most direct route, the Indians turned . . . and made a raid into the settlements to procure a remount."[51]

Had the Indians' pony herd survived Punished Woman's Fork, the Indians actually might have avoided the settlements in northwest Kansas, especially given the wise disposition of their chiefs, and the number of civilian deaths would have been fewer. Another critical factor contributing to the settlement raids was the presence of farmers rather than horse ranchers in Decatur and Rawlins Counties. Most of the farmers owned draft animals; few swift mounts belonged to individual families. The Cheyennes needed fresh horses almost constantly to stay ahead of the soldiers, more horses than people if possible. Since the animals taken from the civilian population were often of a lesser quality, these horses might not outdistance the soldiers' mounts unless they were always fresh, even though the Indians' weight per rider might be less. Consequently, the capture of 200 to 250 *effective* mounts still may have been an insufficient number, though it represented raids on many homesteads. Each raid presented increasing danger for the raiders as the word of the Cheyennes' presence spread among the white population.

Certainly generalized fear and hatred of the whites could account for the inevitable progression from stealing horses to sexual assault and killing and the Cheyennes realized that some of the whites naturally would try to defend their property. Killing and inflicting casualties on the whites meant that not only would retaliation be slower in coming but that communications regarding the Indians' exact whereabouts would be hindered as well. Nevertheless, if the killing of white males presented any strategic advantage to the Cheyennes, it is arguable they recognized it at the time. The sexual molestation of women and children, however, only served in turning the tide of public opinion among Americans against the Northern Cheyennes' cause in the long run.

Many of the dead in Decatur County were buried in Oberlin but later relocated. The raids of 1878 became deeply rooted in the folklore of northwest Kansas, and forgiveness was long in coming. In 1911 the state of Kansas and Decatur County erected a monument in Oberlin to the white victims of September 30, 1878. The monument is twenty-two feet high above its base. On the north, south, and east sides are the names of nineteen of the victims:

John Young
James S. Smith
William Laing Sr.
William Laing Jr.
John C. Laing
Freeman Laing
John Humphrey
E. O. Humphrey

John C. Hudson
George F. Walters
Moses F. Abernathy
Mr.—Lull
Ferdinand Westphalen and son,
John Irwin
Marcellus Felt
John Wright
Edward Miskelley
Frederick Hamper[52]

Today the fine Decatur County Museum displays records and artifacts from what is still known as the *Last Indian Raid in Kansas*.

To be certain, the raids of 1878 were a cultural shock to the citizens of northwest Kansas, every bit as much as the experience at Darlington Agency had been for the Northern Cheyennes. "The 'cumulative communities' there," writes western Kansas historian Craig Miner, "were threatened in their sense of cumulativeness as well as directly by the intrusion of something that, ten years after the last major Kansas Indian raids,[53] seemed, in a fast-changing time, positively antique."[54]

When the military came upon the scene on October 2 or 3, they found not only a psychologically shocked and devastated population, but an angry one as well. The situation was aggravated when many of the survivors fled to the town limits of Oberlin, ostensibly for protection in numbers. One man penned a letter to Governor George T. Anthony asserting, "I am very sorry to say you are censured very much throughout the west as it is not known whether you manifest any interest in behalf of the frontier."[55]

Most settlers pointed fingers at the army's failure to pursue the Ohmeseheso successfully. Writing to a friend on October 6, O. A. Heath was passionate in his anger. "What were the soldiers doing all this time you will ask," he wrote, "following them up Ten Hours Behind (Damn Them) and in all probability the 'Reds' are across the U.P.R.R. [Union Pacific Railroad] and beyond reach at this time. While they were doing their devil's work, General Pope was tele-graphing to Governor Anthony 'not a hostile Indian north of the Atchison Topeka R.R.'"[56]

"Governor, this is a terrible thing," another citizen, John H. Edwards, wrote, "a small force of Indians leisurely making their way for nearly twenty days across the country, and the troops as leisurely following, and not even capturing or killing an Indian and yet, as you are told by the general commanding, not a hostile or Cheyenne Indian within a hundred miles."[57] Years later, feelings against the 4th Cavalry were still being expressed. H. D. Colvin, who had defended his homestead with a revolver and a shotgun, wrote a letter to one editor in which he stated: "Arriving at Keefer's [sic] ranch we met the troops . . . under the command of [Captain] Mauck of the Regular Army, who were *leisurely* [emphasis mine] following the Indians."[58]

Indeed the officers on the scene surely had to have realized the political implications of arriving too late to prevent the raids. For two days troopers aided the homeless and helped bury the dead. Soon officers began to point fingers at one another. First Lieutenant George H. Palmer, 16th Infantry, patrolled around Fort Wallace during the fall of 1878. He blamed the 4th Cavalry for not taking preventative measures after the Battle of Punished Woman's Fork.

> The officer in command at the [Punished Woman's Fork battle] has made a fatal omission of duty in not sending a courier at once to inform us of the battle. If [Captain Clarence] Mauck had sent us word immediately after the fight we would have been in front of the Indians before they crossed [the Kansas Pacific Railroad]. From Fort Wallace to the battlefield is 46 miles. A messenger on a good horse could have brought us the news in 8 hours at most which would have enabled our troops to move in the proper direction . . . and place themselves in front of the Indians. . . .[59]

As far away as Fort Hays, unreasonable fears mounted. On October 3, 1878, Ephriam Goodale, the father of Capt. G. A. Goodale, 23rd Infantry, wrote in his diary: "This morng [sic] at 2 o'clock we were aroused by the guard that Indians were about to attack us and all the post were called up but we were to light no lamps but keep as quiet as possible. Capt. [G.A.] Goodale called his Co. 'K' to arms—stationed guards, etc for 2 hours expecting an attack, but it proved a false alarm!"[60]

The next year when asked by a Senate investigating committee why the 4th Cavalry had not constantly pushed the Indians in their rear and harassed them, Lt. W. E. Wilder gave a direct and accurate answer. "They had this advantage," he told the committee, "they were all the time stealing stock and getting a new mount."[61]

The ultimate scapegoat for the failed campaign, as mentioned earlier, became Capt. Joseph Rendlebrock, who was relieved of command after the Northern Cheyennes crossed into the Military Department of the Platte and forced into immediate retirement because of his actions at the Battle of Turkey Springs, made public at his court martial.

But the Indians, too, would suffer consequences following the raids in northwest Kansas, in the form of changing public opinion among the whites. Arguably, the fighting effort of the troopers during the first two weeks of the odyssey was half-hearted at best, especially considering the Indians' own motivations—the exploitation they had endured at Darlington Agency and their admirable desire to live in their own land. For some soldiers, dying to resist such a cause may not have seemed much of an incentive to shoot at Indians. After witnessing the devastation and suffering in Decatur and Rawlins Counties, however, attitudes changed, at least for a time.

Second Lieutenant Calvin Duvall Cowles, 23rd Infantry and a West Point graduate, has left to history perhaps the best personal account of these changing feelings within the military. He was part of a relief party that came upon the ruins of the burned Laing homestead. "I saw her house in ashes," Cowles wrote. "Many of the settlers were Bohemians who came to this country about a year ago and had never seen an Indian in their lives. Many of the men went out to meet the Indians in a friendly manner. The Indians would come up and shake hands with them and while pretending to offer one hand in friendship would shoot their victim with the other."[62]

Cowles witnessed most of the devastation in Decatur County and later wrote of it to his father in a letter home.

There is no doubt that these Indians were starving and dying of fever and were justified in leaving their reservations peacibly [sic] and going for their old haunts North in a healthy climate where game is abundant. Our sympathies were therefore with them at first but when we reached their trail of murder, rapine [sic] and desolation our blood rose against them and there was not a man who would not gladly have risked his life to avenge the defenceless [sic] men, women & children who had been barberously [sic] murdered and outraged.[63]

As the Indians crossed into Nebraska during the early days of October 1878, the Northern Cheyennes' odyssey would take on an even grimmer character.

CHAPTER SIX

# NEBRASKA

## *Blood on the Snow at Fort Robinson*

*Morning Star said we should be contented, now that we were on our own land. He took us to Fort Robinson where we surrendered to the soldiers. They took from us all of our horses and whatever guns they could find among us. They said then that we must go back to the South, but our men told them it was better to die by bullets.*

—IRON TEETH,
1926

The raids in northwest Kansas focused national media attention on the Northern Cheyennes' odyssey. Reporters from New York, Chicago, Washington, and elsewhere hurried to Omaha now that the campaign promised a good story, reminiscent of the Nez Percé War of the previous year. Carrying dispatches from Capt. Clarence Mauck, William D. Street arrived in Ogallala, Nebraska, from Oberlin, Kansas, on October 3, 1878, after a continuous 140-mile ride. "In a few minutes after my dispatches were sent," Street remembered, "inquiries commenced coming from every direction. From officers in the army, from newspapers and the associated press came dispatches asking [me] for information. It was but meager news that I could give them. I reported about forty men killed; which was not greatly exaggerated."[1]

Soon rumor placed Cheyenne wolves near Julesburg, Colorado, and as far away as Fort Laramie, Wyoming.[2] North of the Sappa, false reports counted one officer, five troopers, and eighteen cattlemen killed in a desperate battle that never even took place.[3] One rancher in extreme northeastern Colorado claimed the Cheyennes made away with fifty of his best horses in the dead of night.[4]

In actuality, the Ohmeseheso moved north swiftly and silently from the Sappa country. Without much rest and traveling mostly at night, the tired people of Little Wolf and Dull Knife crossed into Nebraska and did not stop until they reached the Frenchman's Fork of the Republican River, and then they stopped only briefly. "My friends," Little Wolf said to his people, "we must try to get through here without so much fighting, or we may all be killed. We must go faster."[5]

They crossed the South Platte about noon on October 4, 1878, five miles east of Ogallala, Nebraska. They rode on and crossed the tracks of the Union Pacific railroad, where Lakota scouts for the army soon picked up their trail. Moving on to the North Platte through modern Keith County, they crossed at the mouth of White Clay Creek, then continued to a stream they called White Tail Creek. Always they pushed northwesterly, in the direction of the Sacred Mountain.[6] Fearing discovery by converging troops along the line of the Union Pacific Railroad, the people were at times fearful even of lighting cooking fires. The women, Iron Teeth among them, ignited handfuls of bunch grass and wrapped strips of meat around the smoldering grass, cooking the meat until it was barely edible.[7] When needed, Cheyenne outriders stole fresh mounts. South of the Platte, in Chase County, foragers killed George W. Rowley of Frenchman Falls and took his horses. His body was discovered a week later, riddled with seven bullet holes.[8]

On October 5 William D. Street joined a posse of citizens in Ogallala who set out to locate the Indians between the forks of the

Platte. They surprised a sizable party of foragers butchering a beef on a high bluff. Suddenly, "one of the warriors jumped off his pony and opened fire on our party," Street remembered, "checking our charge in short order. There we were ten to one, but all of one mind when the bullets commenced to sing around our ears, ready to hit. Leading out for a ravine to the left, two men followed me. In a moment we were on the Indians' flank and opened fire on them." But Street and his men soon found themselves outnumbered and broke off the engagement. Returning to Ogallala, they found troops disembarking the train.[9]

Once above the North Platte and away from the settlements, the Indians approached largely uninhabited land and eventually the desolate Sand Hills. Finally, they were out of the way of civilian populations. From here the people became intent on pushing the trek as fast as possible toward the Black Hills. "They seem to have ceased their career of pillage and massacre," declared one eastern newspaper, "being sufficiently intent on taking care of themselves."[10]

But the Cheyennes were not rid of the soldiers, for they had come within the Military Department of the Platte. From his office in Omaha, departmental commander Gen. George Crook quickly took steps to strengthen the northern net, now the army's third line of defense. With Capt. Clarence Mauck still pushing north from Kansas, Crook was hopeful that it would not be long before troops blocked the Cheyennes from all directions. Accordingly, he ordered Maj. Thomas T. Thornburgh to bring his troops from Sydney Barracks to Ogallala at once to pursue the Cheyennes from the rear through the Sand Hills. Thornburgh at the time had four companies, from the 4th, 9th, and 14th Infantries. He ordered five companies of the 3rd Cavalry under Maj. Caleb Carleton to leave Camp, very soon to be designated Fort Robinson, and scout the northern reaches of the Sand Hills in order to intercept the Indians. Reinforced by Capt. Clarence Mauck's 4th Cavalry, Thornburgh would push the Cheyennes into Carleton's cavalry. Thornburgh reached Ogallala about 4:00 P.M. on October 4, missing the Cheyennes by only a few hours, and took up the pursuit immediately.

General George Crook, who eventually worked for Indian rights. Crook was the commander of the Military Department of the Platte, which included Fort Robinson, Nebraska, in 1878–1879. Although he was opposed to sending Dull Knife's contingent back to Indian Territory in autumn 1878, Crook's voice was overruled by superiors in Washington, leading to the terrible slaughter at and around Fort Robinson in January 1879. Courtesy Nebraska State Historical Society.

The next day Mauck's command arrived in Ogallala and took up the trail behind Thornburgh. Crook also alerted several companies of 7th Cavalry then at the cantonment on Bear Butte Creek in the Black Hills,[11] to form a fourth line of defense two hundred miles north of Camp Robinson, in case the Cheyennes broke through the

Sand Hills and into Dakota Territory. General Wesley Merritt and the 5th Cavalry meanwhile set up patrols along the eastern edge of the Big Horn Mountains against the possibility the Cheyennes tried to make it all the way north to the Powder River country.[12]

That morning, not far north of Ogallala, Captain Mauck's soldiers discovered an old Cheyenne man who was weak and had fallen behind the main band. "He was old. And could not go any farther," Lt. W. E. Wilder later told a Senate investigating committee. The soldiers did not harm the old man but rather turned him over to a group of Nebraska citizens riding as a posse behind the troops. "Just as we were leaving," Wilder testified, "we heard a shot, and were told afterward that this Indian had been [killed]. It was reported that the citizens shot him."[13]

About sixty miles north of the North Platte River on October 7, Captain Mauck received a dispatch ordering his troops to Sydney Barracks where some of them would help escort another important band of Northern Cheyennes, under Little Chief, which was still in the North having recently served as army scouts, south to Darlington Agency. The trek of Little Chief's people south under an army guard at the same time that Little Wolf and Dull Knife were moving north is a coincidence of the Cheyenne odyssey that will be examined in a later chapter.[14] The orders to return south as escort to Little Chief's people ended the official role of troops from the Department of the Missouri in the pursuit of the Northern Cheyennes under Little Wolf and Dull Knife. In light of their objective, they had failed miserably.

Meanwhile Maj. Thomas Thornburgh's command was having problems of its own. The Northern Cheyennes always managed to stay ahead of the command, although army scouts, riding in advance, occasionally caught sight of them and presumably exchanged shots. Thornburgh's infantrymen were mounted, but on about October 6, one private from H Company, 4th Infantry, found himself on foot because his horse had fallen and broken its leg. The soldier waited along the trail for Mauck's column, twenty miles in the rear, to rescue him. Before the 4th Cavalry arrived, however, a party of Cheyennes attacked him. The soldier took refuge in a hastily dug rifle pit and held off the Indians for several hours. Bullets cut his clothing but he escaped unscathed. Mauck's column appeared just as a Cheyenne bullet smashed the trigger of the soldier's carbine.[15]

By October 7 Thornburgh's command entered the Sand Hills, and by the tenth they were camped on the Niobrara River north of the Sand Hills, where the troops from Fort Robinson were on patrol. By that time they had abandoned their wagons, which the Cheyennes then pillaged. Most of the Lakota scouts had quit the expedition and gone home. The troops had marched about forty-five miles per day with little food or fresh water. On one occasion they had almost caught up with the Cheyennes, but the Indians escaped through a thick fog. On October 8 Thornburgh crossed Maj. Caleb Carleton's trail out of Fort Robinson. At that point he gave up hope of catching the Indians, figuring that Carleton's 3rd Cavalry was now on their trail.[16]

A special correspondent for the *Chicago Times* wrote from the camp on the Niobrara River that

the expedition will probably be abandoned, it having thus far resulted in utter failure. The march has been through a country, which is a geographical blank, and a desert untenanted by scarcely a living thing. The sand was knee-deep to the horses and was carried by the wind in blinding clouds. The horses [are] so thin that the men almost pulled them over in attempting to mount. The expedition is a complete failure so far as the capture of the renegade Cheyennes is concerned. The savages baffled the troops at every point, and led them into the Sand Hills, from which they might never have emerged.[17]

Somewhere north of the North Platte River, probably in the Sand Hills, but possibly on White Tail Creek in modern Keith County, Nebraska, Little Wolf and Dull Knife parted ways, separating each with their own loyal followers.[18] By most accounts the split resulted from a disagreement between Little Wolf and Dull Knife over the final destination of the Ohmeseheso. Little Wolf, in his role as Sweet Medicine Chief, wishing to proceed on to the Powder River Country where game was abundant, thought it best if the people remained together. But Dull Knife, whose followers had relatives among the Oglalas, wanted to go to the old Red Cloud (White River) Agency near Fort Robinson, where he thought the people would be allowed to remain. Dull Knife did not know that federal reorganization had closed the Red Cloud Agency in Nebraska. The government had only recently relocated Red Cloud's Oglalas, in the spring of 1878, to the Pine Ridge Agency on White Clay Creek, on what remained of the Great Sioux Reservation.

"You can go that way if you wish," Little Wolf told Dull Knife, "but I intend to work my way up to the Powder River Country. I think it will be better for us all if the party is not divided."[19] Dull Knife disagreed. So Little Wolf and those who wished to follow him moved down the Niobrara and back into the Sand Hills, where they spent the early part of the winter undetected, subsisting on wild game and cattle. Whether or not the notion arose that they might have had a better chance in later negotiations if they had not all surrendered together as one group is not known. Whether any disputes over the likely consequences of the Kansas raids weighed into the decision to split up likewise is not known.

In mid-October Dull Knife's followers, about 149, mostly women, children, and the elderly, many of whom were tired of fighting and running, moved toward Chadron Creek. Their destination was the defunct Red Cloud Agency on White River near Fort Robinson, from where, scarcely more than a year ago, they had been taken south to Indian Territory. Wild Hog and his family remained with Dull Knife's group, as did Tangle Hair, the Dog Soldier, and some of his young warriors. Little Shield, Old Crow, Strong Left Hand, Bullet Proof, and Porcupine stayed, too, as did Great Eyes, and Little Finger Nail, who still carried his ledger book of drawings. Roached Hair and Big Beaver, then a boy known as Young Pumpkinseed, also followed Dull Knife.

Iron Teeth, widow of Red Pipe, also followed Dull Knife. She had been sick with dysentery throughout much of the march north and was ready for rest. "I and my family stayed with Morning Star's band," she remembered years later. "As we got [near] to the old Red Cloud Agency my younger son and the oldest daughter set off with some other Cheyennes to go forward to the agency. Some of our friends warned us not to do this, that the Pawnees and Arapahos who belonged to the soldiers would kill them along the way. But they were determined to go. It turned out they did what was best. They got through [all the way to Pine Ridge] without any serious trouble."[20] Remaining behind with Iron Teeth were her two youngest daughters and her eldest son, Gathering His Medicine, now responsible for protecting the family. "[We] had before us many days of hard trail," Iron Teeth reminisced.[21]

Although a few Cheyennes, including Iron Teeth's children and Bull Hump's wife, Dull Knife's daughter-in-law, made it to safety at Pine Ridge Agency, any hope Dull Knife may have entertained regarding Red Cloud's Oglalas coming to his aid was soon dispelled. Indeed, Lakotas now scouted for the army seeking to capture the Cheyennes. "I do not think the Cheyennes will come near us," Red Cloud told a reporter, "but if they do, I will attend to them, as the Great Father asks."[22]

Dull Knife had friends and relatives among the Lakotas who had been relocated to Pine Ridge, and he felt his people would be safe there even if they had to surrender to the soldiers. Not yet knowing that the old Red Cloud Agency had been closed, however, Dull Knife told his followers they would march straight for the old agency grounds. "Now we have again reached our own ground," he told his people, "and from this time forth we will no more fight or harm any white people."[23] Then, on October 23, 1878, while going over a hill not far from the old agency, Dull Knife's Cheyennes ran straight into a patrol of federal troops.

Since early October, Companies B and D of Carleton's 3rd Cavalry, under the direct command of Capt. J. B. Johnson, had been patrolling the White River country around Fort Robinson, anticipating the Cheyennes' advance. By mid-October, Johnson was alerting local ranchers to potential danger. Near Fort Robinson, cattleman Edgar Beecher Bronson, a nephew of famed abolitionist Henry Ward Beecher and cousin of 1st Lt. Fred Beecher, who was killed at the Battle of Beecher Island on September 17, 1868, was visited by Johnson's troops. "Presently [there] arrived before the ranch a sergeant and ten men of Troop B, with two Sioux scouts, Woman's Dress and Red Shirt," Bronson remembered, "the sergeant bringing me a note from dear old [Capt.] Jack Johnson, saying that, while he felt we were quite able to take care of ourselves, it seemed to him expedient to give us reinforcements to help defend our horses. White River was lined with patrols of troopers from the head down to Chadron Creek," Bronson reminisced, "watching for Dull Knife's advance. He could not go south, for Thornburgh lay behind him; he could not go east or west for lack of water—he must come north."[24]

Near evening on October 23, 1878, a snowstorm swept the ridges around Chadron Creek, about seventy miles from Fort Robinson. Through a dense fog, Johnson's troops finally caught sight of Dull Knife's Ohmeseheso. Immediately Johnson ordered his men into a skirmish line.[25] With the soldiers were Lone Tree and Two Lance, both Lakota scouts. With mixed-blood interpreter Long Joe Larrabee, the two Lakotas persuaded Dull Knife's people not to resist. During the ensuing parley with Dull Knife, Wild Hog, and Old Crow, it became apparent to many of the Cheyennes that Wild Hog was now taking a more active role in these negotiations as a spokesman for the younger warriors. Through Larrabee, Captain Johnson explained that the old Red Cloud Agency had been closed and that the Cheyennes would have to go with him to Fort Robinson or fight him.

Reluctantly, the Indians followed the soldiers to their camp on Chadron Creek, where a blazing fire awaited them. The soldiers then distributed bread, bacon, and coffee to the Northern Cheyennes, while others discreetly herded the Indians' horses off to a thicket on the side of the creek. The Cheyennes were by that time desperate for food, "We had been eating our horses that had given out," Wild Hog later testified.[26] That night Capt. J. B. Johnson sent Lakota scouts into Dull Knife's camp to keep them company while secretly counting weapons. Johnson had promised the scouts that all guns they saw would be given to them the next day.[27]

On the morning of October 24, the Cheyennes awoke to find that Captain Johnson had brought in reinforcements from Fort Robinson during the night. The troopers placed artillery on the bluffs above Chadron Creek and pointed the big guns into the Indian camp. Accompanied by Lakota scouts, Johnson entered the Cheyennes' camp that morning and parleyed with both Dull Knife and Wild Hog. Although the chiefs told Johnson they wanted to join the Oglalas on their new agency, Johnson was adamant that they go to Fort Robinson. Only after one warrior drew his bow and a fight almost broke out did the Cheyennes finally agree to give up their guns and horses. Fortunately for the Indians, the troopers did not search the persons of anyone, so a number of rifles and pistols were thus concealed by some of the women in their dresses and blankets. The 3rd Cavalry troopers captured altogether 149 Cheyennes on Chadron Creek. These numbers included 46 men, 61 women, and 42 children. The Indians relinquished 12 rifles, 9 of which were muzzleloaders, 1 shotgun, 4 pistols, and about 15 or 20 bows, along with 131 horses and 9 mules. Captain Johnson allowed the Indians to keep their knives and other tools, including Iron Teeth's precious Elk antler hide scraper.[28]

Later that day Maj. Caleb H. Carlton, the commander at Fort Robinson, arrived at the camp to take charge of the operations. For the next two days, parleys were held with Dull Knife and Wild Hog, the latter becoming increasingly dominant in the negotiations and stating that the Cheyenne men were willing to die on the spot if they could not go to one of the Lakota agencies. As more and more troops streamed into the camp on Chadron Creek from various points along General Crook's northern net, the Ohmeseheso began digging rifle pits and building breastworks, resigning themselves to a fight and indicating to the soldiers that they indeed had not relinquished all of their firearms. On the morning of October 25, two companies of 7th Cavalry brought up a Howitzer from Camp Sheridan, and troopers from Fort Robinson delivered a big Napoleon gun for smashing through the Cheyenne breastworks.[29] "We lay there for several days," remembered Sgt. Carter P. Johnson, 3rd Cavalry, "the Cheyennes throwing up breastworks and preparing to fight."[30]

By the evening of October 25, about eight companies of troops surrounded the Cheyenne camp on Chadron, including at least two of the 7th Cavalry. That evening Dull Knife, Wild Hog, and Old Crow were summoned to the tent of Capt. Hugh Lenox Scott, 7th Cavalry, to meet with reporters and to explain why they had left the Darlington Agency. "They made everybody understand that they had seen the elephant," Scott remembered. "I reported to Colonel Carleton, commanding the post [Fort Robinson], that they would never go back alive."[31]

Sensing the enormous odds against them, however, the Indian chiefs capitulated. They agreed to be escorted into Fort Robinson. The following morning, October 26, the riderless horses of the Cheyennes were driven into Fort Robinson. The people were jammed into army wagons and arrived at the post that evening, in the teeth of a snowstorm. Camp Robinson had been advanced to permanent status and designated as Fort Robinson in the autumn of 1878.[32] Carleton ordered the tired, hungry Cheyennes, now considered prisoners of war, placed in a barracks building at the southeast angle of the parade ground formerly occupied by A Company, 3rd Cavalry. Other barracks used by the post's enlisted men flanked the building. The post stables were behind the Indian's quarters. The fort itself stood on a bench of land to the north, above the valley of the confluence of Soldier Creek and the White River. About a half-mile from here down the valley of White River stood the abandoned cantonment called Camp Canby.[33]

The next morning, October 27, 1878, Major Carleton, through Lakota interpreters and Tangle Hair, who spoke Sioux, told Dull Knife: "Now, the fighting is over. We are friendly with one another.

You must stay here for three months before the government will decide whether to send you south or to send you to the Sioux. While you are here, nothing bad will happen to you, but you must stay for three months. You will have the freedom of the post and may even go off into the mountains, but each night at suppertime you must be here. If one man of you deserts or runs away, you will not be treated like this any longer. You will be held responsible for him." "We are back on our own ground and have stopped fighting," Dull Knife then told his followers. "We have found the place we started to come to."[34] Soon after 1st Lt. Edward B. Moseley, Assistant Surgeon at Fort Robinson, examined the Cheyenne refugees and proclaimed them to be in good health considering their ordeal.[35]

The Northern Cheyennes never enjoyed the "freedom of the post" Carleton had promised. Carleton ordered two searches for weapons, on October 27 and 28. Second Lieutenant George F. Chase conducted the second search in the barracks among the Indians' packs, as the Cheyennes looked on. Chase found only a few old weapons including:

1 Henry Rifle
1 Sharp's Rifle
3 muzzle-loading rifles
1 Springfield Carbine
2 unknown patterns [probably pistols][36]

In any event, it was apparent to Major Carleton and Lieutenant Chase that the twenty-five or thirty firearms confiscated at Chadron Creek and Fort Robinson were not all the weapons the Indians possessed. Eventually Lieutenant Chase discovered a woman hiding a pistol and ordered two guards posted inside the barracks and one outside, night and day, with a lantern always burning inside. Little did the officers realize that the Cheyennes had hidden their remaining few firearms under the floor boards of the barracks or that some women and children wore parts of small arms as jewelry, ready to be reassembled into workable weapons if the need arose.[37]

For almost two months the Ohmeseheso felt optimistic at Fort Robinson. They enjoyed sufficient food rations, and Old Crow, Tangle Hair and others went on jaunts with the 3rd Cavalry, looking for Little Wolf.[38] Although the women were permitted to go to the White River at the edge of the post for water, the men were never allowed out of an enclosure at the rear of the barracks, about the length of the building itself and about thirty yards wide. A slab fence higher than a man's head surrounded the structure.[39]

"They had their dogs with them in the barracks and a heating stove, and were comfortable enough," Sgt. Carter P. Johnson remembered. "They would often stick their heads out of the windows and talk with the guards outside. They had a club, with the end driven with nails, which they had pulled out of the barracks. They would sometimes stick this out and wave it, in fun."[40]

In early December 1878, Gen. George Crook ordered Capt. Henry W. Wessells, 3rd Cavalry, to Fort Robinson from duty near the Rosebud Agency in present day South Dakota. Subsequently, Crook ordered Maj. Caleb Carleton out on an extended scout to find Little Wolf. Carleton had already been in the field for most of November, looking for the Sweet Medicine Chief without success.[41] By December 17 Captain Wessells assumed temporary command of Fort Robinson.

Henry W. Wessells Jr. was born at Sacketts Harbor, New York, in 1846 and was educated in Danbury, Connecticut. On March 1, 1865, he joined the 7th Infantry and served on Reconstruction duty in Florida where he attained the rank of first lieutenant.[42] On December 31, 1870, he transferred to the 3rd Cavalry, where he attained the rank of captain on December 20, 1872. From 1870 to 1878 he served in Arizona, Wyoming, and Nebraska and learned to speak some of the Sioux language.[43]

During his early weeks at Fort Robinson, Wessells became well acquainted with several of the Cheyenne prisoners, especially Dull Knife and his family. He became quite fond of one of Dull Knife's daughters, whom he may have nicknamed "the Princess." Soon, the Cheyennes began calling Wessells "Pose Hausha" (Long Nose).[44]

But forces were at work, even before Dull Knife's surrender on Chadron Creek, to return his people to Indian Territory. The state of Kansas demanded temporary custody of the Indians in order to identify and prosecute those individuals who had allegedly committed the depredations in September and October. But the dogged commitment of the Cheyennes to remain in the North did not go unnoticed. In October, Maj. Caleb Carleton wrote to Gen. Crook, "If [the] prisoners are to go south it will be necessary to tie and haul them."[45] In early November, Red Cloud warned Carleton that the Cheyennes would kill themselves rather that return to the Darlington Agency.[46] On November 11, 1878, the state of Kansas made a formal request for the surrender of the Cheyennes and their removal to Fort Wallace. The request named Little Wolf, Dull Knife, Wild Hog, and Old Crow, the very chiefs who had tried to prevent violence, as the main instigators of the raids.[47]

Finally, on November 22, the Commissioner of Indian Affairs, Ezra Hayt, formally accepted the recommendation of authorities in Kansas and the Secretary of the Interior, Carl Schurz, and the War Department approved it. On December 16, General Crook received a copy of this communication through General Sheridan instructing him to send the Cheyenne prisoners to Fort Leavenworth under heavy guard.[48]

"I may say that my own opinion coincides with that expressed by General Sheridan," Secretary Schurz told the U.S. Senate, "when he says that 'unless they are sent back the whole reservation system will receive a shock which will endanger their stability.' It was, therefore, necessary that the Indians should be taken back to their reservation."[49] No matter how strong the pleas of the Ohmeseheso, in January 1879 the government was not about to ignore the citizens of Kansas and forgive the Indians for killing settlers during their trek north.

By December 1878, Carleton, followed by Wessells, stepped up negotiations to persuade the Northern Cheyennes to accept their fate and move back south. During this time, the soldiers discovered that Dull Knife's son, Bull Hump, had escaped from Fort Robinson.

Although he was later discovered at Pine Ridge visiting his wife and returned to the fort, Bull Hump's escape resulted in the soldiers tightening the guard and restricting the Indians' privileges, further measures designed to persuade the Indians to return south. By midmonth Wessells brought in James Rowland as interpreter to aid the officers in exerting almost daily pressure on the chiefs to return to Darlington Agency. "We will not go there to live," Dull Knife told them through Rowland. "That is not a healthful country, and if we should stay there, we would all die. . . . No, I am here on my own ground, and I will never go back. You may kill me here; but you cannot make me go back."[50]

Later Wessells brought in Lakotas Red Cloud, American Horse, Red Dog, and No Flesh from Pine Ridge to a council with himself, the Cheyenne chiefs, and Capt. P. D. Vroom, 3rd Cavalry. Vroom was a new officer on the scene, now commanding four companies of reinforcements in cantonment at Camp Canby near the post. "We can not help you," Red Cloud told the Ohmeseheso assembled. "The snows are thick on the hills. Our ponies are thin. The game is scarce. You cannot resist; nor can we. So listen to your old friend and do without complaint what the Great Father tells you."[51] After hearing Dull Knife and Wild Hog explain their fears of making a journey south in the dead of winter, Wessells requested clothing and moccasins from Red Cloud's Lakotas for the Cheyennes to use on the journey south. "With their usual generosity they responded at once," Wessells wrote, "furnishing enough for the whole Cheyenne band and some to spare."[52]

Still the chiefs would not consent to go. Realizing the influence of Wild Hog over some of the younger warriors, Wessells began including him more frequently in the parleys in his quarters. "This is our home," Wild Hog told Wessells at one of these parleys, "here we have been raised; here we have buried our fathers and our children and we cannot live in the Indian Territory. If you will allow us to remain we will do anything the Great Father may require of us. We will live like white people, work and wear their clothes. We will never make trouble."[53]

Fort Robinson, Nebraska, as it appeared in 1879 at the time of the Northern Cheyenne's odyssey. The rugged bluff country is visible in the background. Courtesy Nebraska State Historical Society.

Dull Knife's diminishing leadership at this juncture may have been augmented by sickness and fever that befell him toward the end of December. "During these days Dull Knife was very sick," Sgt. Carter P. Johnson remembered, "and on several occasions, two of the [Cheyennes] carried him out naked and rolled his fevered body in the snow. He would lie there in the snow for awhile, naked, and then be carried back. He would not consent to be treated in any other way."[54] But Dull Knife recovered by the first of the year and grew more adamant than ever before. "The only way you can get us there [Darlington Agency] is to come in here with clubs, knock us on the head, drag us out and take us down there dead," he told Wessells around New Year's Day 1879. "We have nothing to defend ourselves with, and you can come in here with clubs and kill us like dogs. If that is not enough, you can cut us up into smaller pieces and feed us to your soldiers."[55]

On January 5, 1879, Captain Wessells cut off food and firewood to the Indians in order to force their compliance. The situation now became a test of wills between the commanding officer at Fort Robinson and the Cheyennes, an impasse that practically assured the violence to come. Wessells later justified his decision by claiming that the action was more humane "than to knock the building down with the field pieces that were standing only a few yards from the prison."[56]

Still the Northern Cheyennes endured as best they could while remaining defiant. Even before Wessells's starvation order the Indians seemed to sense an impending need for food in days to come, and the enlisted men turned their eyes away as they witnessed the daily impoverishment of their wards. "I often saw squaws under the storehouse picking up corn that rattled through the floor," Sgt. Carter P. Johnson remembered, "and there were considerable quantities of it. They would put it in little sacks and carry it into the barracks, as if preparing for some emergency. After the outbreak we found sacks of parched corn on some of the dead."[57]

On January 8 Wessells cut off water to the Northern Cheyennes, who by now were confined entirely to the barracks for fear of violence. Wessells sent a message that the children be sent out to be fed, and although Dull Knife urged his people to let them go, the younger warriors refused. "They would eat their children," one of the Cheyennes shouted to Sergeant Johnson out the window of the barracks, "and when they were consumed [they] would eat their women and it was no use to try to persuade them—they would all die before they would go back south."[58] Although Wessells sent word that the women too might come out and go to Pine Ridge, that only the men must go south, many of the women refused. "We women and children were told we might go to the agency," Iron Teeth remembered years later. "Some of them went there [the sick and infirm], "but most of us went into the prison with the men."[59] All of those in the barracks became more defiant than ever when

Henry W. Wessells, Jr., Brig.-Gen. Retired, photograph taken circa 1901. Wessells, as captain, 3rd Cavalry, was the temporary commander of Fort Robinson, Nebraska, during the dramatic escape of Dull Knife's people in January 1879. From the collection of Henry Wessells III.

the water was cut off. "They tore up the floor and barricaded the windows," Sergeant Johnson remembered, "and kept up a singing . . . almost constantly. At one time we thought, [as we walked] by the door, that they were roasting one of their dogs."[60]

By January 8 the Indians' frustrations were at fever pitch. "One of them, an old fellow known to be crazy, tried to stab the inside guard with a knife," Sergeant Johnson recalled, "but some of the Indians jumped up and restrained him. On another occasion a woman reached out of a window and struck at a guard's throat with a knife. The guards were now afraid to stay inside the building and were withdrawn."[61] On January 9 Capt. Henry Wessells tried to talk to Dull Knife through a window of the barracks, since the chiefs by then refused to come to his quarters, but "Dull Knife's only reply was a sarcastic smile," Wessells later wrote.[62]

Matters were only made worse when Captain Wessells took hostage Wild Hog, Old Crow, and possibly the Elk Horn Scraper headman, Strong Left Hand, as leverage to force the people to agree to return south. Sensing the diminishing leadership of Dull Knife, Wessells sent for Wild Hog on several occasions on January 9. In the morning he had him speak with 1st Lt. C. A. Johnson, 14th Infantry. Johnson tried sympathy. "It makes me feel bad to see you suffering in the way you are," he said to Wild Hog. "I would not have you suffer if I could help it." Then agency representatives from Pine Ridge tried to convince Wild Hog that the women and children could go to Pine Ridge, but Wild Hog remained resolute and returned to the barracks. In the afternoon Captain Wessells sent the interpreter William Rowland for Wild Hog once again, and although some of the younger men did not want him to go, he and Old Crow left the cold barracks one last time.

"Almost as soon as [I] had entered the [post adjutant's] house the soldiers came in and surrounded us," Wild Hog remembered in August 1879. "The commanding officer then said to us, 'Now, we want you to say what you are going to do, right away.' I repeated what we had said before, that the weather was so cold that we should all perish if we tried to make the journey with the snow so deep."[63]

At this juncture, Captain Wessells stood up and said "Will you go or will you not?"[64] When the Indians did not comply, Wessells signaled for the guard to seize Wild Hog. "From the motions of the soldiers I thought they were going to kill me," Wild Hog testified before a Senate Select Committee, "then I concluded I would stab myself. I thought I would rather kill myself than be killed by anybody else. Then the soldiers sprang at me and grabbed my arm and we had a tussle."[65] In the ensuing struggle, Wild Hog, who weighed 250 pounds, pulled his knife and stabbed Pvt. Thomas Ferguson, E Company, 3rd Cavalry, in the sternum, opening a wound about 3/4-inch long and 1/2-inch deep. Other troopers secured Wild Hog's hands and wrestled him to the floor. Private Ferguson was treated by the post surgeon and returned to duty on January 19, 1879.[66]

After the soldiers wrestled Wild Hog down, Wessells ordered him put in irons. "I was myself sitting on a chair, with a soldier guarding me," Old Crow remembered. "When I saw that they had Hog ironed, I said, 'Come and iron me, too'; I let them iron me without any trouble."[67] "Then they put irons on [Strong] Left Hand," Wild Hog testified; "he was the third one ironed."[68]

As the prisoners were led out of the barracks, Strong Left Hand cried out to the Indians in the barracks, "They have got Wild Hog."[69] The prisoners were taken in an ambulance to Camp Canby, a mile from the post, and put in the charge of Capt. Joseph Lawson, 3rd Cavalry, but soon Wild Hog requested to be taken back to the fort to talk to his people. "So we took him up," remembered Sgt. Carter P. Johnson, who was in Lawson's camp, and he talked through the window to them awhile. [He] wanted to go inside but was not permitted to do so. [He] said he wanted to take his family out. He was told he could take out the families of himself [and] Old Crow. . . . He took out a small daughter but none of his children who could take care of themselves including a grown daughter some of the soldiers befriended." They had named her "Blanche" and talked with her often because she could speak, English as well as read and write the language of the Vehoe. "He did, however, take out nineteen old infirm women," Johnson continued, "and they were brought down to our camp with him. He no doubt had method in this knowing that there would be an outbreak and wanting to get the infirm out of the way. I asked him why he did not bring all of his children but he said they were big enough to take care of themselves."[70]

Indeed, Wild Hog's intuition was correct. That evening Wessells made one last attempt to talk Dull Knife out by speaking to him through a crack in the chinking of the barracks logs. Dull Knife told Wessells that he would like to come out but the others would not let him. Then he retired to a corner of the room with the other old people, his leadership over the young warriors irreparably eroded. A similar request was made to Tangle Hair, but the young warriors would not let him go either. Failing in their attempt to weaken the resolve of the people by separating them from their important chiefs, Wessells ordered the barracks secured and the door chained to prevent escape.[71] With Wild Hog in irons the leadership of the young men fell to Tangle Hair, the Dog Soldier.

As darkness swept over the frozen Nebraska plains on January 9, 1879, the Northern Cheyennes prepared for what would become a defining moment in their history. There were 125 of them now locked in the prison barracks at Fort Robinson, Wild Hog having succeeded in removing twenty or so. Forty-four men were of fighting age. They prepared to make a dash for freedom—or death. George B. Grinnell states that it was Little Shield who said, "Now, dress up in your best clothing. We will all die together." Said another, according to Grinnell, "We may as well die here as be taken back south to die there." Yet another Cheyenne, according to Grinnell's interviews, said, "It is true that we must die, but we will not die shut up here like dogs; we will die on the prairie; we will die fighting." So they painted their faces and put on what light war clothing they still possessed, even though there was over a half foot of snow covering the ground and the mercury stood at zero.[72] As Wild Hog remembered of his comrades and family in the barracks, "If they were to die anyway, they [were] determined to sell their lives as dearly as possible."[73]

The Indians had covered the windows with blankets. Now they tore up a board under a wood stove where they had earlier secreted the weapons from the soldiers. They had only a few rifles and about eleven revolvers, reassembled from the small parts that the women and children wore as jewelry. Then the Cheyennes kissed each other for the last time. They piled their parfleches, saddles, and other bulky belongings under the windows, which were located on all sides of the building, so they could quickly escape through them. Little Shield sat in a north window, while Tangle Hair stood by at another.[74]

Some of the soldiers were aware that the Northern Cheyennes were preparing an escape. Pvt. Julius Janzohn, F Company, remembered hearing the Indians "tearing up the floor in the afternoon. We looked in the windows [the Cheyennes had tried as best they could to cover the windows] and saw them making war clubs of the floor boards."[75]

Among the women, Iron Teeth was prepared to face death. She had earlier spread her family blanket over the boards where the few guns and rounds of ammunition were hidden. In the bodice of her dress she concealed a revolver. In her pack was the beloved hide scraper that she would not leave behind for any reason. The "women cut up robes to make extra moccasins," she remembered years later. "I made extra pairs for myself and my three children. . . . each woman held her own pack ready at hand. The plan was to break out just after the soldiers had gone to bed for the night. I gave to my son the six-shooter I had. He was my oldest child, then twenty-two years of age." After thanking his mother for the weapon, Gathering His Medicine took his place at a window with Little Shield, Tangle Hair, and the others.[76]

The men hoped to smash the windows, fell the sentries by firing shots through the broken panes, then help their people escape through the windows and make a dash for the White River.[77] The

THE IMPRISONED CHEYENNES FORTIFYING THEIR TEMPORARY QUARTERS AT FORT ROBINSON.

This drawing of Dull Knife's followers fortifying their prison barracks at Fort Robinson in January 1879 appeared in *Frank Leslie's Illustrated Newspaper*, February 15, 1879. Courtesy Nebraska State Historical Society.

men would seize weapons from the fallen guards and cover the women and children from the front as they fled. A group of warriors would set up a rear guard to keep the troopers busy while the others escaped. If they made it away from the fort, they hoped to obtain horses at the Deadman Ranch, five miles south.

Taps sounded at 9:00 P.M. Soon only a couple of lights burned in the soldier's quarters and in the trader's store. Outside the moon cast a bright glow on the white snow. Anyone caught in the open would make an easy target. Inside the Indians' barracks, 125 sick and hungry people prepared to risk their lives for freedom.

At 10:00 P.M. Little Shield ripped the blankets from a window, smashed the windowpane, and tore out the boards covering the window. He was the first to fire from the west end of the barracks, followed in quick succession by Tangle Hair, Gathering His Medicine, and probably Noisy Walker [Noisy Walking] and Blacksmith. Tangle Hair was the first to jump out of the building. The wife of a warrior named Black Bear was among the first to reach the outside.[78] "My son [Gathering His Medicine] smashed a window with the gun I had given him," Iron Teeth remembered. "We all jumped out."[79]

The opening volley by the Indians was deadly and took the sentries, all 3rd Cavalrymen, by complete surprise, despite their cautious watchfulness on duty that night. Pvt. Frank Schmidt, A Company, screamed as he raised up his hands and fell backwards dead, a bullet in his abdomen. Pvt. Peter Hulse, also of A Company, was struck in the leg almost as quickly. He died of his wounds on January 24. Pvt. Daniel Timmany, E Company, was shot in the arm by a warrior with a revolver at one of the windows, possibly Gathering His Medicine. He later recovered as did Pvt. Edward Glavin, also of E Company, who received a superficial gunshot wound on his right thumb.

Quickly other troopers on guard duty that night opened the door to the guardroom attached to the Indians' barracks. Pvt. James E. McHale was one of these men. He was wounded by a shot

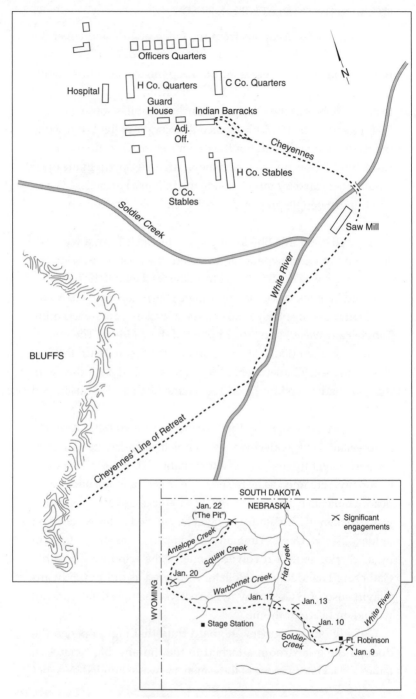

The breakout from the barracks at Fort Robinson.

from a carbine shoved between the logs of a partition. A warrior escaping out the door also wounded Pvt. James Emory of C Company in the guardroom. When Corporal of the Guard Edward F. Pulver, L Company, started to come through the door, a warrior shot him through the window with a revolver. These troopers survived.[80]

Many of the Northern Cheyennes that night were not so fortunate. Within moments after the first volley, sleepy-eyed troopers poured out of their barracks, most in their long winter underwear. They began shooting randomly at the fleeing Cheyennes, often unable or unwilling to distinguish between men and women. Some chased the Indians barefoot across the snow, southeast of the barracks.

The Indians had tied their blankets around their waists and necks in order to leave their hands free. When they escaped from the windows on the east side of the barracks, they rushed south for the bridge below the post sawmill and the confluence of Soldier Creek and the White River. Their intention was to follow the shelter of the White River away from the post. Upon reaching the bridge, many Indians stopped for a drink, their first in two days, but bullets were flying fast. Some of the Cheyennes cut across the bends of the river several times, breaking through ice as they did and soaking themselves in the freezing water. Soon, they began to scatter. Those carrying heavy loads and children on their backs began to fall behind.[81]

Iron Teeth was fortunate. She escaped along White River in to the broken country away from the fort:

My son took the younger of [my] two daughters upon his back. The older daughter and I each carried a little pack. It was expected the soldiers would be asleep, except a few of the guards. But bands of them came hurrying to shoot at us. One of them fired a gun almost into my face, but I was not harmed. . . . For a short distance all of the Indians followed one broken trail toward the river, but soon we had to scatter. My son with the little girl on his back ran off in one direction, while the other daughter and I went in another direction. We had not any agreed plan for meeting again. I and the daughter with me found a cave and crawled into it. We did not know what had become of [my] son and his little sister. A man named Crooked Nose came into our cave. We could hear lots of shooting. Four of my friends were shot to death the night we broke out.[82]

Capt. Henry Wessells heard the first shots. I "had just undressed and was getting into bed when the crack of a carbine was heard and loud it sounded on that still night," he wrote in his journal. "But the stillness was over for more shots were quickly fired followed by the groans of the wounded."[83] By then the fleeing Cheyennes had swiftly moved to the river crossing. Wessells put on his greatcoat and ran out into the night, unarmed. No other officers had yet come out. When Wessells reached the barracks, he found a group of soldiers huddled behind the guardhouse "as if waiting for some officer to command them. [I] ordered them to pursue," Wessells remembered years later, "and shoot down the Indians—which they did, killing both men and women."[84] Then Wessells turned out C Company from their quarters, and they poured volley after volley into the Indians, who were now all out of the prison barracks.[85]

As the people fled toward the river, Tangle Hair and a few of the warriors set up a rear guard to cover them as his Dog Soldiers had often done in past battles with the Vehoe. There were five in the rear guard, including Blacksmith and Noisy Walking. They held their ground for a time and then broke and ran behind the others. All five were shot down. Tangle Hair managed to drag himself to one of the soldier barracks where he was captured and taken to the post hospital after his wounds were dressed.[86] "The soldiers fired on us, and then it was just like shooting cattle," Tangle Hair remembered of this experience, "we dropped dead one after another as we ran. I dodged and doubled as I ran, but was wounded and captured, and brought back to the post."[87] Sgt. John M. Mitchell, M Company, remembered that after the Cheyennes' "rear guard was silenced only half a dozen shots [were] fired by the Indians on the parade ground."[88]

A number of the fleeing Cheyennes headed for the sawmill, southeast along the river and across the bridge on the White River about a mile away. Troopers of C Company soon caught up with some of them. Second Lieutenant J. F. Cummings's mount stumbled into a washout near the sawmill and the officer nearly fell on top of two hiding Cheyennes. They attacked him with knives, the only weapons they had. He killed both with his revolver only to find they were women. A sergeant and several troopers pursued a man and a woman. The Indians turned on the soldiers. The warrior was armed with a revolver, the woman with a piece of iron stove. They were shot down.[89] An unidentified Cheyenne, who might have witnessed this episode, left history the following account.

"Some people who were ahead of me got to the top of [a] hill, but I got out of breath and stopped by a big tree with some other women. One of these was the wife of White Antelope. She was already wounded, and White Antelope was carrying the baby. When the soldiers got up close, White Antelope rushed back on them with a knife and fought for a little while and was killed. When the soldiers had come up close I was shot in the back and in the side of the head and knocked senseless, and knew nothing after that. Two other women were killed there."[90]

Several men and women were caught near the sawmill and were shot down. One woman was found with six bullet holes in her body. Second Lieutenant George F. Chase came upon an old man hiding in the brush along the river. He called out to him, but the man refused to surrender and was shot.[91] This running fight along the sawmill road to the river continued for about a mile. According to a *New York Herald* correspondent who arrived on the scene, "Volley after volley was poured into the fleeing [Cheyennes] and as earnestly returned by the Indians, who sped toward the sawmill, which lies south[east], and their bleeding bodies, mangled and torn, bucks, squaws and papooses all together, literally strewed the road they had selected for their much hoped for deliverance."[92]

Sgt. Carter P. Johnson, now riding with C Company, remembered pursuing the Northern Cheyennes to the river and beyond that night. "We drove them upstream, and they fought stubbornly," he recalled, "fighting as a rear guard for the women and children. We pursued them and killed [and wounded them] scattering twenty-six lying dead [and wounded] between their barracks and the willows along the stream every little ways they would make a stand in the brush and try to stand us off."[93] "They could not be taken," Pvt. James W. Payne, C Company, remembered, "as they were desperate and seemed to want to die rather than surrender. Those who had arms and were wounded continued to fire as long as they could raise up."[94]

Some of the Indians did not get very far from the barracks. Old Sitting Man, who had broken his leg during the trek north, rebroke it when he jumped from the window. He could not move. Knowing the end was near he sat there in the snow on the eastern edge of the parade ground outside the barracks, probably chanting his death song, as a trooper ran up and put the muzzle of his carbine against his head and fired. Survivors remembered seeing the top of Old Sitting Man's head fly off. According to George B. Grinnell, "Later he was seen lying there with the top of his skull beside him in one place, and all of his brains on the snow in another place."[95]

A newspaper correspondent, going over the scene of the fighting the next day, confirmed that some of the killing was at close quarters. "The soldiers . . . were now aroused to the highest pitch of exasperation," he wrote of the fighting on January 9, "and where the first shot did not dispose of the victim, a coup de grace was readily given by final pistol charge."[96] Rancher Edgar Beecher Bronson, who arrived on the scene toward the end of the fighting, later wrote that "many of the dead were powder-burned."[97]

In some cases the soldiers of the 3rd Cavalry showed compassion toward the wounded and the children. Very soon after Tangle Hair was shot, at the beginning of the fight, and brought into the post hospital, he remembered seeing wounded women starting to be brought in to the infirmary.[98] For the next two weeks, Assistant Surgeon Edward B. Moseley and Acting Assistant Surgeon C. V. Pettys administered to the wounded Cheyennes. Moseley kept meticulous records that demonstrate the excellent care given to the wounded Indians as well as the military personnel.[99]

Later that night in the fighting in the bluffs above the river bank, 1st Lt. C. A. Johnson found a baby lying next to a dead woman. He recovered the infant and sent it to his wife at the fort for care. In another instance Capt. Henry Wessells found a child less than two years old and carried it a hundred yards to a place of safety. One correspondent observed that "the men . . . were tender in caring for the squaws if they had done no harm."[100]

Like Iron Teeth, others were fortunate enough to find hiding places. Young Miles Seminole was with his mother when she found refuge in the hollow of a large tree trunk on the river bank. From this spot they heard the struggles along the stream during the night. At one point, a group of soldiers passed within twenty yards of them. The soldiers had with them a young woman they had recaptured.[101]

Shortly after the firing began outside the barracks, Capt. P. D. Vroom's troops at Camp Canby about a mile away, saddled up and quickly reached the scene moving toward the fort and the southernmost bluffs above the river. Vroom ordered Companies A and E across the road leading from the sawmill along the river. Soon Captain Wessells with Companies C and H and 2nd Lt. George F. Chase with F Company closed down the road behind the Indians. The Cheyennes, mostly unarmed, began fleeing into the hills above the western bank of the river. Vroom ordered his left flank up the bluff and then ordered the line forward to cut off the Indians' line of flight. Chase sent some of his men back to the fort, then dismounted and joined the skirmishers on the left.[102]

Here in the hills above the river, a good number of the Ohmeseheso were killed or wounded, including White Antelope and his wife. When the soldiers caught up with the exhausted Indians, they would ask for their surrender, but most refused, fulfilling their pledge to die in the north rather than be returned to Indian Territory. When they refused the offer, they were shot down. Eventually, Lieutenant Chase ordered a rear detail to recover the wounded in the hills and down along the road and take them to the post hospital.[103]

A Cheyenne boy, probably Young Pumpkinseed (Big Beaver), later remembered this time of panic and desperation.

A good many were killed here, but some young men jumped up and ran to and through the line of soldiers who were standing ten or twelve feet apart and so escaped. I was not hit by bullets, but the powder from a close shot had burned me.

"After running a hundred yards, we came to some great sandstone bluffs, in which there were large holes, and into these holes we crept. We could hear the women and children crying, and at last the shooting stopped. Sometime after . . . wagons were heard coming. In the wagons they must have loaded up all that were left alive, for as they went back, women could be heard crying. After this we heard the wagons coming back, and again going away, taking the dead.[104]

Many of those killed or wounded that night along the river and above in the hills were women. Most of the Indians were now in tattered clothing with their blankets tied around them. As Wessells later told reporters, his men often had trouble distinguishing between men and women. Some women fought alongside their men, equally determined also to sell their lives for freedom. Certainly some of these women were easily discernible because they were with children, but they were shot down anyway simply because they were escaping. Captain Wessells remembered seeing an Indian rise up behind a bush. Assuming the Indian was a warrior, he ordered the troopers nearest to him to shoot. A soldier fired and killed the Indian. Examining the body, Wessells found it was that of an eighty-year-old woman who had become exhausted and confused.[105]

Somewhere in the hills above the river, Dull Knife and his family searched for safety. Dull Knife and one of his wives had escaped the barracks with their daughters, their son, Bull Hump, and Dull Knife's father-in-law, Great Eyes. Several other family members followed close behind, but soon the group became separated. Dull Knife, his wife, and Bull Hump found refuge in a hole among the rocks.[106] His younger daughter was not so fortunate. She stopped momentarily, with some other women, to assist several fleeing children.[107] Later, probably the following morning, someone, probably the interpreter William Rowland, found a group of five women who had been shot down together. All were dead except for Dull Knife's daughter, who was severely wounded. Although Rowland tried to speak to her, she breathed her last breath and died as he cradled her in his arms. On her back was a dead child she had tried to rescue. Nearby were the corpses of two or three other children.[108]

Upon hearing the sounds of the fighting that night, neighboring ranchers and other civilians scoured the countryside for the Northern Cheyennes. Among them was Edgar Beecher Bronson, who was fearful that the escaping Indians might try to steal horses from his ranch south of the post. Leaving eight men to guard his ranch, Bronson and a lad named Matthews rode into Fort Robinson to lend assistance. "Half-way to the garrison we could hear heavy firing on our left," he later wrote in his memoirs, "which told us the chase led . . . up the White River Valley." Soon Bronson and Matthews found the trail of carnage leading from the sawmill along the river. "There at our feet, grim and stark and terrible in the moonlight, lay the dead and wounded," Bronson remembered, "so thick for a long way that one could leap from one body to another; there they lay grim and stark . . . lean and gaunt as wolves from starvation, awful with their wounds, infinitely pathetic on this bitter night in their ragged, half-clothed nakedness."

Riding across the trail, Bronson recognized one of the Cheyenne casualties.[109] "He lay on his back, with arms extended and face upturned," Bronson remembered. "In his right hand he held a small knife. . . . As I sat there on my horse . . . believing him dead . . . suddenly he rose to a sitting position and aimed a fierce blow at my leg with his knife. Instinctively, as he rose, I spurred my horse out of his reach and jerked my pistol, but before I could use it he fell back and lay still—dead." Bronson dismounted and took the warrior's knife as a souvenir, cutting the sheath from the Cheyenne's waist.

Soon Lt. George Baxter, leading some half-dressed troopers back to the fort, cut Bronson's trail. "Where are your Indians, George?" Bronson called to him. "Every mother's son gone but those laid out along the trail, old man," he replied. "Then Matt[hews] and I rode on to the post," Bronson recalled, "meeting Lieut. Jim Simpson and Dr. Pettys, out with a waggon [sic] and detail of men, gathering up the dead and wounded."[110]

Late that night, when the fighting stopped, Lt. J. F. Cummings was still in the field looking for wounded. Surprised by two gunshots nearby, Cummings rode forward to investigate. He found about twelve civilians there in the darkness, fully armed. One was J. W. Dear, a post trader since 1874. After Cummings passed these men on the trail he found no more living casualties. "Since there were no soldiers [in the vicinity]," he told an investigating committee of army officers shortly afterwards, "I was convinced that these citizens were killing wounded Indians."[111]

Toward dawn, Lt. Cummings found collaborative evidence to his assertion. First Lieutenant Emmett Crawford, 2d Lt. F. H. Hardie, and 1st Lt. James F. Simpson were in the bluffs at that hour still looking for wounded. They found two women, still alive, whom they carried back to Fort Robinson wrapped in blankets. The officers examined the corpses they came across for evidence of scalping or sexual violations by the soldiers. They found no such evidence, although all the Indians they discovered in the vicinity were dead.[112] During this time, however, the officers discovered three civilians with a buckboard at the base of the bluffs. They were William E. Cook, a division superintendent on the Sidney and Black Hills Express Line, and Henry Clifford, a part-time interpreter at Fort Robinson. The officers heard the third, unidentified man shout to the others from the buckboard, instructing them to bring down blankets from the corpses of the dead Cheyennes. Lieutenant Crawford also heard one of the men say that although he had gotten to the scene too late for the fighting, he had arrived in time to "kill a Squaw."[113]

So the fighting ended in the early morning hours of January 10, 1879. Although some still lay in the bluffs, about twenty-six Cheyennes had already died, fourteen of them men, the remainder women and children. Later on the morning of January 10, two more women and two more children died of wounds in the post hospital. By sunrise close to thirty people were being treated for wounds by Drs. Moseley and Pettys.[114] The frozen bodies of those who died that night "were buried near the post, on the flat," Capt. Henry Wessells remembered.[115] At least they would not have to go south.

## CHAPTER SEVEN

# NEBRASKA

## *Butchery in the Hat Creek Bluffs*

*We stayed in the cave seven nights and almost seven days.
More snow kept falling, it was very cold, but we were afraid
to build a fire. We nibbled at my small store of dry meat and
melted snow for water. Each day we could hear the horses and
the voices of soldiers searching for Indians.*

—IRON TEETH,
1926

During the early morning hours of January 10, 1879, the Cheyennes
who were hiding in the bluffs above White River could still hear
the hoofbeats of the soldiers' horses as the troopers hunted for them.
When the 3rd Cavalrymen recovered frozen corpses from the field,
they brought them back to the sawmill below the fort and laid
them out in rows by sex and age.[1] Shortly before sunrise, 2d Lt. J.
F. Cummings noticed that the civilian interpreter, Henry Clifford,
was still in the hills with a companion. Cummings found Clifford
holding an old warrior and a small child at gunpoint, with a number
of bodies strewn about in the rocks nearby. Clifford told Lt. Cummings that the old man was a Lakota married to a Cheyenne and
that he believed there were still many Cheyennes hiding in the
bluffs. Warning the civilians that no Indians were to be killed

unless absolutely necessary, Lt. Cummings had the old Lakota go through the ravines calling to the Cheyennes in their language, telling them that it would be better for them to come out and surrender than to die fighting.

Returning to the bodies he had discovered in Clifford's presence, Cummings found the first evidence of mutilation and sexual molestation. All of the corpses at that spot in the bluffs had been scalped; one of them had been scalped twice. In addition, the dresses of the dead women had been pulled over their heads exposing their bodies. When the bodies were brought to Fort Robinson, Dr. Moseley found evidence that several of the Indians had been shot after they were dead. One man's face was completely blown away.[2] On February 2 Lt. Cummings testified before a three officer investigating board that it was his most decided opinion the two "citizens were the men who exposed and mutilated the bodies."[3] Henry Clifford denied the accusations, stating that he had found the corpses exposed and mutilated.[4]

Later in the day, 2d Lt. Cummings heard shots near the face of a cliff. Riding up to the rock wall, he discovered a cave; several troopers were bringing a Cheyenne woman, a boy, an adolescent girl, and a small child out of the cave. The boy held a knife in his hand. He was the last male alive, for near the entrance to the cave were the bodies of two young warriors who had refused to surrender. They turned out to be Dog Soldiers, and the woman and the boy were Tangle Hair's wife and son. Cummings returned them to the fort where they were reunited with their wounded father.[5]

About midday, rancher Edgar Beecher Bronson was returning to his ranch from Fort Robinson when he heard the reports of rifles coming from Lt. George Baxter's H Company men up in the bluffs south of the post. Bronson rode to the crest of a nearby ridge and saw Baxter's soldiers formed in a skirmish line. "Dropping behind a tree and looking down-hill," Bronson remembered, "I saw a faint curl of smoke rising from a little washout one hundred yards below me, and, crouched beside the smoldering fire in the washout, a lone

Indian." Bronson supposed the Cheyenne had been heading for his ranch to procure a horse and had been thwarted by frostbitten feet. He later found out the details of this incident.[6]

Observing the smoke, Baxter found the fire and left two troopers at the site. Then he and the remainder of his men rode up a slope to find the trail of the Indians who had been using the fire. When the two troopers guarding the campsite approached the washout in which the fire was located, they discovered a lone warrior concealed on the ground under a gray canvas sheet. Private W. W. Everett called out to him, "Come out and surrender." Suddenly the warrior rose up, threw off the canvas, and fired twice, mortally wounding Everett in the abdomen. Everett died the next day.[7]

After hearing the shooting, Baxter swung his company around along the top of the ridge and opened fire on the old Cheyenne's position. Bronson rode up to Baxter's line in time to see Capt. Joseph Lawson, with reinforcements, near the foot of the ridge. Lawson ordered his troopers to dismount and advance on the warrior in skirmish order. Sixty guns were now aimed at one Cheyenne, an old man determined to live free or die on the spot. "Toward the last I plainly saw him fire his carbine three times with his left hand," Bronson recalled, "resting the barrel along the edge of the washout, while his right hand hung helpless beside him." Soon the man's gun fell silent. He had been hit five times, "once through the right shoulder," Bronson ascertained, "once through the left cheek, once through the right side, and a fourth ball toward the last had completely shattered his right wrist," leaving him to fire with his left hand. The final shot, which killed him, tore off a piece of his skull and ripped into his brain.[8]

Captain Lawson and the other officers that day had to balance the deaths of those Ohmeseheso who had fought to the end, refusing to surrender against impossible odds, with those, mostly women and children, whose lives had been saved. Shortly before the skirmish with the old warrior, Lawson had followed a trail in the snow along White River. Where the tracks ended, one of Lawson's troopers had discovered a small girl about seven years old, sitting alone in the snow, playing with a deck of cards. They gently wrapped her in a blanket and Lawson and his men escorted her back to the fort.[9]

Hiding in another hole in the rocks that day was Iron Teeth's eldest son, Gathering His Medicine, along with his little sister. They had become separated from their mother in the confusion of the previous night near the post sawmill. Sometime on January 10, they heard troopers approaching. Gathering His Medicine was convinced they would be discovered and prepared at once to save his little sister's life. "Lie down, and I will cover you with leaves and dirt," the little girl later remembered her brother telling her. "Then I will climb out and fight the soldiers. They will kill me but they will think I am the only one here, and they will go away after I am dead. When they are gone, you can come out and hunt for our mother."[10]

Gathering His Medicine concealed his little sister, then jumped up from their hiding place and began shooting at the soldiers with the revolver his mother had given him just before the escape from the barracks the night before. But the young Cheyenne was out-gunned and without hope. The soldiers opened up with concentrated volley fire, and Gathering His Medicine was cut down where he stood. The next day, troopers discovered his little sister wandering in the bluffs and carried her back to Fort Robinson unharmed.

Six days passed, however, before the little girl would be reunited with her mother and could tell her the details of the death of Gathering His Medicine. In the hills, Iron Teeth and a man named Crooked Nose hid in a hole in the rocks. On January 10 "we still heard shots," she remembered years later, "but not so many. . . . We stayed in the cave seven nights and almost seven days. More snow kept falling, it was very cold, but we were afraid to build a fire. We nibbled at my small store of dry meat and melted snow for water. Each day we could hear the horses and the voices of soldiers searching for Indians. Finally, [about January 15] a Captain found tracks where we had gone out and back into the cave. He called to us. I crept out. He promised to treat us well if we would go with him. He and his soldiers then took us back to Fort Robinson."

Iron Teeth suffered from mild frostbite on her toes and fingers. The surgeon told her to rub snow on them. Afraid to ask about her son and youngest daughter for fear of letting the soldiers know they might still be at large, Iron Teeth searched for her children among the survivors who had been recaptured. Finally she found her little girl. "I asked her about her brother," Iron Teeth recalled. At first, "it appeared she did not hear me, so I asked again. This time she burst out crying. Then I knew he had been killed. She told me how it had been done."[11]

Unlike Gathering His Medicine, Young Pumpkinseed (Big Beaver) cheated death. After running a gauntlet of bullets the night before to the safety of holes in the cliffs, Young Pumpkinseed and his four companions were discovered by troops about sundown on January 10. They had one rifle and one pistol among them. "The troops began to shoot into the holes where we were and kept shooting," Young Pumpkinseed remembered years later when he was known as Big Beaver, "and presently all had been killed except me. When I looked about and saw that every one of my friends was dead, I did not know what to do. I waited, and at length the soldiers stopped firing."

Young Pumpkinseed then came out of his hiding place to face the soldiers alone, resigned to his death. He began walking toward the soldiers. "A white man called out something and no one fired at me," he recalled. An "officer rode toward me and drew his saber, but did not strike me with it. When the officer had come close to me, he reached out his hand and I stretched out my hand, and we shook hands. The officer called up his soldiers and they surrounded me. I . . . was helped up behind a soldier on his horse and taken into the post."[12]

On the morning of January 10, Capt. Henry Wessells assembled those Cheyennes who had been recaptured the first night and asked them, "Now will you go south?" A wounded girl replied, "No, we will not go back; we will die rather. You have killed most of us, why do you not go ahead now and finish the work?"[13] Beginning that morning, Wessells pressed a relentless war of attrition against those Northern Cheyennes still hiding in the countryside. He alerted agency personnel at Pine Ridge to be on the lookout for any Cheyennes seeking refuge among Lakota friends. Ranchers were told to round up all of their horses and cattle and secure them in order to keep the Cheyennes on foot and without food. Wessells sent troops west up Soldier Creek and southwest along the White River breaks to locate the scattered Indians. Crook, meanwhile, bolstered the effort by ordering additional troops of the 3rd Cavalry to be ready to move to the scene at a moment's notice. Wessells's orders were to give any Indians discovered in the hills and bluffs a fair chance to surrender, and the troops were to fire on them only when they met resistance. Considering the Indians' limited firearms, the cold weather, their lack of adequate clothing, and their relative inability to forage for food, the commander at Fort Robinson thought it would be only a matter of time before they gave up. Little did he realize the determination of these Ohmeseheso to be free or die fighting for the right to live in their beloved north country. Starved and exposed to the elements, some of the people of Dull Knife's band held out for almost two weeks, until January 22, 1879.

"Day after day the fighting went on," Sgt. Carter P. Johnson remembered. "Each time we had them in a tight place Wessells would spend an hour or two calling on them to surrender and not be killed. By this time night would come and he would leave a company on guard and go back to the post, setting out from there again before daylight, to find that the Indians had gone and scattered. We would trail them in the snow and by the middle of [the afternoon] would have them together again, only to repeat the proceedings of the day before."[14]

By mid-January, Wessells had committed six companies (A, C, E, F, H, and L) of the 3rd Cavalry to the field to hunt down the remaining Northern Cheyennes. On the first day, troops of Capt. P. D. Vroom's L Company and elements of A Company guided by

Lakota scout Woman's Dress pressured some of the Indians twenty miles away from the fort along the Hat Creek telegraph road and into bluffs above Soldier Creek. Here the Indians entrenched and held off a charge by the soldiers, mortally wounding Cpl. Henry P. Orr of A Company through the left lung and killing several cavalry horses.[15] Upon hearing the firing of the skirmishers, Wessells rode up with Lieutenant Chase's A Company and parleyed with the Indians, but to no avail. Toward dusk, Wessells ordered a withdrawal back to Fort Robinson. The Indians in the bluffs feasted on horsemeat that night.[16]

By January 11 a party of about eighteen warriors had gathered and entrenched themselves in bluffs above Soldier Creek. Among them was Little Finger Nail, the artist, who still carried his ledger book depicting the exploits of the Northern Cheyennes securely tied to his body. Captain Wessells, riding with Capt. Joseph Lawson's troopers, discovered the Indians in the rocks. Wessells ordered interpreter James Rowland forward to try to convince the Indians to surrender. Reluctantly Rowland approached the Indians, with Wessells by his side. Shots rang out and a bullet whistled between Wessells and Rowland. These warriors would not surrender.[17] The Indians then opened fire on Lawson's troops, killing a horse. During the subsequent return volley, Pvt. Bernard Kelly of E Company was accidentally mortally wounded by one of his comrades.[18] Farrier Peter W. Painter of C Company was shot from his horse, struck in the left shoulder. His wound was slight, and he recovered and returned to duty on February 17. That night, the command returned to Fort Robinson after burning the dead horse to deprive the Cheyennes of food.[19]

Under cover of darkness, the Indians moved back from the bluffs toward the Hat Creek (later called Warbonnet Creek) telegraph road. Second Lieutenant George F. Chase's A Company discovered them in a ravine on the morning of January 12. That day the soldiers pursued the Indians through the rugged Hat Creek Bluffs, occasionally losing the trail, then picking it up again. "We found one moccasin track [in the snow]," Chase remembered,

Woman's Dress (far right) with his family in 1914. Woman's Dress, a Lakota scout for the 3rd Cavalry at Fort Robinson, picked up the trail of Little Finger Nail's refugees, following them to Antelope Creek and the final conflict on January 22, 1879. Courtesy Nebraska State Historical Society.

"evidently made by a lame Indian for we could see the prints of a stick he had used for a cane."[20] Long range shooting was the order of the day. By nightfall Little Finger Nail's party had entrenched in the rugged bluffs at a spot near Hat Creek. The next morning, January 13, 1879, Captain Wessells rode with Lieutenant Baxter's H Company. The troops brought with them a Napoleon artillery piece. By noon the 3rd Cavalrymen began shelling what they thought was the Indians' position. After forty rounds, pickets discovered that the Cheyennes had fallen back unscathed, and after dark the Indians escaped Wessells' grasp once more.[21]

By now the soldiers were pushing Little Finger Nail's party of eighteen starving warriors with their women and children westward. They appeared to be the only Indians not yet recaptured and away from the safety of Pine Ridge Agency. Captain Wessells returned to the fort and came back with a supply wagon and a week's rations. He intended to remain in the field until his business with the Ohmeseheso was finished. By January 16, after losing the Indians' trail regularly for three days, Wessells brought out some Lakota scouts; he was especially hopeful that Woman's Dress and the mixed-blood tracker John Shangreau could locate the Cheyennes.[22]

On January 17 Shangreau picked up the Cheyennes' trail in the bluffs and had come within reach of them when they opened fire on him and the rest of the advance guard of scouts. Shangreau, cut off from Woman's Dress and the other troopers in the advance scout, took refuge behind a tree from where he succeeded in killing a woman in the rocks and a warrior moving towards him.[23] Also in the advance scout was Pvt. Amos J. Barbour of H Company. When the ambush commenced, a Cheyenne shot Barbour from his horse near the Indians' entrenchment. The bullet pierced Barbour's heart, killing him instantly.

Some of the Indians in Little Finger Nail's party rushed forward and retrieved Barbour's body, taking the clothes, except for the bloodstained shirt, as well as the trooper's gun and ammunition. They then scalped Barbour on the right side of the head.[24] The next

morning Wessells took up the pursuit again only to find the Cheyennes had escaped in the night. Shangreau discovered Barbour's
body near the vacated entrenchment, with the scalp laying on a
rock close by. When Shangreau handed Wessells the scalp, Wessells
thought it was a dog skin. When Shangreau explained that it was
the scalp of Private Barbour, Wessells flung it away in frustration
and rage.[25]

Indeed, by this time Wessells felt the pressure of public opinion
mounting against him for his inability to bring less than twenty
tired and half-starved Cheyenne fighting men to bay. Eastern corre-
spondents on the scene were treating the plight of the Northern
Cheyennes with increasing sympathy in the press. One New York
reporter, calling for a federal investigation, wrote, "The Senate had
better begin by inquiring into the reasons why the Cheyennes left
their agency in the Indian Territory."[26] In Washington during mid-
January, Secretary of the Interior Carl Schurz faced an interminable
flow of questions from reporters.[27]

The matter reached the White House, where President Rutherford B. Hayes expressed concern over alleged "unnecessary cruelty"
at Fort Robinson. On January 20, 1879, even before the last of the
Indians had been killed or captured, the army ordered a board of
officers to investigate the treatment of the Northern Cheyenne
prisoners at Fort Robinson. By spring, Secretary Schurz asserted
that "in every respect it would have been better to treat the prisoners well than to treat them harshly."[28]

Dissatisfaction soon reached the Military Department of the
Platte. By January 17 Gen. George Crook decided to remove
Wessells from command at Fort Robinson. Accordingly he ordered
Maj. Andrew W. Evans with two fresh companies of 3rd Cavalry
to march east from Fort Laramie at once to assume command of
the campaign. Evans arrived by stagecoach at Bluff Station on the
Hat Creek telegraph road on January 18, where he presented his
orders to Wessells. By January 20 the combined commands of
Evans and Wessells had pursued the Indian trail, losing it fre-
quently, through more tortuous terrain in the Hat Creek Bluffs, to

"The final fight with the Cheyennes took place on the 22d, fifteen miles from Bluff Station. When the firing ceased the dead bodies of twenty-three Indians were found in the rifle pits occupied by them. This number included seventeen bucks, four squaws, and two papooses. Nine remained, of whom one buck and five squaws were more or less wounded, and three squaws were unhurt." —*Dispatch from Fort Robinson, Neb., to N. Y. Herald.*

BOILED SHOT

CARTRIDGE SOUP

THE LATEST ILLUSTRATION OF OUR HUMANE INDIAN POLICY.

Even political satire in the national media supported the tide of mounting criticism of the army's role in the escape of Dull Knife's followers from Fort Robinson. This cartoon appeared in *Frank Leslie's Illustrated Newspaper*, February 8, 1879. Courtesy Nebraska State Historical Society.

a point not far from the head of Hat (Warbonnet) Creek. Occasionally the Cheyennes fired on the soldiers, and they killed Maj. Evans's horse on the 20th.[29]

Finally Little Finger Nail's party left the shelter of the bluffs for the Antelope Valley, where the snow had melted and they could not be tracked as easily. They hoped to reverse direction and make a forced march eastward to Pine Ridge, but John Shangreau and Woman's Dress found moccasin prints in the soft ground of a prairie dog town on January 21, thereby discerning their line of travel. When Little Finger Nail's people realized they likely would be overtaken, they took refuge in a depression in a dry fork of Antelope Creek (Indian Creek in some accounts), about thirty-five miles northwest of Fort Robinson. It appeared that Capt. Wessells was about to catch his Indians. Mounted, well fed, and dressed for the cold weather in their winter issue coats, the 3rd Cavalry finally had caught up with the ragged band of freezing, hungry Cheyennes, after almost two weeks of frustrating pursuit.

The Indians had traveled through rugged country on foot, through snow and ice, with women and children in tow, fighting off the troopers almost daily. Now they threw up breastworks one last time in preparation for a final battle. This time there were no precipitous rocks or ravines into which they could escape. Captain Wessells later described the Cheyenne defenses at this spot as a natural washout in a "dry creek bed with steep banks."[30] There, on January 22, 1879, about eighteen men and older boys, and about fourteen women and young children crouched in the washout and prepared to die.[31]

At 7:00 A.M. on January 22, Captain Wessells, personally commanding H Company, along with A and E Companies commanded by 2d Lt. George F. Chase and Capt. Joseph Lawson respectively, moved out for the final confrontation with Dull Knife's people. Soon, F Company, now under the command of 2d Lt. John Baxter (officially assigned to the 9th Infantry), would join them. Major Andrew Evans, overall commander of the pursuit, was still camped in the Hat Creek Bluffs with Companies B and D, having been

lured away from Wessells's troops the day before by a couple of
Little Finger Nail's warriors. Wessells took the opportunity to finish
the business personally with the Northern Cheyennes that he had
begun almost two weeks earlier.[32]

Scouts John Shangreau and Woman's Dress and two troopers
rode ahead of H Company. Woman's Dress picked up the trail
once more, heading into a ravine along the dry branch where the
Cheyennes were entrenched. When they rounded a slight bend
and approached what the Cheyennes who remembered this valiant
last stand called "the pit," Little Finger Nail's determined men rose
up and opened fire on the scouts. Behind the breastworks were the
Cheyenne women and children, crimping paper cartridges and
helping to reload what weapons their men possessed. The first
volley brought down Pvt. Henry A. DuBlois's horse. Then a bullet
struck DuBlois through the chest and exited out his back, mortally
wounding him.[33] At the same time, a bullet caught Woman's Dress
in the wrist. Although the wound was not serious, Woman's Dress
"made a big fuss," Captain Wessells remembered, "while being
driven into the post in an ambulance."[34]

When they heard the shooting, Wessells's troops rode quickly to
the scene and dismounted about five hundred yards below the
Cheyennes' position, returning fire to cover the fleeing scouts.
Wessells decided to attack the pit from three directions, pouring
crossfire into the Cheyennes' breastworks. He ordered Second
Lieutenant Chase with A Company to hold the middle in front of
the pit while he and his own company, along with H Company,
took up a position to the northwest of Chase. Captain Lawson's E
Company moved into position on the opposite side. Second Lieutenant John Baxter arrived with F Company sometime after the
initial deployment and took up position between Lawson and
Chase. Although the companies were not at full strength, there
were now 147 soldiers and 5 officers amassed against 18 Cheyenne
fighting men.[35]

That morning the troopers fired continuously into the pit while
gradually advancing to within about one hundred yards of the

rim. Finally, Captain Wessells sent a runner to direct Chase to move A Company into a better position for a direct assault. Wessells planned to bring H Company up the line to reinforce Chase on the right, but to Chase's dismay, he found his new position to be too exposed. Suddenly a bullet struck Sgt. James Taggert in the neck, killing him instantly. More bullets started singing off rocks and kicking up dirt all around the troopers of A Company. Chase decided he could not afford to wait in this new position for H Company to reinforce him, so he formed his men into skirmish order and gave the order to charge the pit. Quickly the dismounted soldiers advanced; the Cheyennes held their fire until the troopers were within thirty yards of the breastworks. Then Little Finger Nail's men stood up and rained lead into Chase's ranks. Private George Nelson fell within twenty yards of the pit, killed instantly by a bullet that tore through his liver, but A Company held and advanced to the crest of the pit. Again the Cheyennes fired in unison, almost into the faces of the advancing troopers. Farrier George Brown broke through to the rim of the pit and fired down into it, then suddenly fell, cut down point-blank by a carbine ball. He yelled and made an attempt to throw off his cartridge belt but soon lost consciousness and dropped dead, his body sliding down the angled slope of the breastworks.[36]

During this fighting, which lasted about forty-five minutes, 2d Lt. Francis Hardie noticed Little Finger Nail with the ledger book of drawings still strapped to his waist. Hardie, who coveted such trophies, turned to a trooper next to him and said, "I want that book if we come out all right."[37] Company A moved to within five yards of the pit and fired several volleys into it before falling back. Some of these bullets struck their mark, tearing flesh, and screams emanated from the Cheyennes' breastworks.[38]

After ordering a cease fire, Captain Wessells called out for the Indians in the pit to surrender. The reply was a rapid series of rifle reports from the warriors in the pit. Then the guns fell silent for a time. During this lull in the fighting a young girl raised a carbine over the rim of the breastworks as a signal to the soldiers that she wanted to come out. Sgt. Carter P. Johnson remembered hearing her crying from the pit. But she never had the chance to escape, for in the next instant her mother caught her by the hand and slit her throat, screaming that they would never surrender.[39]

Captain Wessells and Second Lieutenant Chase mounted a second assault of the pit with selected troopers from Companies A and H. As Wessells and Chase led their skirmishers, a shot rang out from the Cheyenne position. A pistol ball struck Wessells in the head at the same instant he fired at the Indian shooting at him. The ball opened a three-inch wound in the temporal muscle on the right side of Wessells head, bringing him to his knees by the force of the blow. Troopers escorted Wessells to the rear where Acting Assistant Surgeon C. V. Pettys dressed the superficial scalp wound.[40]

Chase continued the attack, leading the 3rd Cavalrymen to the edge of the pit once more; they would fire a volley, move back a few yards to reload, then charge again. During this action, Sgt. Willard D. Reed, H Company, advanced to the rim of the pit. He had his knee on its edge and, while firing a shot into the pit, was struck in the left thigh by a carbine ball from a weak charge that had been reloaded by one of the Cheyenne women. Reed eventually recovered from the shallow flesh wound.[41]

"They now began firing at us from above [the rim of the pit],"
Sgt. Carter P. Johnson remembered, "and were firing lively, but we could not just see their exact position. Finally one of them jumped up and ran [to another position]. We finally charged right upon them, firing at each other not farther apart than twenty feet."[42]
Again, the troopers heard the shriek of a small girl as another mother cut her daughter's neck and then stabbed herself rather than surrender to the soldiers.[43]

Toward the end of the fighting, three warriors jumped up from the pit and appeared either to be trying to escape through the gauntlet of bullets or to charge the soldiers in an act of suicide. One had an empty revolver, the other two were armed only with knives. As they came through the black, acrid smoke of the battle, they were met with a hailstorm of bullets. All of them went down, shot to pieces by the disciplined volley fire of the soldiers at almost point blank range. Then there was no more firing from the pit.[44] By now Captain Lawson had advanced with E Company. Lawson may have been the first officer to look into the pit after the fighting ceased. There he saw the bullet-torn bodies piled and bleeding on top of one another. Many of the corpses were riddled with bullets. Some were stripped for the final battle and several were dressed, in the words of one soldier, in "regular store clothes."[45]

The soldiers found a little girl still alive in the bottom of the pit, protected under the corpses. Soon they found more survivors beneath the dead—seven women and children, all but three wounded. John Shangreau and some of the troopers gave them cups of water to drink.

Among the living was the small girl whose mother had cut her in the neck before stabbing herself. They also found the older girl whose throat had been cut by her mother when she had tried to surrender. Fortunately the knife had not struck a vital artery. Her mother also was still alive although bleeding profusely. When Second Lieutenant Chase offered to assist the mother, she grasped his hand and spit into his face in one last act of hatred and defiance. That night she died in the post hospital. Also among the wounded was Wild Hog's daughter, whom the soldiers had nicknamed Blanche. Wild Hog had not evacuated her from the barracks on January 10 when he had been allowed to take out his family, stating that she was old enough to take care of herself. She had a gun shot wound in the arm and would survive.[46]

While removing the bodies of the dead from the pit, the troopers came upon the corpse of Little Finger Nail with his ledger book of art depicting the fighting of the Northern Cheyennes still strapped to his body. In one end of the book was a hole torn by a carbine ball. The ball had passed completely through the book, mortally wounding Little Finger Nail. A trooper removed the book from the body and gave it to 2d Lt. F. H. Hardie.[47] Only one warrior was found alive in the pit, his leg shattered by bullets. Acting Assistant Surgeon Pettys tried to dress his wounds, but the brave Ohmeseheso

This ledger book, carried by Northern Cheyenne warrior Little Finger Nail, contains colorful crayon drawings of the exploits of the Northern Cheyennes. Some speculate that these drawings were made while the Indians were confined to the barracks at Fort Robinson, Nebraska. Negative #327518, Courtesy the Library, American Museum of Natural History.

told Pettys through an interpreter that he wanted to die and then be thrown back into the pit with the bodies of his friends. He died the next day.[48]

Officially, of the thirty-two Northern Cheyennes found in the pit, seventeen men, four women, and two children were killed in that last stand of January 22, 1879. Captain Lawson's troopers buried

This ledger book was taken from the body of Little Finger Nail following the assault on the Cheyennes' crude defensive position on Antelope Creek, January 22, 1879. The hole in the cover of the book is where a bullet passed through, killing Little Finger Nail. Compare the entry position of the bullet into the cover with the position of the hole through the pages within the ledger (previous photograph). The bullet must have entered the cover of the book at an extreme angle from directly above Little Finger Nail as he was fighting in the "pit" on Antelope Creek. Today the Little Finger Nail Ledger Book is housed in the Gallery of the American Indian at the American Museum of Natural History in New York City. Negative #321322, Courtesy the Library, American Museum of Natural History.

them in the pit where they fell. The next day one man, one woman, and one child died of wounds. Altogether, from January 10, 1879, through January 23, 1879, a total of sixty-four Northern Cheyennes lost their lives in the fighting around Fort Robinson. The 3rd Cavalry recaptured seventy-eight, leaving seven unaccounted for and presumed dead, including Dull Knife and his immediate family. Among Dull Knife's people at Fort Robinson, one-half had perished or suffered wounds.[49] Below is a partial list of those Cheyennes treated for gunshot wounds in the Fort Robinson Hospital until January 24, 1879. The list, reconstructed from Dr. Moseley's records, is woefully incomplete. It does not include those persons who died of wounds in the field nor does it include those such as Iron Teeth who were treated for frostbite or superficial wounds and released immediately. The report also does not include some of the Cheyennes, such as Tangle Hair and his companions, who were treated on the night of January 10 immediately following their rear guard action near the post barracks.

1. Yellow Woman (died)
2. Short Woman
3. Red woman
4. Buffalo Girl (5 years)
5. little boy (7 years)
6. Stub Foot (16 years)
7. Big Head
8. Medicine Robe (old woman)
9. Medicine Woman
10. Little Bear (10 years)
11. Moccasin Woman (50 years)
12. Lost Woman
13. Medicine Girl (6 years)
14. Lame Girl (6 years)
15. little girl (5 years, died)
16. baby girl (1 year, died)
17. White Antelope the Northerner (died)

18. woman (died)
19. Noisy Walker (Noisy Walking)
20. Baby girl (6 months, died)
21. Wild Hog's daughter "Blanche"
22. boy
23. girl[50]

Eleven soldiers of the 3rd Cavalry were killed in the various engagements between January 9 and January 22. They are listed below with their company, in order of their deaths.

1. Pvt. Frank Schmidt, "A"
2. Pvt. Peter Hulse, "A"
3. Pvt. W. H. Good, "L"
4. Pvt. W. W. Everett, "H"
5. Cpl. Henry P. Orr, "A"
6. Pvt. Bernard Kelly, "E"
7. Pvt. Amos J. Barbour, "H"
8. Farrier George Brown, "A"
9. Sgt. James Taggert, "A"
10. Pvt. George Nelson, "A"
11. Pvt. Henry A. DuBlois, "H"

In addition, one officer, Capt. Henry Wessells, and nine enlisted men were wounded.[51]

Following the action at Fort Robinson, a three-officer investigating board convened at the post on January 21, 1879, concluding on February 7, 1879. This committee found no wrongdoing on the part of the officers and men at Fort Robinson in relation to allegations from Washington of unusual cruelty practiced against the Northern Cheyennes at Fort Robinson.[52] Asked by the investigating board if he knew of the killing of *any* Cheyennes who had not shown resistance, Captain Wessells answered, "none whatsoever."[53] The adjutant general authorized veterans of the fighting to wear a special war chevron on their uniform sleeve,[54] and on April 17,

Even Frederic Remington, who glorified the exploits of the frontier army in his illustrations, could not escape the grim reality of the fight at "the pit" on Arickaree Creek on January 22, 1870. The troops could be killed by the enemy or froze, frozen.

1879, Sgt. William B. Lewis of B Company received the Medal of Honor for "conspicuous bravery and personal gallantry" under fire in the fighting around Fort Robinson in January 1879.[55]

Among the great battles in which men and women have chosen to give their lives for principle and freedom rather than submit to oppression, the self-sacrifice of Dull Knife's followers at Fort Robinson must be considered one of the most extraordinary acts of valor in American history. The Indians who fell in the terrible pit on Antelope Creek symbolize displaced peoples everywhere whose sense of home and desire for independence transcends the love of life. They died with honor, and their sacrifice *is* remembered.

Since September 1878, the Ohmeseheso had trudged close to a thousand miles trying to reach their homelands near the Sacred Mountain, where Sweet Medicine had consecrated their sacred covenants. Throughout their quest, they had grown weary of trying to convince both Indian bureau personnel and the army that they would rather die than return to Indian Territory. The United States ignored their determined pledge, refusing to believe its sincerity, until January 9, 1879. On February 7, 1879, a dumbfounded board of officers at Fort Robinson finally admitted that "the statements of the Indians were not brag . . . they literally went out to die."[56]

CHAPTER EIGHT

# Montana

## *Little Wolf Comes Home*

*Our hearts looked and longed for this country where we were born. There are only a few of us left, and we only wanted a little ground, where we could live.*

—LITTLE WOLF,
1879

Among the seven Northern Cheyennes missing after the fighting north of Fort Robinson was Dull Knife. Capt. Henry Wessells presumed that he and the six others had died of exposure among the frost-laden rocks of the Hat Creek Bluffs. But Wessells was mistaken. Dull Knife, his wife Pawnee Woman, and his son, Bull Hump, and another woman, probably Bull Hump's wife, had remained concealed in the bluffs for ten days, surviving on what little food the women in the party had in their packs. Finally, they left the bluffs and began making their way northwest toward Pine Ridge, traveling at night and hiding during the daylight hours.

Eventually, Dull Knife and his family reached the home of Gus Craven, whom Dull Knife knew and trusted because Craven was married to a Lakota Woman. By now the members of this small party had become emaciated, having been reduced to eating their moccasins. From his house, Craven secreted the family to the home of the interpreter, William Rowland. Finally, Rowland slipped Dull Knife and his family in among Red Cloud's Lakotas on the Pine Ridge Agency, where a lodge was set up for the old council chief under an out-of-the-way bluff on Wounded Knee Creek.[1] Soon thereafter Dull Knife learned what had happened to the others at Fort Robinson. He must have reflected on his fate there on the lonely bluff—how he had been unable to save his people and how they had died while he had lived.[2]

Behind, at Fort Robinson, Dull Knife had left two daughters and a son among the dead. Earlier, possibly at Punished Woman's Fork, one of his wives, Little Woman, had been killed by a stampeding horse. During the past year, Dull Knife had lost all of these family members.[3] Capt. Henry Wessells learned of Dull Knife's fate and visited him at Pine Ridge Agency. Wessells inquired about the daughter he had grown fond of at Fort Robinson. Jokingly, as he had often done at the post, Wessells asked Dull Knife if he were going to give him his daughter. "No," replied Dull Knife. "The one you wanted—you killed." Wessells claimed he was so broken up on learning of her death that he was moved to tears.[4]

Of the seventy-eight Northern Cheyennes who were recaptured and returned to the prison barracks at Fort Robinson, seven who were suspected of committing, permitting, or instigating the depredations upon civilians in Kansas in February 1879 were taken south by the army to stand trial. They were Wild Hog, Tangle Hair, Strong Left Hand, Old Crow, Porcupine, Noisy Walker (Noisy Walking), and Blacksmith. Including their families, twenty Indians returned south.[5]

The remaining fifty-eight Ohmeseheso left Fort Robinson in early February. Because many of the warriors were dead, the government decided to allow their surviving family members to stay in the North with the Oglalas at Pine Ridge. They were loaded into wagons and escorted to that agency by Lt. G. W. Dodd. Among these refugees were Iron Teeth and her daughters. Years later she remembered that when she was released from the post hospital and returned to the barracks, she had expected "that the soldiers would come out at once into the prison and shoot all of us." "But they did not. Instead, a few days later we were taken to the Pine Ridge Agency and were put among the Oglala Sioux."[6] Her son, Gathering His Medicine, had died so that his sister might live to find a home in the north country. Now his mother and sisters were finally close to that goal, even if they had to share an agency with Red Cloud's approximately seven thousand Lakotas.[7]

For the army, the defeat of Dull Knife's people at Fort Robinson did not end the Cheyenne campaign that had now dragged on for almost five months. About October 29, 1878, wolves (or scouts) from Little Wolf's band found out that Dull Knife and his people had been captured. An account states that one of these wolves, who may have been a warrior named Bird, was captured. The next day this scout, with a detachment of troops under Maj. Caleb Carleton, rode out of Fort Robinson in search of Little Wolf.[8] Captain Hugh L. Scott, 7th Cavalry, also scouted the area around Chadron Creek, with Old Crow as his guide, but Little Wolf and his people were long gone by November 1, 1878. "I returned to Fort Robinson, without Old Crow's seeing even a track," Scott remembered, "convinced that Little Wolf had never been in that region."[9] By the end of January 1879, Little Wolf and his followers were still making their way north.

Little Wolf decided to take his people back into the rugged Sand Hills, where they could hide and hunt in preparation for the coming winter. At first they stayed on the move, being careful to camp in favorable defensive spots in case of attack by troops. In one of these camps, Little Wolf's band was joined by about seven more Northern Cheyennes, including Black Coyote; his wife, Buffalo Calf Woman, a woman warrior who had distinguished herself at the Battle of the Rosebud; his mother; and four others. Black Coyote and his party had left Darlington Agency after Little Wolf and Dull Knife and had followed their trail to this point. Black Coyote informed Little Wolf that soldiers were tracking them, so the band scattered, only to come back together in small groups in the winter days that followed. On another day, Little Wolf's camp was joined by Black

Horse, Mad Hearted Wolf, and Whetstone, three warriors who had escaped Darlington Agency even before Little Wolf's and Dull Knife's exodus. The trio claimed that on their way north they had several times narrowly escaped recapture by the whites.[10]

Near the lower fork of the Niobrara River, the Cheyennes discovered a sheltered valley where they camped for much of the winter virtually undetected. There they built lodges of brush and tree limbs, hunted wild game, and occasionally shot cattle that had wandered far across the open plains.[11] Sometime during the winter, Black Horse and a party of foragers ranged to the vicinity of the North Platte River to replenish the pony herd. Black Coyote and others joined them a few days later, about thirteen foragers in all. Hitting isolated ranches, they managed to put together a small herd. In their haste to get away, Black Horse nearly froze trying to cross the ice-choked North Platte River on foot, because his horse refused to enter the frigid water. In one instance, the party discovered a white man unsuspectingly riding toward them. "Let us go to that high point," Black Coyote told his friends, pointing to an adjacent hill, "wait for him, and shoot him off his horse as he comes over the point." After killing the man, the warriors charged down the hill and counted coup on him.[12]

At another ranch, Black Horse and his companions chased a white settler into a house. A gun battle ensued as the Cheyennes surrounded the house and poured lead in through the windows. Thinking he had killed the man inside, Black Horse entered the house only to be shot down by the man, who was still very much alive. Black Horse dragged himself through the door to safety, and the other warriors set fire to the house. Soon two whites fled the blazing building and were shot and killed by Black Horse's men.[13]

According to white observers, the outriders killed four whites in January 1879, although the sources do not agree on the exact locations or dates. The foragers killed James Ashbaugh and Frank Moorehead and burned their ranch on either January 23 or 29. Two other cattlemen, named Briggs and Bosler, were also killed in a winter line camp at about the same time. On January 31, a group

of Cheyenne outriders, again most likely Black Horse's men, surrounded the ranch of a man named Wetherhill; they helped themselves to provisions, asked directions, and rode off without killing
anyone. Altogether the Indians eventually made off with about
eighty horses.[14] Perhaps identifying the Cheyennes' situation with
the Nez Percé War two years earlier, newspaper reporters who
described these incidents in early 1879 erroneously claimed that
Little Wolf's people were trying to reach Canada to join Sitting
Bull's refugees from the Great Sioux War, just as the Nez Percé had
so valiantly tried to do in 1877. Black Horse recovered from his
wounds, cared for by his relatives, but soon after these events, Little
Wolf's people found six companies of 5th Cavalry pursuing them.[15]

Shortly after Black Horse and his foragers returned to the valley,
Little Wolf decided to move northwest toward the Black Hills to
evade these troops. He and his followers crossed the White River
into the badlands near the Black Hills. Now they were near Noahavose, the Sacred Mountain, but they did not linger, for the Black
Hills were populated with whites who had followed the gold rush
a few years earlier. On they went toward the Little Missouri and
the Powder River–Tongue River Country that Little Wolf so dearly
loved. When they crossed over into present-day South Dakota, they
found themselves within the jurisdiction of the Military Department
of Dakota, commanded by Brig. Gen. Alfred H. Terry. Soldiers of
the 2nd Cavalry now would be coming down from a northwesterly
direction to intercept them.

Despite Little Wolf's leadership, somewhere near the Little
Missouri River in the late winter of 1879, domestic violence broke
out among the Ohmeseheso. The aging chief, Black Crane, who
was married to a younger woman, became jealously enraged at
Black Coyote, who he thought was paying too much attention to
his wife. In a fit, Black Crane came at Black Coyote with a knife,
whereupon Black Coyote grabbed his gun and shot Black Crane
through the heart, killing him instantly. Black Crane's son, Red
Robe, who was also present, shot Black Coyote in the arm and
received a slight arm wound himself from Black Coyote's return

fire. As was customary, Little Wolf banished Black Coyote from the camp because he had murdered of one of his own people. Black Coyote's wife, Buffalo Calf Road Woman, and a few of his friends, including Whetstone, rode off with him.[16] Some of the women in Black Crane's family were so enraged that they went to Black Coyote's campsite, possibly before Black Coyote was banished by Little Wolf, and threw his baby daughter over a snowbank. The infant survived, however, grew to womanhood, and married.[17]

Unbearable stress, it seems, eventually overcame a few of Little Wolf's people during the grueling journey north. Wooden Leg related to Thomas B. Marquis the story of a man who became psychotic on the journey north and began beating and clubbing all the members of his family. "An adult daughter, screaming and struggling to get away from him, stabbed him with her sheath knife. He let loose of her, walked away staggering, and dropped dead." Although the young woman was grief-stricken over killing her own father, the chiefs sympathized with her and she was not punished.[18]

Little Wolf probably never entertained serious thoughts of joining Sitting Bull and his Lakotas in Canada. Their line of march shows that the Northern Cheyennes were, by the end of winter 1879, headed toward the old Tongue River Cantonment, located on the Yellowstone River just west of Miles City, Montana, and two miles above the mouth of the Tongue River. Here Little Wolf briefly had been a scout for the army, and here Two Moon's people still lived. Little Wolf probably figured he could talk the government into letting them stay if he and his warriors agreed to join the Indian scouts once again. He did not know that the name of Tongue River Cantonment had been changed on November 8, 1878, to Fort Keogh.[19]

Elements of the 2nd Cavalry were now stationed at Fort Keogh. When the word spread that Little Wolf's people had broken out of the Sand Hills and were headed northwest, the Department of Dakota mobilized. On February 22, 1879, Brigadier General Terry, the departmental commander, ordered Lt. William P. "Philo" Clark to move down and intercept the Northern Cheyennes. Clark had organized the company of Indian scouts in 1877 and thus knew and respected Little Wolf from the time they had spent together at Fort Robinson, before the Indians' removal south. The Cheyennes in return respected Clark, whom they called "White Hat," as an officer of honesty and integrity. Clark, a New Yorker, graduated twenty-sixth in his class at West Point in 1868. He spent his entire service in the West on the northern plains. For a time during the Great Sioux War, he was acting aide de camp to Brig. Gen. George Crook. After he organized the Indian scout company, made up of Indians from several tribes, Clark, at this time, became an expert on American Indian sign language, and he hoped someday to publish his knowledge of the subject in a book.[20]

Lieutenant Clark had Companies E and I, 2nd Cavalry, under his command, including an artillery squad manning a rapid fire Hotchkiss gun and four Lakota scouts. He took ten wagons, forty pack mules, and a consignment of Sibley tents in case of an extended bivouac in the field. He arranged for ranchers and drivers on the Bismarck to Fort Keogh mail route to keep him informed of any sightings of the Cheyennes.

On his way down the Yellowstone, Lieutenant Clark posted a picket made up of one noncommissioned officer and three men on Sheridan Buttes near the mouth of Powder River and then established a base camp on the Yellowstone near the mouth of O'Fallon's Creek. From there his soldiers began scouting the tributaries for any sign of the Ohmeseheso. Clark's troopers suffered from the elements during the last week in February as the temperature dipped to thirty-three degrees below zero. On February 27 the temperature rose and the ice broke on the Yellowstone River. The stream rose six feet, stranding the 2nd Cavalrymen temporarily on the bluffs above O'Fallon's Creek. On March 4 they moved back to the Powder River in an attempt to cross, but the ice had broken there too, leaving an impassable "wide gorge of ice on the banks."[21]

On March 8 Clark sent two Lakota scouts, along with mixed-blood interpreter Billy Jackson and a man named Fleury, to search between the Powder River and the Little Missouri River for the Cheyennes. Then Clark's command moved down the Powder River and went into camp again. On March 17 Clark requested some Cheyenne scouts from Fort Keogh to help persuade Little Wolf to surrender, and six arrived at his camp on the nineteenth. Clark had also requested a mixed-blood interpreter called Seminole, who knew both the Cheyenne and Lakota languages, so that there would be no misunderstandings among his Indian scouts, but Seminole was no longer employed by the army. Clark sent for him anyway, paying Seminole's salary at his own personal expense.

Lieutenant Clark, through Seminole, told his Cheyenne scouts that he hoped they would be able to persuade Little Wolf to surrender. He told them he would recommend that the Ohmeseheso remain in the North and that if they gave up their ponies and guns he would not fight them. "One of the headmen replied that to shoot these people [Little Wolf's] would be like going back and firing at the children in his own lodge," Clark reported. "[T]he other, Brave Wolf, said that he was a soldier, and though he had kin in [Little Wolf's] village, he would do as he was ordered."[22]

About March 22, one of the Lakotas who had been sent to scout the Little Missouri returned and reported that he, along with Fleury and Jackson, had been captured on the twentieth by Little Wolf's people near the mouth of Box Elder Creek. He told Clark that he and the other captives had made the Cheyennes believe they had stolen government stock and were on their way to refuge with Sitting Bull in Canada. He also reported that they told Little Wolf they would talk to Sitting Bull and make the Northern Cheyennes welcome among his Lakotas. The next day the scout escaped and rode back to the 2nd Cavalry camp, covering 125 miles in 24 hours. Clark broke camp and marched 22 miles toward Box Elder Creek and went into camp about 11:00 P.M. Shortly thereafter, Fleury and Jackson came riding in, after escaping from Little Wolf's camp and riding 90 miles that day.[23]

On March 23 Lieutenant Clark left his wagons and crossed the Yellowstone, carrying rations enought for eight days. He marched forty-five miles. The next morning he sent out three Cheyenne and two Lakota scouts to try to locate Little Wolf's camp; Little Wolf was waiting for them. Indeed, he had moved his camp to a more defensible position to await the soldiers. After a march of thirty-five miles on the twenty-fourth, the two Lakotas returned to Clark's command and reported that they had discovered the trail and that the three Cheyenne scouts were following it up.

On the morning of March 25, after a march of three miles, two of Clark's Cheyenne scouts rode in with three of Little Wolf's people, who told Clark that Little Wolf had agreed to his terms. Little Wolf requested that Clark camp where he was and told Clark that the Cheyennes would move up to his location, but Lieutenant Clark refused. Instead he sent Brave Wolf and Young Two Moon, two of his Cheyenne scouts, to inform Little Wolf that he should come out to meet with him. Brave Wolf delivered the message, later informing Clark that he had told Little Wolf: "I love the soldiers of Keogh; I go with them to fight all their enemies, and if you will not listen you will force me to fight my own people, for you are my kinsfolk."[24]

Meanwhile, Little Wolf's warriors built breastworks at their camp in case of trouble. Little Wolf came out and met Lieutenant Clark about a half mile from the camp. He told Clark that he was glad to see him again and that he wished to meet his terms. Later Clark went into the Cheyenne camp unarmed and told Little Wolf that his people would have to give up their arms immediately and that their ponies must be relinquished when they arrived at Fort Keogh. With Seminole interpreting, Little Wolf rose and made his surrender speech to Lieutenant Clark:

> Since I left you at Red Cloud [Agency] we have been south, and have suffered a great deal down there. Many have died of diseases, which we have no name for. Our hearts looked and longed for this country where we were born. There are only a few of us left, and we only wanted a little ground, where we could live. We left our lodges standing and ran away in the night. The troops followed us. I rode out and told the troops we

did not want to fight; we only wanted to go north, and if they would let us alone we would kill no one. The only reply we got was a volley. After that we had to fight our way, but we killed none who did not fire on us first. My brother, Dull Knife, took one-half of the band and surrendered near Camp Robinson. He thought you were still there and would look out for him. They gave up their guns, and then the whites killed them all. I am out in the prairie, and need my guns here. When I get to Keogh I will give you the guns and ponies, but I can not give up the guns now. You are the only one who has offered to talk before fighting, and it looks as though the wind, which has made our hearts flutter for so long, would now go down. I am glad we did not fight, and that none of my people or yours have been killed. My young men are brave, and would be glad to go with you to fight the [Sitting Bull] Sioux.[25]

Clark compromised and allowed the Northern Cheyennes to keep their arms for hunting until they reached the army supply wagons. Little Wolf agreed. Clark issued rations to the Indians while his medical officer tended their sick and wounded, including Black Horse. The Cheyennes surrendered thirty-one guns, twenty rifles, and eleven revolvers. Clark made a final check for arms just before arriving at Fort Keogh, but he found no more.[26]

Lieutenant Clark and Little Wolf's people arrived at Fort Keogh about noon on April 1, 1879. Of the nearly 300 Northern Cheyennes who had started out from Darlington Agency, 114 now surrendered with Little Wolf. There were 33 men, 43 women, and 38 small children. When Clark rode into the fort, the "troops were all out," wrote one reporter, "the cannon thundered, the band played 'Hail to the Chief,' and men, women, and children crowded around him with their hearty congratulations."[27] Lieutenant Clark commended the work of his Cheyenne and Lakota scouts and reported no casualties on either side.[28]

But Clark's pronouncement of a bloodless coup was premature. Missing among the 114 Ohmeseheso who surrendered to Clark at

Box Elder Creek were Black Coyote, who had been banished for killing Black Crane; Black Coyote's wife, Buffalo Calf Road Woman; his friend Whetstone; and perhaps about five others who chose to follow Black Coyote into exile.[29] On February 22, 1879 these Cheyennes killed two white hunters, named Furgeson and Thompson, near the trail to Rapid City.[30] They also may have been responsible for the death of a stage driver near Miles City.[31] On April 5, 1879, four days after Little Wolf's people arrived at Fort Keogh, Black Coyote and his companions killed and scalped Pvt. Leo Bader, E Company, 2nd Cavalry, and wounded a signal sergeant named Kennedy. The two soldiers were working on the telegraph line along the Deadwood Road in the vicinity of Mispah Creek, about forty-five miles from Fort Keogh, at the time of the attack. They were eating their lunch when Black Coyote and his companions surprised them. The Indians killed Bader instantly. They shot Kennedy in the hip, but he was able to crawl to safety and hold the Indians at bay with his revolver until three citizens traveling the Deadwood Road came along and drove off the Cheyennes. The civilians took Kennedy, exhausted from loss of blood, into Fort Keogh, where he recovered in the post infirmary.[32]

Immediately, Maj. George Gibson dispatched from Fort Keogh a detachment from B Company, 2nd Cavalry, with Indian scouts, under the command of Sgt. T. B. Glover to pursue Black Coyote's party. The scouts struck the trail at Mispah Creek and caught up with Black Coyote about eighty miles from the fort. The Indians surrendered on sight. They had with them at the time of their capture Private Bader's horse, his carbine, some of his clothing, and his scalp.[33]

Little Wolf, upon hearing of Black Coyote's arrest, showed no mercy. "Your laws punish such crimes," he said, "hang them or prison them for life. I never want to see their faces again. They knew I had made peace with you and they killed your soldiers."[34] Black Coyote's party were turned over to civil authorities and tried for murder between May 27 and June 5, 1879, in Miles City. Three, including Black Coyote and Whetstone, were convicted and received the death sentence. They awaited execution in the Miles City jail, which would soon be used for the incarceration of many Cheyennes accused of crimes during the early reservation period. The Indians called the jail the "red house" because it was made of bricks.[35] But Black Coyote, Whetstone, and the other condemned man would cheat the executioner. All three hanged themselves in their jail cells about June 7, becoming in all likelihood the last casualties of the Northern Cheyenne odyssey.[36]

In the weeks following his surrender, Little Wolf's greatest ally became his captor, Lieutenant Clark. Although the State of Kansas argued for Little Wolf's extradition to stand trial for atrocities committed there, and others urged that the Indians be returned to Darlington Agency as an object lesson, Clark maintained the right of the Ohmeseheso to have a home in the North. "They are weary with constant fighting and watching," Clark asserted. "They want peace, rest, and a home somewhere in this country where they were born and reared."[37]

Clark's arguments were heard only because he made them at the opportune time. By the spring of 1879, after pursuing the Indians for eight months and twelve hundred miles, through three military departments, the army was embarrassed and weary of the Cheyenne odyssey. The departmental commander, Gen. Alfred H. Terry, endorsed Clark's report and the report of Clark's commanding officer, Maj. George Gibson. Terry advised Washington, "I think that, for the present at least, these Cheyenne prisoners should be left at Fort Keogh. I have no doubt that we shall be able to make great use of them in case active hostilities with the Sioux should be renewed."[38]

The army and the Indian bureau concurred, and shortly thereafter, Little Wolf enlisted as a sergeant in Lieutenant Clark's Indian scouts. Clark and Little Wolf became friends, and Little Wolf aided Clark in his research for a book on Indian sign language. Wrote one reporter shortly after the surrender, "Little Wolf is happier at Keogh than he has been in a long time."[39] Although Little Wolf knew the arrangement made with the whites that spring was temporary

General Nelson A. Miles, pictured here later in his career, exercised his influence in Washington to keep Little Wolf's people in Montana in 1879, near Fort Keogh. Miles envisioned an "Indian Territory of the North" similar to the Indian Territory, which later became Oklahoma, for all the tribes of the northern plains, a vision that was never realized. Courtesy Kansas State Historical Society.

and tenuous, he had ensured that his followers would never again be returned to the hated Indian Territory. More trouble lay ahead, combined with personal tragedy, but by April, 1879, the Sweet Medicine Chief had brought 114 of his people home to their beloved Montana lands.

## CHAPTER NINE

# KANSAS

## State of Kansas v. Wild Hog, et al.

*Dusky Demons*
*The Cheyenne Robbers and Murderers Fall at Last into the*
*Hands of the Civil Authorities*
*That They Will Never Again Ravish Women and Kill*
*Children Is a Certainty.*

—*LEAVENWORTH TIMES,*
February 16, 1879

The early days of 1879 were busy ones for the Sheriff of Ford County, Kansas, William Barclay "Bat" Masterson. On January 7 he returned to Dodge City from Trinidad, Colorado, after extraditing the infamous horse thief Dutch Henry. Early February found him en route to Fort Leavenworth to receive the Northern Cheyenne prisoners Wild Hog, Old Crow, Tangle Hair, Noisy Walker (Noisy Walking), Strong Left Hand, Porcupine, and Blacksmith. The Indians had been accused of high crimes and misdemeanors against the people of the State of Kansas and were being turned over by the army to the civil authorities to stand trial in Dodge City for first degree murder.[1]

Since the capture of Dull Knife's followers on Chadron Creek in the autumn of 1878, both federal and civil authorities in Kansas had pressured the military to extradite the "perpetrators" (without any genuine plan to identify specific individuals). U.S. Attorney George R. Peck told Kansas governor George T. Anthony in December 1878, "A prompt and vigorous prosecution of the perpetrators of these outrages would serve as a warning against their repetition,"[2] but it is difficult to tell whether Kansans were more interested in preventing recurrence of future raids or in seeking revenge during the winter and spring of 1878–79. In late January 1879 the three member Board of Officers at Fort Robinson, assigned to investigate the treatment of the Cheyenne prisoners, tried to identify those responsible for the raids. Maj. A. W. Evans, 3rd Cavalry; Capt. John Hamilton, 5th Cavalry; and Lt. Walter Schuyler, 5th Cavalry, questioned Wild Hog, Old Crow, and an unnamed Cheyenne Woman. The Indian chiefs stated they could not control the young men, and they denied personal participation in the raids. All three testified that they had remained in the main camps while the foragers were out looking for food and horses. They claimed that Dull Knife's leadership had eroded among his followers during the journey and that few of the young warriors respected his wishes. They all agreed that the "young men" who committed the depredations were now with Little Wolf's band, not with Dull Knife's.[3]

Only a short while before, Lieutenant Schuyler had written to General Crook asserting that although "the Squaws refuse to talk [for fear of repurcussions to their families] . . . Wild Hog, [Old] Crow and [Strong] Left Hand . . . say that all the young men, including those of their party, were actively engaged in the Kansas outrages, though old men tried to restrain them; probably at least fifteen of those lately in prison here were engaged in those massacres."[4] But despite the demands of the Kansans, the Board of Officers that adjourned on February 7 recommended that "no further action should be taken."[5]

By the early months of 1879, the army began to change its tune about the Northern Cheyennes. The sensational press coverage the Hat Creek Bluffs fighting received in the East helped the army to recognize the extent of the Indians' suffering. The army had always blamed the short-sighted Indian Bureau policies for the conditions at Darlington Agency as the cause of the Cheyenne odyssey. In later months at least, those officers in the West, especially Colonel Miles and Lieutenant Clark at Fort Keogh, would become the Northern Cheyennes' close allies in their cause of remaining in the North.[6]

The people of Kansas were not to be denied, however. Already Governor George T. Anthony had cited the precedent of *State of Texas v. Satanta* (1872), in which individual Indians stood trial in the civil courts. General of the Army, William T. Sherman, had endorsed the idea.[7] On January 15, 1879, Ford County attorney Michael W. Sutton wrote to the new governor, John P. St. John, enclosing copies of warrants for the arrest of the Indians. General Philip Sheridan, division commander, upheld Sherman's earlier endorsement, even though the decision probably was unpopular with the commanders of the Department of the Platte and the Department of the Missouri, Gen. George Crook and Gen. John Pope, respectively.[8]

The seven Northern Cheyenne prisoners and their families left Fort Robinson on Tuesday, February 4, 1879. Capt. P. D. Vroom with two companies of the 3rd Cavalry escorted them to Sidney Barracks on the Union Pacific Railroad, where they arrived on February 8. The Indians, heavily ironed, entrained the next morning escorted by Lt. Morris C. Foote and nine men of the 9th Infantry. The train trip east took two days, and the prisoners arrived at Fort Leavenworth early on the morning of February 11. They spent that day in the post guardhouse.[9]

The next morning, Sheriff Bat Masterson, Deputy Sheriff C. E. Bassett, James Masterson, A. J. French, and Kokomo Sullivan, all of Ford and Meade Counties, arrived at Fort Leavenworth to "identify" the prisoners. Their qualifications for doing so, stated one newspaper, were that "these gentlemen are all old timers on the plains, and are familiar with Indians and Indian ways." The seven prisoners were indicted for the first-degree murder of cattleman Washington O'Connor in southwest Kansas. Sullivan, who resided in Meade

County in September 1878, had escaped the Cheyenne raiders,[10] but his friend Washington O'Connor was killed. Apparently no one questioned Sullivan to see if he had witnessed O'Connor's death and therefore could positively identify all seven of the accused. A group of horrified settlers, presumably including Sullivan, had witnessed O'Conner's death on the open plains, albeit from a bluff some distance away.

"DUSKY DEMONS," cried the *Leavenworth Times* as Masterson took charge of the prisoners. "The Cheyenne Robbers and Murderers Fall at Last into the Hands of the Civil Authorities. That They Will Never Again Ravish Women and Kill Children Is a Certainty."[11] A crowd of curious citizens gathered at the railroad depot to see the spectacle as the Northern Cheyenne prisoners were escorted, heavily ironed, onto the Kansas Pacific train for their journey to Dodge City to stand trial. "Their eyes betokened curiosity," wrote one reporter, in the racist language of the era, "to see the devils who had desolated so many homes, and the firm set lips of the 'old timers,' when their names were mentioned, indicating anything but a friendly feeling." While waiting in the station to board the train, the Leavenworth County sheriff, a man named Lowe, compassionately brought the Indians clay pipes and tobacco. As a gesture of thanks "Wild Hog, took a piece of silver, cut to represent the sun and attached to a chain from his neck, and handed it to Mr. Lowe, who read the words 'Wild Hog' that were engraved on one side."[12]

In Topeka a crowd of one thousand people turned out to see "real live wild Indians."[13] The prisoners arrived in Dodge City on the seventeenth. The reporters from western Kansas were more familiar with Indians than were the journalists of more settled eastern Kansas, where conflict between whites and Indians was a thing of the past. Consequently, they were not as curious, but their reactions were nevertheless critical and biased, toward both the Indians and eastern Kansans who did not live in fear of Indians. "The Sheriff of Leavenworth County and the Marshall and Mayor of Lawrence, wrote a Dodge City reporter, "were more eager to pay homage to the stinking savage than render assistance to the officers. The ill-treatment and discourtesy by these officers is roundly condemned by Sheriff Masterson and party."[14]

A Dodge City reporter wrote, concerning the prisoners' welfare in the hands of the Leavenworth County sheriff, "We have saved the labor of interviewing Mr. Lo, because we believe his broken English would afford little knowledge of his depressing condition. We know the prisoners will be kindly treated and amply provided for. An Indian is contented with a full stomach and plenty of tobacco. These luxuries will not be denied them. They will go far to render their condition comfortable, and thus allay any apprehension regarding an escape." The reporter observed of eastern and western Kansans, "How different with the people who have more knowledge of savage crimes and butchery. Not a ripple of excitement was observed as the Indian prisoners entered [Dodge City]."[15] One observer, however, "thought it strange that the citizens of Dodge City had not formed a necktie party for the entertainment of the whole [group] of savages."[16]

In June 1879 a formal indictment was filed in the 9th District Court of the State of Kansas for the murder of Washington O'Conner. Sometime during the process, for unspecified reasons, charges were dropped against Old Crow. Because of his advanced age and an endorsement by the army of his distinguished service as an Indian scout, Old Crow probably was not likely to be convicted.[17]

Salina attorney J. G. Mohler was appointed legal counsel for the Northern Cheyenne defendants. Representing the people of Ford County as prosecutor was Michael W. Sutton, whose "recent successful prosecutions," claimed one reporter, "have brought the admiration of law-abiding people and the terror of evil doers." H. B. Gryden and H. D. Johnson of Dodge City assisted Sutton.[18]

The trial convened on June 24, 1879, with Hon. Samuel M. Peters of the 9th Kansas District Court presiding. Immediately defense counsel Mohler petitioned for a change in venue on the grounds that Judge Peters had been, since sitting on the bench, in close "social contact" with the people of his district, including the

Michael W. Sutton, "The Terror of Evil Doers," was the district attorney for Ford County, Kansas, who prosecuted seven Northern Cheyennes for the murder of cattleman Washington O'Conner in the case of *State of Kansas v. Wild Hog, et al.* After the judge granted a change of venue from Dodge City to Lawrence, however, Sutton lost interest in the case. About the same time, he began a romance with Florence Clemmons from New York. Wild Hog and the six other accused Indians benefited from Sutton's marriage to Clemmons at about the time the trial moved to eastern Kansas. Courtesy Kansas State Historical Society.

aggrieved parties. Therefore, Mohler asserted, the defendants were incapable of getting a "fair and impartial trial before him in said district." Mohler claimed that the Cheyennes likewise could not get a fair trial in two other judicial districts in western Kansas.

J. G. Mohler, defense attorney for the Northern Cheyennes. Mohler secured a change of venue from Dodge City to Lawrence, then forced a dismissal of charges against the Indians on a nolle prosequi when the prosecution failed to provide any witnesses. Courtesy Kansas State Historical Society.

Although Bat Masterson and others gave sworn statements that in their belief Judge Peters was not "prejudiced" toward the defendants, Peters's sense of duty prevailed. To the horror of western Kansans, he granted a change of venue to the 4th Judicial District of Douglas County.[19]

With the case moving east, citizens in the western portion of the state feared that the Cheyennes would never be convicted. Stated one southwest Kansas newspaper: "This is generally considered the last of the Indian farce. The prospect for convicting them at this term was not very flattering, even at this distance from the scene

Extradited Cheyennes on trial in Kansas. This photograph was taken in Dodge City, Kansas, on April 30, 1879, probably at the request of Franklin Adams, first secretary of the Kansas State Historical Society. The photographer probably was J. R. Riddle, who donated a stereograph of the original plate to the Kansas State Historical Society. First row, left to right: Wild Hog, George Reynolds (interpreter), probably Noisy Walker (Noisy Walking), Blacksmith; second row, left to right: Tangle Hair, Strong Left Hand, Old Crow, Porsupine, rear: Franklin Adams. Courtesy Kansas State Historical Society.

of the outrages. Now that they are allowed to be taken three hundred miles away all hope of conviction is lost."[20]

In July 1879 the Indians went to Lawrence, Kansas, to stand trial in the 4th District Court, with Hon. N. T. Stephens, presiding. As western Kansans had feared, however, sentiment among the people of Lawrence and Topeka for prosecuting Wild Hog and his companions was ambivalent at most. Succumbing to changing attitudes of the army and the northeastern press, eastern Kansas newspapers began to detail not the alleged crimes but the grievances of Old Crow and Wild Hog, especially the conditions at Darlington Agency.[21]

Indeed, before the trial began in Lawrence on October 13, defense attorney Mohler saw the army as his ally in winning acquittal for his Northern Cheyenne clients. During this time, he issued subpoenas to over forty individuals, mostly army officers and government officials, including Maj. Gen. John Pope, commander of the Department of the Missouri; Col. Nelson A Miles, 5th Infantry, who favored keeping the Northern Cheyennes in the North; and Secretary of the Interior Carl Schurz. Mohler intended to build his case on the grievances that led the Cheyennes to leave Darlington Agency in September 1878. His instructions to the Secretary of the Interior were to bring "any and all Treaties made between the Government of the United States and the . . . Northern Cheyenne[s]."[22]

Meanwhile, the prosecution was having trouble locating witnesses who had the time or resources to travel to Lawrence from western Kansas. Sutton complained that the change of venue made it impossible for him to obtain witnesses, since they were scattered all over the United States. He informed Kansas attorney general Willard Davis that he did not think he could continue to prosecute the case.[23] Historian Todd D. Epp has advanced the argument that perhaps the Northern Cheyenne defendants owed their greatest debt of gratitude to Miss Florence Estelle Clemons of Gloversville, New York. Miss Clemons fell in love with Ford County district attorney Mike Sutton in Dodge City during late summer 1879, while visiting at the home of her uncle, A. B. Webster. Perhaps by autumn 1879, Sutton, "the terror of evil doers," was more concerned with the attentions of his intended bride than prosecuting the Northern Cheyennes. The couple were married October 1, 1879, and honeymooned in Kansas City and St. Louis, returning to Dodge City on October 9, only four days before the trial. This was the critical time period during which to locate survivors of the raids and bring them to Lawrence.[24]

Sutton failed to appear in court on October 13, and there were *no* witnesses. One newspaper quipped, "No one present seemed to have charge of the prosecution."[25] An attorney named Jetmore took over the doomed case and asked the court for a continuance of one week. Sensing victory, Mohler demanded to go to trial immediately, and Judge Stephens denied the motion for a continuance. Because the denial virtually destroyed the prosecution's case, for they had no witnesses, Jetmore filed a nolle prosequi. Judge Stephens accepted the motion and dismissed all charges against the Northern Cheyenne defendants, turning them over (including Old Crow) to John D. Miles, the Cheyenne agent at Darlington Agency, for their return to the Cheyenne and Arapaho reservation in Indian Territory.[26]

Although it may appear, perhaps surprisingly, that justice was served in the *State of Kansas v. Wild Hog*, as the Indians received all legal safeguards from a change of venue to the right to subpoena,[27] the reasons for the arraignment of these particular men in civil court in the first place must be questioned. Even if they had been involved in the depredations in western Kansas in the fall of 1878, there was little chance that the prosecution would find witnesses who could identify any of them as the individuals who committed specific acts of barbarism or property destruction. In addition, the consistent testimonies of Old Crow and Wild Hog during government hearings revealed that they were the very men who had pleaded with the younger warriors *not* to kill peacefully disposed civilians. If the government wanted to hold the chiefs and headmen, as representative war leaders of the Northern Cheyennes, accountable for their warriors' actions on vague charges of war crimes or the like, something it probably could not have done constitutionally, then the proper venue would have been a military tribunal, not a civil court. In one sense then, the case of *State of Kansas v. Wild Hog*, in retrospect, appeared indeed to have been a trial of revenge, despite the outcome.

By the autumn of 1879, federal government officials were focused more on remedying the grievances of the Northern Cheyennes at

This photograph of the Cheyennes on trial was taken in Lawrence, Kansas, in October 1879 by W. H. Lamon following a change of venue granted the Indians. Although no identifications accompany the photograph, the children in front are probably Wild Hog's, and the women are probably the wives of other Indians on trial. Second row, left to right: Porcupine, unidentified woman, Old Crow, Wild Hog; top row, left to right: unidentified woman, probably Noisy Walker (Noisy Walking), Strong Left Hand, unidentified man, Blacksmith, Tangle Hair, unidentified woman.

Darlington Agency and on deciding where the northerners should permanently live than they were on seeking revenge for the crimes against citizens of western Kansas. It was doubtful that Wild Hog and his six codefendants understood the legal specifics of why they were not hanged, but in any event, the dismissal of charges against these men likely was just. We will never know if the defense would have made distinctions between "innocent" settlers and those who were aiding the military by trying to shoot the Cheyennes. That the *actual* perpetrators of the crimes committed against defenseless civilians went unpunished, however, is certain.

To at least some degree, Wild Hog and Old Crow probably helped refocus the issue away from the Kansas raids and onto the grievances of the Indians. Not only had they testified before the Board of Officers at Fort Robinson in January, prior to their return under guard to Kansas, but they subsequently gave more detailed testimony to the Senate Select Committee in Lawrence, Kansas. Collectively their testimonies voiced the Northern Cheyenne perspective on the Cheyenne odyssey; their words were carefully transcribed by a stenographer, unedited save original translation by the sworn interpreter, Ben Clarke.

On February 12, 1879, Sen. William B. Allison submitted a resolution to the U.S. Senate for the creation of a select committee to examine the removal of the Ohmeseheso from the North to Darlington Agency in Indian Territory in 1877. By autumn 1879, given the recent events of the Cheyenne odyssey, the committee decided to study the reasons the Indians had fled Darlington to return north. When Wild Hog, Old Crow, and the other prisoners were brought to Lawrence, the committee traveled there to hear their testimony. The testimonies of agency personnel and officers in the Department of the Missouri were heard at Fort Reno. Members of the committee present in Lawrence were Senators S. J. Kirkwood, Jon T. Morgan, H. L. Dawes, J. E. Bailey, and P. B. Plumb.[28]

Wild Hog's testimony was passionate, and his words have been widely quoted in recounting the history of the Northern Cheyennes. Although Wild Hog's name does not appear on the rolls of the Northern Cheyenne Indian Reservation in Montana during the 1880s, indicating that he may have remained at Darlington Agency following the trial, his contribution in turning official opinion finally toward allowing his people to live permanently in the North is undiminished.

Citizens of western Kansas who lost family and property to the Cheyenne raiders were more successful in garnering some compensatory recognition from the state government, even though most of the claims were never paid. Upon the recommendation of Kansas governor John P. St. John, the state legislature approved, during the early congressional session of January 1879, Senate Joint Resolution 1, "relating to the losses sustained by citizens of Kansas by the invasion of Indians" in 1878. Accordingly, Governor St. John appointed a committee of three men to serve on the commission. They were R. E. Stevenson of Olathe (chairman), A. W. Mann of Burr Oak, and W. R. Adams of Larned. The men were to hear claims in Dodge City, Hays, and Norton Center. After hearing the claims, the commissioners audited them, drafted a report on July 1, 1879, and submitted the final document to Governor St. John.[29]

Of 116 claims presented, 26 were rejected because of lack of evidence or the commission's lack of statutory authority to pay for the items or persons claimed. The 90 claims that were approved totaled $101,766.83, at an average of $1,130 per claim.[30] The heaviest claims were paid to cattle ranchers in southwest Kansas. The three highest payments were $17,760 to Evans, Hunter, and Evans of Ford County; $14,091 to Smith and Savage of Gove County; and $13,700 to J. L. Driskill and Sons, Ford County.[31] These ranches were profit-making businesses, so the possibility exists that some of these claims were inflated. Table 9.1 illustrates the claims by county.

## TABLE 9.1
### Claims and Rewards

| COUNTY | No. OF CLAIMS | LOSS CLAIMED | REWARD ALLOWED |
|--------|---------------|--------------|----------------|
| Barber | 3 | $ 2,410 | $ 1,023 |
| Comanche | 12 | 53,639 | 27,208 |
| Clark | 6 | 16,743 | 7,955 |
| Meade | 3 | 315 | 240 |
| Ford | 7 | 56,670 | 34,920 |
| Foote | 1 | 100 | 75 |
| Hodgeman | 19 | 8,398 | 245 |
| Ness | 16 | 2,315 | 415 |
| Sheridan | 5 | 20,428 | 15,819 |
| Decatur | 31 | 11,830 | 6,704 |
| Rawlins | 13 | 9,798 | 7,162 |

SOURCE: Table compiled by Ramon Powers, "The Kansas Indian Claims Commission of 1879," *Kansas History* 7 (autumn 1984): 204.

These claims for property loss in modern courts of law would indeed prove interesting. As historian Ramon Powers, the scholar who has studied the Indian Claims Commission most meticulously, has pointed out, the "pioneers of civilization on the frontiers such as western Kansas were reassured that the government would compensate them for the risks of life and property." Yet in reality, only a portion of the settlers who filed claims eventually received compensation.[32]

The claims filed varied in scope and amount—with some people filing for goods damaged and others for loss of life. Julia Laing of Decatur County filed a claim including $12 for twelve dresses and $15 for library books. J. H. Cruzen's claim included $25 for one and one-half acres of pumpkins, and George Street of Decatur County claimed $191.05 for sixty-two items including twenty-five cents for a stolen box of matches. Susana Walters of Decatur County filed for $5,000 for the loss of her husband, Frederick, and Mary Abernathy asked for $3,000 for the death of her husband, Moses. Mary Hammper requested $6,000 for the death of her husband. In perhaps the most odd claim by modern norms, Frank Vocasek of the Bohemian immigrant settlement in Rawlins County, requested $2,000 for his having been psychologically "damaged" because of the rape of his wife. He claimed that *he* had suffered great mental anguish and ostracism from his (male) neighbors that forced the family to move to a new locale, but he asked for no compensation for the suffering incurred on the part of his wife.[33]

The government of Kansas did not pay these claims with state funds. The approved claims were submitted to the Secretary of the Interior of the United States for payment of damages by the federal government. Federal records show that only 26 of the 116 approved claims were ever paid by the federal government, for a total of $10,327.45 by 1884. Until the courts overturned the practice, federal Indian depredation claims were paid out of tribal appropriations, a situation that arguably compounded the shortages and consequent problems at agencies like Darlington, problems which originally caused the Northern Cheyennes to leave.[34]

By 1879 Little Chief became another voice for the eventual resettlement of the Northern Cheyennes in the North. He and his band of Northern Cheyennes, many closely tied by marriage and kinship to the Lakotas, were sent to Darlington Agency from Montana in October 1878, at the very time Little Wolf's and Dull Knife's people were fleeing north. During the autumn of 1878, there was little dissention among government officials regarding the plan for eventually concentrating all Northern Cheyennes in Indian Territory. Allowing bands such as Little Chief's to remain in the North while Little Wolf's people were captured and returned to Darlington Agency would have caused more problems than it would have solved.

The army rounded up the band in December of 1877 following the Great Sioux War and brought them to Fort Abraham Lincoln in Dakota Territory. They were then enlisted as scouts, and during the early summer of 1878, some of them aided elements of the 7th Cavalry on an expedition to the Black Hills to locate a site for Camp Ruhlen, which became Fort Meade on December 30, 1878.[35]

Following this endeavor, with Sitting Bull safely out of the way in Canada and more than sufficient numbers of Northern Cheyenne scouts from Two Moon's band stationed with Col. Nelson A. Miles at Tongue River Cantonment, the army and the Indian Bureau agreed to move Little Chief's band south in the late summer of 1878.[36] Although officers in the Departments of the Platte and the Missouri hoped Little Wolf's northern-moving group and Little Chief's southern-moving group would not cross paths, they felt that removal of Little Chief's people to Indian Territory at that time would help serve notice to all Cheyennes of the government's intention to concentrate them at Darlington Agency. The close affinity of Little Chief's people with the Lakotas at Pine Ridge might also have influenced the decision regarding the timing of the removal. Many, perhaps most of Little Chief's people were married to Lakotas or were half-Lakota. Allowing them to remain at Pine Ridge would strenghten the claims of other Cheyennes with kinship ties to Lakotas to remain in the North. Of course the irony of allowing Two Moon's band to remain at Fort Keogh as scouts was never brought to the attention of Congress or the Indian Bureau at the time since Indian scouts might prove useful in the event of Sitting Bull's return to the United States from Canada.

On July 24, 1878, Gen. Alfred H. Terry ordered Companies H and L of the 7th Cavalry to escort the Indians from Fort Lincoln to Sydney Barracks, Nebraska. The colonel of the 7th Cavalry himself, Samuel D. Sturgis, was in command of the operation, with Capt. Frederick Benteen actually in charge of the escort as far as Sydney Barracks, Nebraska. At Bear Buttes, Dakota Territory, the expedition was joined by K Company under 2d Lt. H. M. Creel and Colonel Miles's frequent chief of scouts and interpreter, Ben Clarke, who would take personal charge, speaking for the Indians all the way to Indian Territory.[37] Although dispatches from Gen. George Crook reminded the command to keep a watchful eye for Little Wolf's and Dull Knife's people, the trip to Sydney Barracks was relatively uneventful. "They are all apparently in good spirits and seem to enjoy the trip," one reporter with the command noted.[38] The command arrived at Sydney Barracks on September 16, 1878.

At Sydney Barracks the escort was transferred to four companies of the 4th Cavalry. Maj. Clarence Mauck, who had unsuccessfully pursued Little Wolf's and Dull Knife's people north through Kansas into Nebraska, would have company in the form of Little Chief's Indians on his return trip south to Indian Territory. They left Sydney Barracks on October 20, 1878.[39] The journey had been uneventful to this point, except when the expedition had neared the vicinity of Pine Ridge. Many of these Indians had affinity with the Lakotas there and wished to remain. Chiefs Iron Shirt and Black Wolf declared they wanted to stay with the Lakotas and would go no farther south. The Indians were allowed to retain their firearms, and they may have been told at this juncture or even earlier that if they did not like life at Darlington Agency, they could return north. In any case, events proceeded without incident for a time after the Indians left Nebraska. The command moved on through Forts Wallace, Dodge, Camp Supply, and on to Indian Territory. The command arrived at the Cheyenne and Arapaho reservation on December 9.[40]

Just prior to the arrival of Little Chief's band at the agency, as the expedition camped on the North Canadian River, an event took place that almost resulted in violence. Major Mauck received orders from Gen. John Pope, commander of the Department of the Missouri, that the Indians were to be disarmed before coming on to the agency. Agent John D. Miles had made his concern known to Pope that the Cheyennes should not be allowed to keep their weapons. On the morning Major Mauck carried out the order (probably December 8, 1878), tension spread throughout the camp. "We moved up our four troops of dismounted cavalry and ranged them on two sides of a trapezoid, so that they should not fire into one another," an unidentified officer wrote for an address before the Order of Indian Wars in 1928. "The Indians came out of their camp and faced us. Grim looking warriors they were, with their carbines and Winchesters at full cock."[41]

The officer was convinced the Cheyennes thought Mauck was going to rob them for his own personal gain. Iron Shirt in particular threatened violence. Finally a mediator, probably 2d Lt. H. M. Creel, settled the three-hour stand off. Although he was a member of the 7th Cavalry, Creel was fluent in the Cheyenne language and thus accompanied the expedition the full distance to Darlington Agency.[42]

Major Mauck turned over Little Chief's 186 people to agent Miles at Darlington Agency on December 9. They joined 640 northerners who already were enrolled and who had not followed Little Wolf and Dull Knife north three months earlier. Soon Little Chief's people began to make the same complaints Little Wolf's people had the year before. The southerners ostracized the northern children and did not allow them to attend their day schools. Provisions were scarce. The land was poor, the climate unhealthy. Little Chief's people uttered what had now become a mantra among the northerners, that General Miles and others in Montana had promised them they could return north if they did not like Darlington Agency.[43]

Little Chief, within a short time, began echoing Little Wolf's complaints: "A great many have been sick; some have died. I have been sick a great deal of the time since I have been down here—homesick and heartsick and sick in every way. I have been thinking of my native country and the good home I had up there where I was never hungry, but when I wanted anything to eat could go out and hunt buffalo. It makes me feel sick when I think about that, and I cannot help thinking about that."[44]

Hoping to avoid another debacle like the Little Wolf–Dull Knife exodus, the Indian Bureau and Congress were eager to appease Little Chief. Even though Little Chief had promised not to leave for the North, agent Miles knew that such outspoken opposition to remaining in Indian Territory might inspire others to follow the example of Little Wolf and Dull Knife. Once the news got out that Little Wolf's band was to remain for the time being at Fort Keogh, many northerners of Little Chief's band became even more resistant to assimilation. Finally in May of 1879, Little Chief and five other northerners traveled to Washington to meet with President Hayes and Secretary of the Interior Schurz.[45]

Although no immediate actions were taken, by 1881, with Little Chief and many of his followers keeping up their complaints, and with the ever-present voice of Wild Hog back at Darlington Agency, it became painfully obvious to the Indian Bureau and the army that they had made a mistake in trying to concentrate Northern Cheyennes and Southern Cheyennes in Indian Territory. During the summer of 1881, the Commissioner of Indian Affairs invited Little Chief to come to Washington with a delegation of Lakotas from Pine Ridge to discuss the possibility of all Northern Cheyennes moving back north. Plans were finally set in motion to allow all northerners the right to return to their beloved homelands.[46]

## CHAPTER TEN

# EPILOGUE

## A Reservation in the North

*All the right was on the side of those Indians.*
—HENRY W. WESSELLS JR., BRIG. GEN. RETIRED,
1924

There is little doubt that the attention generated in Washington and around the nation by the self-sacrifice of Dull Knife's people at Fort Robinson helped sway Americans' opinions in favor of the Cheyenne crusade to settle on a reservation in the North. The Northern Cheyenne scouts under Two Moon and White Bull, joined by Little Wolf's followers in the spring of 1879, remained at Fort Keogh, Montana, until 1882. In May and June of that year, the government moved these Indians about ninety miles south of Miles City, Montana, onto a small reserve on Rosebud Creek and the Tongue River. From there they endeavored to gain recognition for these lands, expand them, and persuade Washington to resettle in the North all Northern Cheyennes who wished to live there.[1]

Dull Knife's eighty-five followers increased to more than one hundred after the dismissal of charges against Wild Hog and the others who had been sent to Kansas for trial. Although many writers have made the assumption that Wild Hog eventually returned to the North, there is no official record of his name at either Pine Ridge or Fort Keogh. Sgt. Carter P. Johnson, F Company, 3rd Cavalry, however, remembered meeting Wild Hog in Sydney, Nebraska, in 1883, on his way to Pine Ridge during the last significant move north of Northern Cheyennes from Darlington Agency.

Johnson had been present at the fighting on Antelope Creek in 1879 and had ensured that Wild Hog's daughter, "Blanche," had received treatment for her arm wound following the fighting at the "pit." "He was delighted to see me," Johnson recalled, "and took great pride in showing me this Indian woman whom he informed me was the girl Blanche. His esteem seemed to consist of the fact that I had bandaged this girl's arm, and nothing else, and from the fact that he was under the impression that I had made some effort to have her spared and brought in."[2]

The agent for the Lakotas complained that, during their stay at Pine Ridge, the Ohmeseheso were not industrious and were "a constant source of grief" because all they did was mourn the losses of their relatives at Fort Robinson. At the request of Col. Nelson A. Miles at Fort Keogh, the Indian Bureau finally gave the approval for Dull Knife's people to relocate to Fort Keogh, Montana, in November 1879.[3]

In 1881 Little Chief traveled to Washington with a delegation of Lakotas and won permission to move from Darlington Agency in Indian Territory to Pine Ridge Agency. Because many of Little Chief's people, like Dull Knife's followers, had kinship ties with the Lakotas through marriage, many of his band preferred that agency to Fort Keogh. Prior to the establishment of the 1882 reserve on Rosebud Creek, the ranks of the Indian scouts at Fort Keogh filled up, resulting in reduced incentive for some to move there. On October 6, 1881, Little Chief and his followers left Indian Territory along with 82 Ohmeseheso who, against government orders, departed with him to settle at Pine Ridge. This move occurred despite the objections of Pine Ridge agent Valentine T. McGillicuddy, who did not like the Northern Cheyennes. After Little Chief's transfer, 684 Northern Cheyennes remained at Darlington

Agency. Approximately one-half of these hoped to return north while the other half wished to remain in Indian Territory because of family ties with the Southern Cheyennes.[4]

In 1883 Congress authorized the transfer of the remaining Northern Cheyennes at Darlington Agency who wished to go to Pine Ridge. On September 1, 1883, 360 of them arrived at Pine Ridge Agency, bringing the numbers there to almost 1,000.[5] Among those who returned north in 1883 were Wooden Leg and most likely Wild Hog and his family. But the prejudice of Agent McGillicuddy toward the Cheyennes at Pine Ridge continued. Leaders at the Montana reserve, with the support of Gen. Nelson A. Miles, who envisioned an Indian Territory of the North, put pressure on Washington to unite all Northern Cheyennes in Montana.

A series of presidential executive orders and directives between 1884 and 1900 brought most of the northern people together in the Tongue River country. President Chester A. Arthur, in 1884, signed the order recognizing the reserve on Rosebud Creek. In 1886 under the auspices of the Interior Department, lands along the Tongue River were withdrawn from white homestead entry and given to the Northern Cheyennes. In 1900 another executive order enlarged and confirmed the reservation. The name was changed from Tongue River Reservation to Northern Cheyenne Indian Reservation. During these years, many northerners at Pine Ridge and elsewhere moved to the new reservation. Among them were Iron Teeth and her surviving family members.

During a time when reformers and the federal government preached allotment, assimilation, and the break up of tribal lands, the Northern Cheyenne reservation properties actually increased to about 460,000 acres by 1900. Much of this had to do with the determination of Indian leadership and the efforts of some of the old soldiers such as Gen. Nelson A. Miles, who had once fought them. During the last two decades of the nineteenth century, the struggles of the Northern Cheyennes shifted from fighting soldiers to waging legal combat with Montana ranchers who resented the Tongue River grasslands being designated reservation property.

In essence the confirmation of the Northern Cheyenne Indian Reservation constituted a final admission of failure on the part of the federal government to concentrate all Cheyennes in the South. Certainly, allowing the Ohemeseheso to remain in the North ended any further exodus from Indian Territory through settled lands. That situation, with resulting bloodshed, had been repeated between 1867 and 1879. States historian Orlan J. Svingen: "What satisfied the Indian Office sparked rebellion among dissatisfied Cheyennes. Government and military leaders remained inflexible to the Indians' arguments and failed to respond until scores of Cheyennes had perished in 1878 and 1879. Only then did officials realize the magnitude of the Indian opposition to removal."[6]

Indeed, the sacrifice of Northern Cheyennes who made the heroic odyssey north in 1878–79 ultimately was not in vain. By the turn of the twentieth century, they had lost their independence on the open plains but had realized their desire to live in their beloved north country. Not all tribes by 1900 could claim such good fortunate. Still, the Northern Cheyenne Indian Reservation remains much smaller than the adjacent Crow Reservation.

For many of the old veterans of life on the open plains and the Cheyenne odyssey of 1878–79, however, life on the reservation, even in their northern homelands, did not bring satisfaction, for their life on the land they had once known was gone forever. Dull Knife, who had lost a wife, three sons, and two daughters in a single year, remained embittered for the remainder of his life. He only survived Fort Robinson by four years and died in his seventies, in 1883, at the home of his son, Bull Hump.[7]

Many of Dull Knife's direct descendents have established and maintained close kinship ties with the Pine Ridge Lakotas. George Dull Knife survived Wounded Knee in 1890 and toured Europe with William F. Cody's Wild West Show. Guy Dull Knife fought in World War I although the United States did not yet consider him a citizen. Guy Dull Knife, Jr., fought in Vietnam and is a talented artist. In their homes from South Dakota south to Loveland, Colorado, the Dull Knifes have remembered the stories of their ancestor's experience in the Cheyenne odyssey, and they remain a visible, historically important American family.[8]

Today, Dull Knife Memorial College on the Northern Cheyenne Indian Reservation at Lame Deer, Montana, stands as a testament to the leadership of this renowned Old Man Chief of the Cheyennes. "We can no longer live the way we used to," Dull Knife said of his short time on the reservation. "We cannot move around no more the way we were brought up. We have to learn a new way of life. Let us ask for schools to be built in our country so that our children can go to these schools and learn this new way of life."[9]

The later life of Little Wolf was marred by tragedy. After 1879, rivalry and political friction arose between the followers of Two Moon and those of Little Wolf, and consequently between their two respective warrior societies, the Kit Foxes and the Elk Horn Scrapers. Not yet as well known as Dull Knife, because of the publicity of the fighting at Fort Robinson, Little Wolf was bypassed by the soldiers at Fort Keogh, and Two Moon, the Kit Fox headman, was elevated to the position of "head chief" at the fort, an honor not accorded legitimacy by Cheyenne tradition. Perhaps remembering his people's past life on the buffalo plains, Little Wolf grew increasingly moody and alienated.

A warrior named Starving Elk would suffer the effects of Little Wolf's depression. Many years earlier, Little Wolf had suspected Starving Elk of having kindled more than a passing interest in one of his wives. By the time of the odyssey north, Starving Elk apparently had struck up a close friendship with Little Wolf's daughter, Pretty Walker. Some Indians thought Starving Elk was still enamored of Little Wolf's wife. As Sweet Medicine Chief, Little Wolf could not show anger over such gossip.

But only a short time living near Fort Keogh had changed Little Wolf. Although he continued his friendship with Lt. W. P. Clark, and even collaborated with him on his book on American Indian sign language, Little Wolf, like so many others on the reservation, also acquired an addiction to whiskey. On the cold night of December 12, 1880, he stumbled drunkenly into the trading post of Eugene

Lamphere on Two Moon Creek, where many of the Indians had set up winter camp. He spotted a group of men and women in the store gambling for candy. Among them was his daughter Pretty Walker, and with her in the group of gamblers was Starving Elk. After Little Wolf went into a rage, Lamphere and some embarrassed Cheyennes tried to calm him and remove him gently from the trading post. "I will kill you," Little Wolf screamed at Starving Elk, as Starving Elk tried to take him gently by the arm and escort him out the door.

Little Wolf stumbled out the front door and the customers thought the matter was over, but shortly Little Wolf returned with a rifle. He entered the store, shouldered the weapon, and opened fire at almost point-blank range, killing Starving Elk instantly. The acrid smell of gunpowder, the loud report of the rifle, combined with the sight of the murdered Starving Elk lying on the floor, sobered Little Wolf almost immediately. "I am going up on that hill by the bend of the creek," he said somberly in anticipation of revenge by Starving Elk's family. "If anybody wants me I'll be there." With his wife, he kept up a lonely vigil on the hill for two days.[10]

Realizing Little Wolf's significant stature among his people and fearing trouble, the army whitewashed the murder. When Capt. G. N. Whistler at Fort Keogh wired the commander of the Department of Dakota, Gen. Alfred H. Terry, asking what to do, Terry, although he had no objection to turning Little Wolf over to civilian authorities if they so demanded, replied succinctly, "The difficulties surrounding the disposition of Little Wolf, if caught, are so great, [we] better not find him."[11] When Little Wolf turned himself in to Captain Whistler on December 15, Whistler simply told him, "You are no longer chief of the Cheyennes."

"It is true and just," Little Wolf replied.[12] Civilian authorities likewise did not request justice for Little Wolf in civil courts. Friends persuaded Starving Elk's family not to seek revenge on the Sweet Medicine Chief, although they did burn his lodge and his wagon. Tensions subsided over time. Many years later, Starving Elk's

Little Wolf and his wife in old age on the Northern Cheyenne Indian Reservation in Montana. George B. Grinnell was visiting him and took this photograph. Courtesy of the Southwest Museum, Los Angeles, negative #20604.

brother, Bald Eagle said, "Little Wolf did not kill my brother. It was the white man whiskey that did it."[13]

But Little Wolf never forgave himself. Although he was not formally banished by his people, he exiled himself along the wilds of Rosebud Creek. In later times he told close friends that he had loved Starving Elk as a brother. Few, except for whites, would smoke with him. Occasionally he did odd jobs while his wives washed clothes for settlers. Although other Cheyennes moved near him after the expansion of the reservation in 1884, he remained quiet and aloof among his people. Settlers remembered him as a gentle and dignified old man who loved children. He was a familiar figure in southern Montana by the turn of the twentieth century.[14]

Little Wolf's leadership and his vision for his people effectively ended with his surrender. In 1892 the renewal of the chiefs' council was long overdue, having been interrupted by the odyssey and the reordering of life on the new reservation. Ashamed and embarrassed, Little Wolf did not attend the ceremonies to name his successor and pass on the chief's bundle containing the holy symbols of the prophet Sweet Medicine. The council sent a runner for Little Wolf, for only he could name a successor. "I've done wrong," Little Wolf told the runner. "I killed a man, and I don't think I ought to sit with the chiefs." "We need you," the council replied. "We can't proceed without you." After a day Little Wolf came to the council for the last time to take his place as Sweet Medicine Chief. Although he could not smoke the pipe with others, he named Sun Road as his successor. Sun Road accepted the office without taking the actual Sweet Medicine bundle from Little Wolf. "I didn't want to say it," Sun Road later confessed, "but he wears that medicine over his shoulder slung under his left arm. I think it has begun to smell." Although there was talk in the council of doing away with the Sweet Medicine bundle, a chief named Grasshopper blocked the action by accepting the bundle from Little Wolf. Years later when Grasshopper died, the bundle was gone. Some suspected he had buried it long before his death.[15]

Little Wolf died in relative obscurity in 1904, ironically the same year that Young Chief Joseph (Hin-mah-tooyah-lat-kekt) of the Nez Percé died. Little Wolf, in later life, was never accorded as much adoration by whites as Chief Joseph was for the other great odyssey of Indian peoples in the 1870s. But Joseph died at Colville,

Washington, not in his homeland of the Wallowa Valley. Little Wolf died in his beloved Tongue River country, albeit reimagined according to the Euro-American vision of geographical borders. Unlike Joseph, although his exploits were heroic, Little Wolf and not Joseph, had led his people directly in both council and battle against the whites during their long trek—and unlike Joseph, he had brought his people home.

For years into the twentieth century, however, Little Wolf was not held in especially high regard by many of the Cheyennes, mostly the younger generations who had not experienced the odyssey of 1878–79. Because of the publicity surrounding the fighting near Fort Robinson, the name of Dull Knife was ubiquitous in the early literature of the Cheyenne odyssey, while Little Wolf remained a shadowy figure. During Little Wolfs' later years, the interest generated by only a few whites over his life kept his reputation as an important chief alive. Undoubtedly, much of this credit must be given to ethnohistorian George B. Grinnell. Little Wolf and Grinnell met often and enjoyed smoking together as Little Wolf recounted stories. Little Wolf became one of Grinnell's sources for his work on the Cheyennes, and Grinnell, more than any contemporary, made Americans aware that Little Wolf, not Dull Knife, had been the principal leader of the Ohmeseheso on the trek north. In a letter to a friend in 1925, Grinnell paid Little Wolf the ultimate tribute. "I knew old Little Wolf almost intimately," he wrote. "Toward the end of his life . . . I disregarded the tribal feeling about him and used to pass him my pipe to smoke. I consider him, I think, the greatest Indian I have ever known."[16]

In 1917, following a legal battle with Little Wolf's daughter, Grinnell brought the bodies of both Little Wolf and Dull Knife from burial places in the mountains and had them interred in the cemetery at Lame Deer, Montana.[17] Today the modest graves are adorned with small American flags, that snap in the ever present wind, celebrating the lives of two significant Americans whose love of freedom and sense of place continue to symbolize resistance and the self-determination of a great people.

In his old age, Little Wolf continued to denounce the raids made by younger warriors on settlers in Kansas during the autumn of 1878, as did other Cheyenne veterans of the odyssey who testified at government hearings in 1879. Fearful, no doubt, of retribution to their families if they did not denounce the raids, those who gave their stories to the whites claimed only that Dull Knife's influence (not Little Wolf's) had eroded by the time the Indians left Darlington, and as a result, many unnamed younger warriors had become unruly. So too has Northern Cheyenne oral tradition guarded knowledge of the matter through the years. The sole exception to these secrets may be a deed committed by Black Coyote. As the murderer of Black Crane, of Pvt. Leo Bader of the 2nd Cavalry, and of several civilians, Black Coyote, who had left Little Wolf's band as an outlaw, hanged himself in the Miles City jail. But Black Coyote may have become a scapegoat for the Northern Cheyennes as they were pressed over the years for information regarding the Kansas killings.

Nevertheless, in later years Cheyenne oral historian John Stands In Timber recalled being told that Black Coyote and Vanishing Wolf Heart had shot and killed Anton Stenner of Rawlins County, Kansas, while out on one of the raids the chiefs had forbidden. According to Stands In Timber, Stenner had befriended Little Wolf in earlier years, and Little Wolf had recently visited the Stenner homestead, either shortly before or at the actual time Black Coyote sneaked up on the house from behind some bushes and shot the farmer. Stands In Timber did not relate what Little Wolf's reaction was, if indeed he was present at the Stenner homestead at the time of the killing, an unlikely scenario given Little Wolf's denunciation of the raids. This account also differs widely from others recalling Stenner's death.

Stands In Timber met Anton Stenner's grandson in the early twentieth century. Young A. C. Stenner was then a resident of Powell, Wyoming. When Stenner told about his grandfather's death, Stands In Timber recalled the story of Black Coyote. "The Cheyennes had a ceremony for [A. C. Stenner] later on," Stands In

Timber recalled before his death in 1967. "[They nick-] named him [Stenner] Little Wolf, and adopted him into the tribe."[18]

But in northwest Kansas, traditions of bitterness die hard. To this day a Kansas state historical highway marker stands on U.S. 36, east of the cemetery and the stone memorial in Oberlin commemorating those civilians who were killed in 1878. The highway marker is titled "Last Indian Raid in Kansas" and relates how the Northern Cheyennes, "harassed only by a small troop detachment and cowboys . . . moved through Kansas killing and plundering."

Little Wolf's compassionate friend and captor, Lt. William P. Clark, passed away early in life, snuffing out a promising military career. Promoted to Captain, 5th Cavalry, on January 25, 1881, he was transferred to army headquarters in Washington, D.C., where he compiled a detailed map of the Big Horn Mountains. He died in Washington at age 39, on September 22, 1884, one year after the death of Dull Knife.[19]

Second Lieutenant John Baxter, who led Company F, 3rd Cavalry, in the final assault of Little Finger Nail's people in the "pit" on January 22, 1879, remained in the West. He left the army shortly after the Cheyenne odyssey and prospered in the cattle business. In 1886 he became governor of Wyoming Territory, but he served only one month. President Grover Cleveland removed him from office because of allegations he had illegally fenced in public lands for use by his cattle business.

Although he has been vilified in popular revisionist literature of the mid to late twentieth century for the slaughter of Dull Knife's people at Fort Robinson, Capt. Henry W. Wessells achieved a distinguished military career in the U.S. Army. He remained in the 3rd Cavalry and succeeded Anson Mills as its commanding officer in 1898. He was seriously wounded in the Battle of San Juan Hill, Santiago de Cuba, July 1–2, 1898, while supporting Col. Theodore Roosevelt's Rough Riders. After having his head bandaged, he continued fighting. Roosevelt paid tribute to Wessells in his memoirs of the "Rough Riders."

In May 1899, Lieutenant Colonel Wessells took the 3rd Cavalry to the Philippines during the insurrection that year. He was promoted to Colonel on February 2, 1901, and not long thereafter retired with disabilities incurred in the line of duty. He kept a lengthy diary of his service in the Philippines, which, at the time of this writing, has not yet been fully transcribed by his grandson, Henry Wessells IV. The army advanced Wessells to the rank of Brigadier General, U.S.A., retired, on April 23, 1904. He lived in Washington, D.C., after retirement, where in 1927 he was awarded the newly authorized decoration of the Silver Star for his conduct in Cuba during the Spanish American War. He died on November 9, 1929, at age eighty-three.[20]

Wessells's memoirs give historians little insight into how, in later years, he reviewed his own command decisions at Fort Robinson in January 1879. In his final comments to the Senate investigating committee that year, Secretary of the Interior Carl Schurz criticized Wessells's actions: "I am of the opinion that in every respect it would have been better to treat the prisoners well than to treat them harshly. I think that freezing and starving them was not the way to reconcile them to their fate . . . . the way to avoid trouble would have been to separate the unruly persons from the rest, and to treat all as kindly as possible."[21]

In all of his brief accounts of the fighting at Fort Robinson, Wessells related details of his command in military fashion, with little editorial commentary. Five years before his death, however, Wessells wrote to author E. A. Brininstool describing his actions at Fort Robinson in 1879 for one last time. He concluded his correspondence with the revealing statement: "All the right was on the side of those Indians."[22]

On Tuesday, March 22, 1898, at about 3:50 P.M., a fire consumed the old barracks at Fort Robinson, from which Dull Knife's people had escaped almost twenty years earlier. Two small girls, ages two and four, the daughters of a Buffalo Soldier, Sgt. Harry Wallace, C Troop, 9th Cavalry, were burned to death. Their charred remains were discovered on the bed where they had sought safety. The fire was determined to have started in the girls' room but its source remains a mystery.[23] In the 1980s, archaeologists from the Nebraska State Historical Society excavated the site of the old barracks, which dated from 1874. They unearthed a belt plate from a soldier's uniform, several unfired .45 caliber rounds, possibly hidden by Cheyenne prisoners in 1878–79, and a child's porcelain doll, scorched by fire.[24]

In his lifetime, Porcupine helped destroy a Union Pacific train in Nebraska in 1867, fought the Buffalo Soldiers in Kansas, and survived the carnage at Fort Robinson. He was placed on trial for his life in the Kansas courts and later became a spiritual leader for his people. In 1889 Porcupine visited the messiah prophet, Wovoka, and became a practitioner of the Ghost Dance, which he preached among the Northern Cheyennes without much success. The Ghost Dance doctrine held the vestige of bygone visions of the land and universe, shared now by only a few survivors of the older generations on the reservation. He died on the Northern Cheyenne Indian Reservation at age eighty-one in 1929.[25]

In 1995, an English professor from Vermont, Alan Boye, set off on foot with descendants of Dull Knife's people to retrace the Northern Cheyennes' thousand-mile journey north. Boye thoughtfully recorded his companions' impressions of the hardships their ancestors must have endured on the historic odyssey of 1878–79 in his book *Holding Stone Hands*.[26]

Indeed, Cheyenne people of today remember their history. Like other peoples in America and around the world who share the common cultural bond of past great journeys, the Northern Cheyennes experienced a defining, unifying moment in the odyssey, and the old stories and people are remembered with pride and respect, as in any nation that honors its heroes. Yet in a larger sense, the Cheyennes share an even wider cultural bond, which illuminates our modern historical understanding as many of them seek to place their stories into the panorama of American history. The story of the epic Northern Cheyenne journey is part of the great, diverse record of people in North America whose separate stories total our shared history. But continuing to relate only the suffering and hardship endured by a society without larger understanding is no longer sufficient. Modern Americans must cease to isolate the Indian Wars as oversimplified examples of atrocities, violence, and institutionalized injustice. We must no longer consider simply "Indian History" or simply "military history." Sorting out atrocities or injustices by group, for the purpose of using them as a measure against opposing groups, leads to separate ownership of what is, in reality, the shared history of Indian and non-Indian peoples. Only by finally bringing the Indian Wars into the full context of the American story can we take the step of unifying our American history into a whole record of a bonded past, rather than continuing to view it as the segmented record of many separated pasts.

The story of the odyssey of the Northern Cheyennes is too complex and disturbing in its inconsistencies to isolate as simply the cultural-historical property of either the Cheyennes, the Kansas settlers, or the federal government. In total, the odyssey of the Northern Cheyennes created seemingly inexplicable and unnecessary suffering for a variety of Americans—Indians, whites, African Americans, and persons of mixed ancestry. To isolate their stories in attempts to sort out simple notions of right and wrong is to further confuse an already obfuscated and traditionally isolated period in American history. The pain and suffering, triumph and tragedy of all of these Americans ground them in a common American history that is impossible to truly understand from the many separate points of view. Future students of history can use this basic truth either to continue stressing our disunity as a people or to seek meaningful understanding of events for the purpose of forging unity among all Americans. We all remember our heroes, for they shared common, not isolated, experiences. The stories of loyalists are equally as important as the stories of patriots in understanding the complex nature of the Revolutionary War. The stories of slave owners as well as slaves are necessary to comprehend the hypocritical nature of slavery. Confederate and Union

Tangle Hair, in old age, is pictured here with his granddaughter on the Northern Cheyenne Indian Reservation in Montana. Tangle Hair and several other warriors fought a rearguard action at Fort Robinson on the night of January 9, 1879, which enabled women and children to escape from the barracks and make their way to the White River. He was wounded in the action and was later extradited to Kansas to stand trial with Wild Hog and the others. Photo by E. C. Grinnell. Courtesy of the Southwest Museum, Los Angeles, negative #42791.

soldiers have long shared the human drama of the Civil War. From Oberlin, Kansas to the Northern Cheyenne Indian Reservation in Montana, it has been close to half a century since the last Indian and white survivors, children at the time of this epic event in American history, passed from the stage. How will they be remembered?

In 1954, Little Wolf's daughter, who was a child at the time of the trek north, died on the Northern Cheyenne Indian Reservation. She was the last survivor of the epic Cheyenne odyssey of 1878–79.[27] Among the adult generation who made that historic trek, one of the last survivors was Iron Teeth—the wife of Red Pipe, who was killed in the village in the Big Horns in November 1876, and the mother of Gathering His Medicine, who was killed in the Hat Creek Bluffs in January 1879.

Iron Teeth lived well into her nineties. Her remarkable life began in a time when Indians lived mostly unassailed by whites and extended to the age of the automobile and the airplane. Between 1926 and 1929, living alone in an isolated shack on the Northern Cheyenne Indian Reservation, she told the story of her life to a physician for the Northern Cheyennes, Dr. Thomas B. Marquis. Her account is the most complete record left to history of the Cheyenne odyssey through the eyes of a woman. For years, her story remained obscure in the historical record. Iron Teeth remembered stories told to her by her grandmother, who recalled a time before the Cheyennes migrated to the Great Plains. Iron Teeth herself remembered planting corn in the Black Hills as a girl, before the tribe completely abandoned agricultural practices because of raids on their fields by enemies.

But mostly she remembered her husband, killed in the Great Sioux War, and her son, killed three years later in the Cheyenne odyssey. Many of her friends too were killed at Fort Robinson. Throughout her long life she kept treasures given to her by her family. "This [buffalo] hide-scraper I have is made from the horn of an elk my husband killed just after we were married," she told Marquis. "He cut off the small prongs and polished this main shaft." Her beloved scraper had been among her belongings when the Ohmeseheso left Darlington Agency. "It was in my little pack when we broke out from the Fort Robinson prison. It has never been lost. Red Pipe was the only husband I ever had," she remembered. "I am the only wife he ever had. Through more than fifty years I have been his widow. When I die, this gift from my husband will be buried with me."

Like others of her generation, impoverished, alienated by the reservation system she could not accept, and consumed by memories of the old life that no longer offered her sustenance, Iron Teeth

Iron Teeth at age ninety-two is pictured here in 1926 with her beloved elk antler hide scraper. At the time of this photograph, she was being cared for medically by Dr. Thomas B. Marquis in her isolated cabin on Rosebud Creek, located on a remote section of the Northern Cheyenne Indian Reservation. Marquis visited her on several occasions during the fall of 1926 to record the story of her long life. Courtesy Montana Historical Society, Helena.

tried to cope through her last years. Once, a missionary who took an interest in her gave her a dog to keep her company, but "I killed the dog," she told Marquis, "ate some of the meat, and dried the remainder of it." Occasionally she gathered chokecherries in the spring and dried them in the old way to ward off hunger. "I used to smoke tobacco," she remembered. "But several years ago I quit. I decided it was not good for the heart and it also costs too much money."

By the late 1920s, Iron Teeth had little remaining besides her memories, yet her attitude had mellowed. "I used to hate all white people," she recalled, "especially their soldiers. But my heart now has become changed to softer feelings. Some of the white people are good, maybe as good as Indians."

Iron Teeth concluded her talks with Marquis on a cold November day, fittingly with memories of her son, one of the heroes of the Cheyenne odyssey. "We called him Mon-see-yo-mon—Gathering His Medicine," she told him. "Lots of times, as I sit here alone on the floor with my blanket wrapped about me, I lean forward and close my eyes and think of him standing up out of the pit and fighting the soldiers, knowing that he would be killed, but doing so that his little sister might get away to safety." Her last words to Marquis, perhaps better than any complex chapters in the historical record, give a proper tribute to the heroes of the Cheyenne odyssey. Eloquently, this remarkable woman has given voice to the memory of a people who have not vanished from the pages of American history, a people determined to command dignity from their fellow Americans. Pulling her blanket around her head, perhaps with the scent of wood smoke rising from the blackened flue of her dilapidated cabin, she asked simply: "Don't you think he was a brave young man?"[28]

# NOTES

## PREFACE

1. See Grinnell, *Fighting Cheyennes*, 383–435; Marquis, *Wooden Leg*, 310–47; John Stands In Timber and Liberty, *Cheyenne Memories*, 226–37; and Powell, *People of the Sacred Mountain*, 2: 1153–264.

2. *Indian Raid of 1878. The Report of the Commission Appointed in Pursuance of Senate Joint Resolution No. 1*, hereafter cited as Senate Resolution No. 1, 1–3.

3. Powers, "Why the Northern Cheyenne Left the Indian Territory, 72–81. See also Powers, "The Northern Cheyenne Trek Through Western Kansas."

4. Johnson, "Cheyennes in Court," 6–12. See also Epp, "*The State of Kansas v. Wild Hog, et al.*," 139–46.

5. For an interesting evaluation of Grinnell's transcriptions of Cheyenne oral history, see David Fridtj of Halaas, "Beecher Island Re-examined." See also a review of *The Battle of Beecher Island and the Indian War of 1867–1869* by John H. Monnett, in Colorado Heritage (summer, 1993): 45–46.

## INTRODUCTION

1. The classic account of the Dull Knife battle of November 25, 1876, taken from Indian testimony by ethnologist George Bird Grinnell, is found in Grinnell, *Fighting Cheyennes*, 359–82. One of the more interesting accounts from the military perspective was written about twenty years

after the fight by Lt. Henry H. Bellas, 4th Cavalry. It may be found in Greene, ed., *Battles and Skirmishes of the Great Sioux War*, 167–85. For an enumerated quartermaster's list of 7th Cavalry items found in Dull Knife's village, see Wheeler, *Buffalo Days*, 144–45.

2. Keenan, "They Fought Crook and Custer."

3. Marquis, "Red Pipe's Squaw," 208. In this version of Iron Teeth's memoir, she refers to her husband as "Red Ripe." Later renderings of her story (including those by Peter John Powell) give his name as Red Pipe, the name used in this book. Both Iron Teeth's and Beaver Heart's testimonies are excerpted in Greene, *Lakota and Cheyenne*, 113–20.

4. Wheeler, *Buffalo Days*, 143–44.

5. Marquis, "Red Pipe's Squaw," 118.

6. Wheeler, *Buffalo Days*, 145n.

7. The terms *Omisis* and *Ohmeseheso* require some explanation. Originally the Ohmeseheso, or Northern Eaters, constituted the largest Cheyenne band in the north. Today many scholars use the term *Omisis* to denote the entire group of Northern Cheyennes, while others use *Ohmeseheso*. In actuality, in 1878–79, not all northerners were members of the Eaters band. Some, including Little Wolf, were northern Suhtai, or So'aeo'o. A few Southern Cheyennes numbered among Little Wolf's and Dull Knife's people. In recent years the renowned Cheyenne scholar Father Peter John Powell has used *Ohmeseheso* to indicate the Northern Cheyennes as a whole. Out of respect and admiration for his scholarship, I apply the same meaning in this work. See Powell, *People of the Sacred Mountain*, 1: xxxviii.

8. Grinnell, *Fighting Cheyennes*, 400.

9. Marquis, *Wooden Leg* , 320.

10. Marquis in *Wooden Leg* estimated 284, while a Senate Select Committee reported 353.

11. Marquis, *Wooden Leg*, 399

12. Ibid.

13. Ibid., 418–20.


## CHAPTER 1

1. Bourke, *Diary*, vol. 19, 1, 853–55.

2. Report of Asst. Surgeon J. H. Patzki, U.S. Army, "Fort Fetterman, Wyoming Territory," 362.

3. About forty-five lodges under White Bull (Ice) and Two Moon surrendered to Miles on April 22, 1877, at the Tongue River Cantonment

in Montana, renamed Fort Keogh on November 8, 1878, to honor Capt. Miles Keogh, who was killed at Little Big Horn. Frazer, *Forts of the West*, 82. See also Powell, *People of the Sacred Mountain*, 2: 1087–128. The Cheyennes called the Tongue River, Elk River. Some of these Cheyennes served as scouts for the army in the Nez Perce War.

4. Powell, *People of the Sacred Mountain*, 2: 1383 n. 2.

5. Biographies of Little Wolf, Dull Knife, and others, written by Eastman in his classic, *Heroes and Great Chieftains*, are readily available on the fine Cheyenne Tribe genealogy web site. <http://www.mcn.net> (Timothy D. Cook, owner; Glenn Walker, compiler). Eastman claims that Little Wolf was about thirty–five at the time of the Cheyenne odyssey in 1878–79. In a biography written in 1978, however, historian Gary Roberts asserts that Little Wolf was past thirty at the time of his first encounter with the whites in 1856. This would have made him over fifty in 1878. See Roberts, "Shame of Little Wolf," 38. Powell states that Little Wolf was born in 1830. See Powell, *People of the Sacred Mountain*, 2: 1419. For short biographies of both Dull Knife and Little Wolf, see Hoig, *Peace Chiefs of the Cheyennes*, 123–37.

6. Eastman, "Little Wolf," at <http://www.mcn.net/~hmscook/roots/cheyenne.html>.

7. Roberts, "Shame of Little Wolf," 38.

8. Ibid., 39.

9. Little Wolf's nephew, Young Little Wolf, claims that Little Wolf was headed to the village on the Greasy Grass to persuade the Indians there not to fight, an action that angered some of the Lakotas, who later threatened Little Wolf's life. See Camp, Interview with [Young] Little Wolf, Northern Cheyenne Indian Reservation, Walter M. Camp Manuscript Collection. Transcript in Hammer, ed., *Custer in '76*, 632–33.

10. Roberts, " Shame of Little Wolf," 38.

11. Powell, *People of the Sacred Mountain*, 1: xvii–xviii.

12. Bourke, *Diary*, vol. 19, 1, 856–57.

13. Hoebel, *Cheyenne Indians of the Great Plains*, 1–2.

14. The best source on early Cheyenne trade relations is Jablow, *Cheyenne in Plains Indian Trade Relations*.

15. West, "Called Out People," 15. West's contentions that Cheyennes as well as whites were excessive consumers of the environment of the Great Plains may be explored further in West, *Contested Plains*.

16. For an examination of the environmental effects the Euroamerican settlement of that area of Kansas had on the Tsis tsis tas, see Monnett, *Massacre at Cheyenne Hole*.

17. It is not the purpose of this work to examine in depth the ethnology of the Tsis tsis tas. Such an effort would be painfully redundant, for the Cheyennes are one of the most studied peoples in North America. Standard works on the Cheyennes as tribe include but are in no way limited to the following studies.

Beginning in the early twentieth century, ethnologists interviewed elderly tribe members and recorded their stories. One of the first resulting works was George A. Dorsey's, *The Cheyennes*. The classic works remain George B. Grinnell's, *The Fighting Cheyennes*, *The Cheyenne Indians: Their History and Ways of Life*, and *By Cheyenne Campfires*.

For information on the southern people, see George Bent (Grinnell's chief informant) in George Hyde, *The Life of George Bent Written From His Letters*, edited by Savoie Lottinville. Unfortunately, these early studies, as well as some modern ones, are filtered through the cultural lenses of the white ethnologists who wrote them, and often their interests followed white society's fascination. Later works, arguably more objective, include Hoebel, *The Cheyennes*, and Stands in Timber and Liberty, *Cheyenne Memories*.

Perhaps the best secondary source is Cheyenne historian Father Peter John Powell's, *People of the Sacred Mountain*. Also valuable is Powell's, *Sweet Medicine: The Continuing Role of the Sacred Arrows, the Sun Dance, and the Sacred Buffalo Hat in Northern Cheyenne History*.

18. Bourke, *Diary*, 19: 1905.

19. Ibid., 1906.

20. Powell, *People of the Sacred Mountain*, 2: 1146.

21. Marquis, *Wooden Leg*, 303–304.

22. Malinowski, ed., *Notable Native Americans*. Short profile of Dull Knife's life by John D. McDermott, 133.

23. See <http://www.mcn.net/~hmscook/roots/cheyennes.html>.

24. Malinowski, ed., *Notable Native Americans*, 133. For Dull Knife's early exploits and his actions in the Great Sioux War, see also McDermott, ed., *Papers of the Dull Knife Symposium*. Later, Iron Teeth's account was republished in Marquis, *Cheyennes of Montana*, 52–81. Marquis interviewed Iron Teeth in 1926 when she was ninety-two. The original transcripts are in Marquis, "Indian Diaries," entries for Oct. 15–20, 25, 29, and Nov. 6, 1926.

25. Although not readily available, the most complete transcript of Iron Teeth's reminiscences is Marquis, "Red Pipe's Squaw," reprinted in Marquis, *Cheyenne and Sioux*, Ronald H. Limbaugh, ed., 25.

26. Ibid., 26.

27. Dusenberry, "Northern Cheyenne," 28.

28. Kappler, ed., *Indian Affairs*, 2: 1012–23.

29. Ramon Powers, "Why the Northern Cheyenne Left the Indian Territory," 73.

30. Covington, "Causes of the Dull Knife Raid," 14.

31. Powers, "Why the Northern Cheyenne Left Indian Territory," 73.

32. Ibid., 74.

33. Hyde, *Spotted Tail's Folk*, 229–30.

34. Spotted Tail made the visit for the Lakotas and rejected the idea of his people moving south for any reason.

35. Powell, *People of the Sacred Mountain*, 2: 1149–50.

36. Covington, "Causes of the Dull Knife Raid," 15. Many of the northerners already settled at Darlington Agency had relatives among the Southern Cheyennes.

37. Powers, "Why the Northern Cheyenne Left Indian Territory," 75.

38. Marquis, *Wooden Leg*, 308–309.

39. Marquis, *Cheyenne and Sioux*, 19.

40. Powell, *People of the Sacred Mountain*, 2: 1151.

41. *Testimony Taken by a Select Committee of the Senate Concerning the Removal of the Northern Cheyenne Indians*, 160, hereafter cited as *Senate Report 708*.

42. Ibid., 224–25. See also Powell, *People of the Sacred Mountain*, 2: 1385 nn. 55–56.

43. Marquis, *Wooden Leg*, 309.

44. Ibid.

45. Marquis, *Cheyenne and Sioux*, 19.

46. Marquis, *Wooden Leg*, 310.

47. For comparison of Lawton's remarkable physique and personality see Miles, *Personal Recollections*, 487; and Daly, "The Geronimo Campaign," 249.

48. Henry Ware Lawton (1843–1899) is best known for his actions against Geronimo in Mexico in 1886. In that campaign, one of Captain Lawton's officers persuaded Geronimo to surrender to Gen. Nelson A. Miles, the action that ended the conflict with the Chiricuahua Apaches. Promoted to Brigadier General, Lawton then became Major General of Volunteers in 1898. His maneuvers in Cuba, at the Battle of El Caney during the Spanish American War, won him additional acclaim. Lawton was killed in action at San Mateo during the Philippine Insurrection on December 19, 1899. See Altshuler, *Cavalry Yellow and Infantry Blue*, 198–99.

49. Powell, *People of the Sacred Mountain*, 2: 1151.

50. Covington, "Causes of the Dull Knife Raid," 15.

51. Marquis, *Wooden Leg*, 315.

52. *Senate Report 708*, 160.

53. Ibid. Various writers over the years have placed the numbers between 927 and 937.

54. Covington, "Causes of the Dull Knife Raid," 15.


## CHAPTER 2

1. *Senate Report 708*, 35. This entire report, taken by a Select Committee of the U.S. Senate of the 46th Congress following the Cheyenne odyssey, remains the most valuable original source detailing the suffering of the Northern Cheyennes at Darlington Agency in 1877 and 1878. The testimonies of Wild Hog and agent John D. Miles are especially illuminating.

2. Powell, *People of the Sacred Mountain*, 2: 1154.

3. *Senate Report 708*, 5–6.

4. Ibid., 15.

5. Seeger, *Early Days Among the Cheyenne and Arapahoe Indians*, 48.

6. Covington, "Causes of the Dull Knife Raid," 16.

7. House, *Annual Report, Commissioner of Indian Affairs (1878)*, xxii.

8. Seeger, *Early Days*, 48.

9. *Senate Report 708*, 90.

10. House, *Annual Report, Commissioner of Indian Affairs (1877)*, 85.

11. This argument is made in Powers, "Why the Northern Cheyenne Left Indian Territory," 79.

12. For this argument, see Dusenberry, "Northern Cheyenne," 28. Compare also the disastrous results of the concentration policy on the San Carlos Apache reservation in Arizona during the 1870s with the results of a similar policy at Darlington Agency.

13. Covington, "Causes of the Dull Knife Raid," 16.

14. Kappler, *Indian Affairs*, 1: 189.

15. *Senate Report 708*, 109.

16. *New York Herald*, Feb. 14, 1879, 126.

17. Powers, "Why the Northern Cheyenne Left Indian Territory," 77.

18. *Senate Report 708*, 83.

19. Ibid., 36.

20. Ibid., 6.

21. Ibid., 36.

22. Ibid., 161.

23. Ibid., 262, 272, xvi.

24. Ibid., 63–64. For an excellent synopsis of the food shortage in 1877–78, see also Powers, "Why the Northern Cheyenne Left Indian Territory," 77–78, and Covington, "Causes of the Dull Knife Raid," 16–17.

25. House, *Annual Report, Commissioner of Indian Affairs (1878)*, xxii; *Senate Report 708*, 176.

26. *Senate Report 708*, 8, 37.

27. Quoted in Powers, "Why the Northern Cheyenne Left Indian Territory," 79.

28. Marquis, *Cheyenne and Sioux*, 19–20.

29. Powell, *People of the Sacred Mountain*, 2: 1156.

30. House, *Annual Report, Commissioner of Indian Affairs (1877)*, 95.

31. Ibid.

32. House, *Annual Report, Commissioner of Indian Affairs (1878)*, 54.

33. Grinnell, *Fighting Cheyennes*, 385. By way of comparison, Mackenzie calculated twenty-five Northern Cheyennes killed in the attack on the camp in the Big Horn Mountains on November 25, 1876. See AGO, *Chronological List of Actions*, 63.

34. *Senate Report 708*, 4; Powell, *People of the Sacred Mountain*, 2: 1157.

35. House, *Annual Report, Commissioner of Indian Affairs (1878)*, 67.

36. For a sketchy comparison of reservation disease statistics during this time, see Crockett, "Health Conditions in Indian Territory," 34–35.

37. House, *Annual Report, Commissioner of Indian Affairs (1878)*, 295.

38. Marquis, *Wooden Leg*, 320.

39. *Senate Report 708*, 27; Marquis, *Cheyenne and Sioux*, 20.

40. Marquis, *Wooden Leg*, 320.

41. Quoted in Grinnell, *Fighting Cheyennes*, 398.

42. *Senate Report 708*, 5.

43. Marquis, *Cheyenne and Sioux*, 20.

44. Powell, *Sweet Medicine*, 197. See also Powell, *People of the Sacred Mountain*, 2: 1157.

45. Marquis, *Wooden Leg*, 320–21.

46. See Little Wolf to George B. Grinnell, Oct. 9, 1897, George B. Grinnell Papers. This material is published in slightly modified version in Grinnell, *Fighting Cheyennes*, 401–405.

47. July 4th is Grinnell's date. He may be mistaken. The events following Little Wolf's first meeting with agent Miles likely happened in a much shorter period of time, probably between the last week in August and the first week in September. The Cheyennes left Darlington on September 9, 1878.

48. Powell believes that Dull Knife was with Little Wolf at this first confrontation, as were Wild Hog, American Horse, and nearly all the warriors. See Powell, *People of the Sacred Mountain*, 2: 1158.

49. Grinnell, *Fighting Cheyennes*, 401–402.

50. Ibid., 402.

51. Ibid.

52. Powell identifies these three men as Black Horse, Mad Hearted Wolf, and Whetstone. Powell, *People of the Sacred Mountain*, 2: 1158.

53. *Senate Report 708*, 61.

54. Little Robe of the Southern Cheyennes and others visited President Grant in Washington in 1873. Little evidence exists that Little Wolf was with them. These words may well be Grinnell's alone.

55. Grinnell, *Fighting Cheyennes*, 402–403.

56. George Bent to George Hyde, Nov. 13, 1913, George Bent Papers. For extended commentary on the events of September 5 through September 9, 1878, see Powell, *People of the Sacred Mountain*, 2: 1387–88 n. 39.

57. *Senate Report 708*, 278.

58. Ibid., 403. See also Covington, "Causes of the Dull Knife Raid," 20. Powell estimates 284 Northern Cheyennes left Darlington Agency on September 9, 1878. See Powell, *People of the Sacred Mountain*, 2: 1160.

## CHAPTER 3

1. House, *Annual Report, Secretary of War (1878)*, 44.

2. Heitman, *Historical Register and Dictionary*, 1: 823.

3. Wright, "Pursuit of Dull Knife," 145 n. 19a.

4. House, *Annual Report, Secretary of War (1878)*, 45.

5. For an examination of the circumstances that led to this power balance shift, see Monnett, *The Battle of Beecher Island and the Indian War*, 75–110.

6. For a short analysis of this plan, see Wright, "Pursuit of Dull Knife," 145–47.

7. Sheridan's correspondence with his department commanders is dispersed profusely throughout the adjutant general's files in National Archives and Records Administration (hereafter referred to as NARA) RG 94. Pertinent correspondence regarding his orders in the Northern Cheyenne pursuit, however, is conveniently organized in the Campbell (pen name, Stanley Vestal) Papers. See also Lt. Gen. P. H. Sheridan, *Record of Engagements with Hostile Indians*, 79. For a synopsis of the entire episode, see Brininstool, *Dull Knife*, 12–13.

8. There is some disagreement over this site. According to Little Wolf in 1897, the camp was on the Little Medicine Lodge River. See Little Wolf to Grinnell, Oct. 9, 1897, George B. Grinnell Papers. Virtually all white sources place the site at Turkey Springs, on the north side of the Canadian. General Sheridan fixed the site 10 miles north of the Cimarron

and 35 miles east of Camp Supply on the Fort Dodge road. See *Army and Navy Journal* 16 (Sept. 28, 1878): 118. As with the Sand Creek Massacre, the location of some battle sites on the open plains have become confused over time.

9. Marquis, *Cheyenne and Sioux*, 20.

10. Ibid.

11. *Senate Report 708*, 62–63.

12. This warrior is not to be confused with the esteemed Crooked Lance, the Northern Cheyenne Roman Nose killed at the Battle of Beecher Island in Colorado Territory on September 17, 1868. Noisy Walker (Noisy Walking) the Dog Soldier is not to be confused with Noisy Walking, son of White Bull (Ice), killed at Little Big Horn.

13. Powell has done a good job compiling the names of some of the warriors identified as having made the flight north in 1878–79. See Powell, *People of the Sacred Mountain*, 2: 1160–62.

14. Marquis, *Wooden Leg*, 321, 323.

15. This mild irony was pointed out by Powell, *People of the Sacred Mountain*, 2: 1162.

16. Virtually all white sources including military reports place the contact between Rendlebrock's troops and the Indians at around 9:00 A.M. Grinnell, the major Indian source for the Battle of Turkey Springs, however, places the time late in the afternoon of the second day. Grinnell must be mistaken, or more likely his informant, Little Wolf, who remembered the event nineteen years later, was mistaken. The battle was fought on the 13th, meaning that the Cheyennes had been traveling since the night of the 9th or 10th, three full days prior to the battle. See Grinnell, *Fighting Cheyennes*, 404.

17. Grinnell, *Fighting Cheyennes*, 404.

18. This anonymous account is titled "The Great Cheyenne Chase: A Truthful Account by a Dragoon Who Participated in It." It is possible that the manuscript originally was prepared for sale by an officer. Officers occasionally moonlighted anonymously as journalists for eastern publications. There is no record of this report ever being published, and the author has never been identified. It may be the work of Capt. Sebastian Gunther, who moonlighted for *Army and Navy Journal*. In the article he wrote for that publication on the Battle of Turkey Springs, all officers but himself are identified by name.

19. Grinnell, *Fighting Cheyennes*, 404–405.

20. Stands In Timber and Liberty, *Cheyenne Memories*, 233.

21. Wright "Pursuit of Dull Knife," 147.

22. "Great Cheyenne Chase," 1.

23. *Army and Navy Journal*, Aug. 10, 1878, 150.

24. "Great Cheyenne Chase," 1.

25. *Army and Navy Journal*, Aug. 19, 1878, 150.

26. "Great Cheyenne Chase," 1.

27. Wright, "Pursuit of Dull Knife," 148 n. 29.

28. Little Wolf to Grinnell, Oct. 9, 1897, George B. Grinnell Papers. For casualty reports, see also the Report of Capt. W. G. Wedemeyer, Oct. 26, 1878, Walter Campbell Papers, box 120, folder 2.

29. *Wichita Weekly Beacon*, Sept. 25, 1878.

30. Wright, "Pursuit of Dull Knife," 153–54.

31. Report of Capt. Wedemeyer, Walter Campbell Papers. According to Wedemeyer, two additional unnamed men were killed about the same time as Bristow and Clark, but the allegation is unsupported by any other credible source.

32. Ibid. See also Grinnell, *Fighting Cheyennes*, 406; and Powell, *People of the Sacred Mountain*, 2: 1164.

33. Colcord, "Reminiscences of Charles F. Colcord," 16. Colcord claimed that eight people were killed by the Cheyennes about the same time that he found the bodies of Bristow and Clark. The others were Jim Lawson, Frank Dow, Tom Murray, an unnamed "horse wrangler," a "Cook," and a boy named Cotton. Colcord does not identify the locations of these other killings, but they likely occurred in southwest Kansas rather than Indian Territory. Ibid., 11–12.

34. A photo of the cemetery site is available in the Cherokee Strip Volunteer League's, *Battle of Turkey Springs*, a brochure commemorating the one hundredth anniversary of the Battle of Turkey Springs.

35. See, for example, Grinnell, *Fighting Cheyennes*, 413. "They [the young men] did not tell me much of what they did," Little Wolf told Grinnell, "because they knew I would not like it. "

36. John J. Bourke to Asst. Adj. Gen., Dept. of the Platte, Oct. 15, 1878, Omaha Barracks, Nebr., copy in Walter Campbell Papers, box 120.

37. Grinnell, *Fighting Cheyennes*, 413.

38. Powell, *People of the Sacred Mountain*, 2: 1164.

## CHAPTER 4

1. William H. Hemphill to John P. Hatch, Nov. 1878, NARA, RG 393, microfilm publication M989.

2. AGO, *Chronological List of Actions*, 68.

3. "Great Cheyenne Chase," 2.

4. Charles E. Morse to Post Adjutant, Sept. 27, 1878, NARA, RG 393.

5. Ibid.

6. Colcord, "Reminiscences of Charles F. Colcord," 14.

7. Wright, "Pursuit of Dull Knife," 149.

8. "Great Cheyenne Chase," 2.

9. *Topeka Capitol*, Jan. 3, 1910.

10. *Army and Navy Journal*, Oct. 26, 1878.

11. Charles E. Morse to Post Adjutant, Sept. 27, 1878, NARA, RG 393.

12. Grinnell, *Fighting Cheyennes*, 407.

13. Charles E. Morse to Post Adjutant, Sept. 27, 1878, NARA, RG 393.

14. *Army and Navy Journal*, Oct. 26, 1878.

15. Grinnell, *Fighting Cheyennes*, 407.

16. *Senate Report 708*, 129.

17. Charles E. Morse to Post Adjutant, Sept. 27, 1878, NARA, RG 393.

18. AGO, *Chronological List of Actions*, 68. Grinnell relates the unsubstantiated killing of two soldiers in the Sand Hill fight. See Grinnell, *Fighting Cheyennes*, 407.

19. Berryman, "Early Settlement of Southwest Kansas," 569.

20. Colcord, "Reminiscences of Charles F. Colcord," 14–15.

21. Pickering, "Administration of John P. St. John," 389.

22. AGO, *Chronological List of Actions*, 68.

23. Grinnell, *Fighting Cheyennes*, 407–408.

24. The most straightforward secondary accounts of the Sand Creek skirmish are Wright, "The Pursuit of Dull Knife," 149–50; and Powers, "Northern Cheyenne Trek," 12–14. For comparison, see also the testimony of Lt. W. E. Wilder in *Senate Report 708*, 127–36. The fullest account from the Cheyenne perspective is Powell, *People of the Sacred Mountain*, 2: 1164–66.

25. Grinnell, *Fighting Cheyennes*, 408.

26. Marquis, *Cheyenne and Sioux*, 20.

27. Charles E. Morse to Post Adjutant, Sept. 27, 1878, NARA, RG 393.

28. "Great Cheyenne Chase," 2.

29. Cullum, *Biographical Register*, 2: 382–83.

30. Punished Woman's Fork of the Smoky Hill River, or Punished Woman's Creek in modern Scott County, Kansas, has been known by many names. Once confusingly referred to as White Woman's Creek, it also was known as Famished Woman's Fork, then Beaver Creek (not to be confused with the northern Beaver Creek in the Republican Valley), and finally, Ladder Creek, which appears on modern highway maps. See Rydjord, *Kansas Place Names*, 477.

31. Account of Old Crow in *Senate Report 708*, 20–21.

32.  *Hays (Kansas) Daily News*, Nov. 20, 1966.

33.  Brown, "Life and Adventures of George W. Brown," 136.

34.  George W. Brown, quoted in Kittie Dale, "Last Kansas Indian Battle at Squaw's Den," *Hays (Kansas) Daily News*, Nov. 20, 1966.

The "Squaw's Den Battleground," often referred to locally as "Battle Canyon," is located about fourteen miles north of Scott City, Kansas, on the way to Scott Lake State Park. This is public access. For further information, including directions to the site, contact the Scott City Chamber of Commerce by E-mail at: <sccc@ruratel. net>.

35.  Sebastian Gunther in *Senate Report 708*, 150.

36.  Ibid., 129.

37.  "Great Cheyenne Chase," 2.

38.  W. E. Wilder in *Senate Report 708*, 129–30.

39.  *Army and Navy Journal*, Oct. 26, 1878.

40.  Grinnell, *Fighting Cheyennes*, 409.

41.  Ibid. Recorded Cheyenne reminiscences of Punished Woman's Fork are sadly lacking. Little Wolf's and Tangle Hair's selective comments to Grinnell are all too brief, and no other Cheyenne participant elaborated to the Senate Select Committee, either after the event or to journalists in later years. Apparently, Little Wolf did not consider the fight of major importance, or perhaps he considered it a tragedy rather than a victory because of the critical loss to the 4th Cavalry of the pony herd and the stores of dried meat and other provisions.

42.  *Army and Navy Journal*, Oct. 26, 1878, 185. See also the *New York Tribune*, Sept. 30, 1878; and *Harper's Weekly* 22 (Oct. 19, 1878): 827. Lewis's military record is found in William H. Lewis, 4820 ACP, 1878, NARA, RG 94, 9W3/19/27/D/box 534 and microfilm ms 250–63, microfilm publication T837.

43.  AGO, *Chronological List of Actions*, 68. Although the adjutant general's report cited here lists one enlisted man killed, five wounded, and no Indians killed or wounded, virtually all reports by officers participating in the battle assert only two enlisted men wounded, none killed, and either one or two Cheyennes killed.

44.  Brown, "Life of George W. Brown," 136.

45.  Malinowski, ed., *Notable Native Americans*, 134.

46.  Brown, "Life of George W. Brown," 136–37.

47.  Ibid.

48.  *Senate Reoprt 708*, 150. Mauck officially reported that 62 ponies were killed—17 in the battle and 45 shot in the canyon—on September 28. See Clarence Mauck to John A. Pope, Sept, 28, 1878, AGO Letters Received, NARA, RG 94.

49. Ibid., 130.

50. Brown, "Life of George W. Brown," 137. See also Wallsmith, "Centennial 1878–1978," 5; and Kansas State Historical Society, Scott County Clippings Scrapbook, vol. 1, 1888–1967, ms K 978. 1: sco. 8, 53–54.

51. *New York Herald*, Oct. 10, 1878.

52. Brown, quoted in the *Hays (Kansas) Daily News*, Nov. 20, 1966.

53. Powers, " Northern Cheyenne Trek," 15. See also Kansas State Historical Society, *Eighteenth Biennial Report*, 30–31.

54. Colcord, "Reminiscences of Charles F. Colcord," 12.

55. Collins, *Indians' Last Fight*, 251–52.

56. Kansas State Historical Society, *Eighteenth Biennial Report*, 31.

57. Collins, *Indians' Last Fight*, 256.

58. Ibid., 251.

59. *Russell (Kansas) Reformer*, Feb. 4, 1898.

60. For example, see the *Dodge City Times*, Sept. 14, 1878.

61. Papers of Gov. George T. Anthony, Kansas State Historical Society. The political fallout from the Cheyenne odyssey through southwest Kansas is examined in depth in Powers, "Northern Cheyenne Trek," 15–16.

62. Bratt, *Trails of Yesterday*, 75–77, 227.

63. Colcord, "Reminsicences of Charles F. Colcord," 10–11.

64. William H. Hemphill to John P. Hatch, Nov. 1878, Fort Dodge Post Records.

## CHAPTER 5

1. Keith, "Dull Knife's Cheyenne Raid," 116–17.

2. *Senate Resolution No. 1*, 3.

3. *Dodge City Times*, Nov. 2, 1878.

4. Miner, *West of Wichita*, 110.

5. Cutler, *History of the State of Kansas*, is full of interesting facts regarding Decatur and all other Kansas counties. This entire resource is available on the Internet via the Kansas Collection, created in part by Professor Lynn Nelson of the University of Kansas, through the Kansas Heritage Server, at: <www.ukans.edu/carrie/kamcoll/books/cutler/>. Scroll to "Chapters by County," and click on "Decatur"(eleven pages).

6. Laing, "A Tale of Horror," 1–2, reprinted in *Omaha Weekly Republican*, Nov. 22, 1878. "Although [Cheyenne women were] known for their chastity [and their men respected it], white women were a different matter," wrote Cheyenne historian Peter John Powell in *People of the Sacred*

*Mountain* vol. 2, 869. Cheyenne attitudes regarding chastity and rape of the unchaste are also explored in one of the best concise ethnologies of the Cheyennes, E. Adamson Hoebel's *The Cheyennes: Indians of the Great Plains*, 95–96.

7. Ibid., 3.

8. "Billy O'Toole's Story of the Raid," hereafter referred to as Interview with Billy O'Toole, edited by George Nellans, 2.

9. Ibid.

10. *Kansas City Star*, Sept. 23, 1962.

11. Interview with Billy O'Toole, 2.

12. Records of the (Kansas) Governor's Office, Gov. John P. St. John, 1879–83, Correspondence Received; State Department, Commission to Examine Claims: Indian Raid of 1878 (Topeka: 1879), folder 18, hereafter referred to as "Claims 1878."

13. Sutton, "More About the Dull Knife Raid," 25.

14. *Kansas City Star*, Sept. 23, 1962.

15. Wallsmith, "Centennial," 6.

16. Claims 1878, folder 21.

17. Wallsmith, "Centennial," 8. John Stands In Timber claimed that Stenner was killed by Black Coyote, who had left Darlington Agency after Little Wolf and Dull Knife. See Stands In Timber and Liberty, *Cheyenne Memories*, 234.

18. *Kansas City Star*, Feb. 24, 1938.

19. Hayden, *The Time That Was*, 25.

20. Wallsmith, "Centennial," 7–8.

21. Hayden, *The Time That Was*, 26–27.

22. *Kansas City Star*, Sept. 23, 1962.

23. Ibid.

24. O. E. Heath to W. L. Saunders, Oct. 6, 1878, Meridian, Kans. This letter was discovered in an old trunk by Marie Dunn and published in the *Emporia Times*, July 26, 1956. Some of the best concise accounts by surviving eyewitnesses are found in Foster, "Last Indian Raids," 140–50.

25. *Kansas City Star*, Sept. 23, 1962.

26. *Oberlin Times*, Sept. 10, 1909.

27. *Kansas City Times*, May 28, 1939.

28. Lockard, *History of the Early Settlement*, 203.

29. Ibid., 204.

30. Ibid., 204–205.

31. Foster, "Last Indian Raids," 147.

32. Keith, "Dull Knife's Cheyenne Raid," 118.

33. Ibid., 117.

34. Wallsmith, "Centennial," 7.

35. Greene and Wright, eds., "Chasing Dull Knife," 32–33.

36. Interview with Billy O'Toole, 2.

37. Sandoz does not state in her short note to herself where this incident occurred. It may well have happened in southern Nebraska in early October, 1878. When Mrs. Grantham related the incident, she was a resident of Lexington, Nebraska. Mari Sandoz Collection, Pt. 2: Research Files, box 25, file 26: item no. 1, n.d.

38. Grinnell, *Fighting Cheyennes*, 413.

39. For extensive evaluations of the Sappa Creek fight in 1875, see Monnett, *Massacre at Cheyenne Hole*, and Chalfant, *Cheyennes at Dark Water Creek*.

40. Street, "Cheyenne Indian Massacre," 373.

41. Street, "Incidents of the Dull Knife Raid."

42. Lockard, "The Battle of Achilles," 29.

43. Lockard, *History of the Early Settlement*, 204–205.

44. Mari Sandoz Collection, Pt. 2: Research Notes, box 29, folder 2.1: item no. 3. Sandoz also cross-referenced the 1908 Street article in Constable, "History of Rawlins County," 36–40.

45. Hyde, *Life of George Bent*, 369.

46. Powell, *People of the Sacred Mountain*, 2: 1171.

47. Ibid., 1390 n. 36.

48. *Senate Report 708*, 21.

49. Powers, "Northern Cheyenne Trek," 11.

50. *Senate Report 708*, 132.

51. Dodge, *33 Years Among Our Wild Indians*, 592. See also Papers of Richard Irving Dodge, Everett D. Graff Collection, 38–40.

52. Kansas State Historical Society, *Eighteenth Biennial Report*, 21–22.

53. The so-called Great Solomon raids by the Dog Soldiers in 1868.

54. Miner, *West of Wichita*, 118.

55. Kansas State Historical Society, *Eighteenth Biennial Report*, 29.

56. *Emporia Times*, July 26, 1956.

57. Kansas State Historical Society, *Eighteenth Biennial Report*, 28.

58. *National Tribune*, Oct. 19, 1911.

59. Greene and Wright, eds., "Chasing Dull Knife," 27, 30.

60. Goodale, ed., "A Civilian at Fort Leavenworth and Fort Hays," 147.

61. *Senate Report 708*, 135.

62. Jordan, Jr., ed., "A Soldier's Life on the Indian Frontier" 155.

63. Ibid., 154.

## CHAPTER 6

1.  Street, "Incidents of the Dull Knife Raid," 7.
2.  *Rocky Mountain News*, Oct. 11, 1878.
3.  *Army and Navy Journal*, Oct. 12, 1878.
4.  Dale, ed., *Frontier Trails*, 27.
5.  Grinnell, *Fighting Cheyennes*, 409. The major Cheyenne source for the capture of Dull Knife and the subsequent outbreak from Fort Robinson is Grinnell. His interviews with Tangle Hair and others apparently intrigued him so much that almost all of the detailed notes from his field books were included in *The Fighting Cheyennes*.
6.  Ibid.
7.  Learning of this from his grandmother, Medicine Woman, who was with Little Wolf and Dull Knife in 1878, Henry Tall Bull related the story to Powell in 1959. See Powell, *People of the Sacred Mountain*, 2: 1390 n. 40.
8.  *Daily Nebraska State Journal*, Nov. 1, 1878.
9.  Street, "Incidents of the Dull Knife Raid," 8.
10. *Army and Navy Journal*, Oct. 19, 1878.
11. Originally called Camp Ruhlen, this post's name was changed to Fort Meade on December 30, 1878. Camp Robinson, likewise, was advanced to permanent status in autumn 1878 and received official designation as a fort on Deccember 30.
12. Gen. George Crook, Dept. of the Platte, to Gen. Philip Sheridan, Div. of the Missouri, Oct. 28, 1878, *Fort Robinson Post Returns* NARA, RG 393, Special Files, Cheyenne Outbreak, 1878–79, M1495, roll 6.
13. *Senate Report 708*, 132.
14. Ibid., 130.
15. Crook to Sheridan, Oct. 28, 1878, *Ft. Robinson Post Returns*, NARA, RG 393: Special Files, Cheyenne Outbreak.
16. Ibid.
17. *Omaha Daily Bee*, Oct. 16, 1878.
18. The exact location of this split is disputed. Little Wolf told Grinnell it occurred on the Niobrara River, but Big Beaver told Grinnell it was south of the South Platte, not far north of Punished Woman's Fork. Tangle Hair placed it on Birdwood Creek, north of the Platte and near where, in 1830, the Skidi Pawnees captured *Maahotse*, the sacred arrows. At least one white account stipulates that the separation did not take place until the Indians were on Chadron Creek, on about October 23, 1878. See Powell, *People of the Sacred Mountain*, vol. 2: 1390 n. 51.
19. Grinnell, *Fighting Cheyennes*, 410.

20. Marquis, *Cheyenne and Sioux*, 21.

21. Ibid.

22. *Army and Navy Journal*, Oct. 12, 1878.

23. Grinnell, *Fighting Cheyennes*, 414.

24. Bronson, *Reminiscences of a Ranchman*, 160–61.

25. *Daily Nebraska State Journal*, Oct. 26, 1878.

26. *Senate Report 708*, 22.

27. Proceedings of a Board of Officers, hereafter referred to as Board of Officers, Dept. of the Platte, Records of the Adj. General's Office, 1780–1917, NARA RG 94: AGO 1878, file no. 8705, reproduced on roll 449, 4–15, 53–54. The same record is located in Proceedings of a Board of Officers, Dept. of the Platte, Special Orders No. 8, Records of the U. S. Army Continental Commands, NARA, RG 98: 4–15, 53–54. All official supporting documents in relation to the Indian escape from Fort Robinson also are located in Letters Sent from the office of the Secretary of War to the Commissioner of Indian Affairs, NARA, RG 94, AGO, 1879, on microcopy 666, roll 30.

28. Ibid., 53–54, 20–23.

29. Ibid., 20–25, 52–57

30. Interview with Sgt. Carter P. Johnson, Sept. 9, 1913, Ellison Manuscript Collection, Denver Public Library, manuscript no. 8, box 26, folder 14: 1.

31. Scott, *Some Memories of a Soldier*, 98.

32. Orders issued by Gen. P. H. Sheridan on December 30, 1878, made the designation official. See Buecker, *Fort Robinson and the American West*, 123. See also Grange Jr., *Fort Robinson*, 217.

33. For Fort Robinson's vivid history, see Buecker, *Fort Robinson and the American West*, and Schubert, *Buffalo Soldiers*.

34. Big Beaver to Grinnell, Aug. 10, 1911, Field Notebooks.

35. Board of Officers, 134–35.

36. Ibid., 29. An excellent study of post Ordinance Reports yielded a complete analysis of the guns confiscated: Buecker and Paul, "Cheyenne Outbreak Firearms," 2–12. The authors stipulate that some of the confiscated guns were given to Lakota auxiliaries.

37. Board of Officers, 50.

38. Grinnell, *Fighting Cheyennes*, 417–418.

39. From the journal of Captain Henry W. Wessells, in the possession of Henry W. Wessells IV. Portions of this journal are published in Wessells IV, "Hard Military Service," 601–605. Henry W. Wessells IV, Managing Editor of AB Bookman Publications, is the great-grandson of Capt. Henry W. Wessells, Jr., commander of Fort Robinson in 1879.

40. Interview with Sgt. Carter P. Johnson, 2.

41. Crook to Asst. Adj. Gen., Div. of Mo., Dec. 12, 1878, *Ft. Robinson Post Returns*, NARA, RG 393: Special Files: Little Wolf Papers, Crook Letterbooks, vol 1.

42. Wessells, Jr., Enlistment Papers, NARA, RG 94, AGO: entry 91, 1st series, box 817.

43. Wessells Jr., 2403 A.C.P. File, 1891, NARA, RG 94, AGO: 9W4/7/9/E/box 17.

44. Gen. Wessells, Outbreak of the Cheyennes at Fort Robinson, unpublished interview with Henry W. Wessells, Ellison Manuscript Collection, 1, 4, n.d.

45. Carlton to Crook, Oct. 31, 1878, *Ft. Robinson Post Returns*, NARA, RG 393, Special Files: Cheyenne Outbreak.

46. Letters Received by the Office of the Adj. General, Main Series, 1871–80. NARA, RG 94, Div. of the Missouri, roll 449, file 8705, item 9095.

47. Ibid., item 9421.

48. Ibid., items 9983, 10209.

49. *Senate Report 708*, 251.

50. Grinnell, *Fighting Cheyennes*, 418.

51. Bronson, *Reminiscences*, 167–68.

52. Wessells IV, "Hard Military Service," 604.

53. Ibid.

54. Interview with Sgt. Carter P. Johnson, 4.

55. Board of Officers, 75–76.

56. Wessells IV, "Hard Military Service," 604.

57. Interview with Sgt. Carter P. Johnson, 4.

58. Ibid., 3.

59. Marquis, *Cheyenne and Sioux*, 21.

60. Interview with Sgt. Carter P. Johnson, 4.

61. Ibid., 3.

62. Wessells, IV, "Hard Military Service," 604.

63. *Senate Report 708*, 12.

64. Wessells, interview, 2.

65. *Senate Report 708*, 12.

66. Grange, Jr., "Treating the Wounded," 278.

67. *Senate Report 708*, 22. Wild Hog claimed Old Crow was put in irons first.

68. Ibid., 12.

69. Grinnell, *Fighting Cheyennes*, 419.

70. Interview with Sgt. Carter P. Johnson, 4.

71. Board of Officers, 80–81.

72. Grinnell, *Fighting Cheyennes*, 420.

73. *Senate Report 708*, 12.

74. Grinnell, *Fighting Cheyennes*, 421,426.

75. Board of Officers, 141. See also Angeline Johnson's reminiscences in Twitchell, ed., "Camp Robinson Letters," 95.

76. Marquis, *Cheyenne and Sioux*, 22.

77. The exact escape route of the Northern Cheyennes from Fort Robinson has been the subject of some controversy in the past. Some popular accounts have placed the route directly up the barren ridge, about two miles from the fort. Cheyenne accounts place the escape corridors along Soldier Creek and White River and to the hills and bluffs on the west side of the river. In 1987, the University of South Dakota, in conjunction with the Northern Cheyenne Tribe and Dull Knife College, conducted archaeological research in both locations. Artifacts were found along the water drainage courses but not on the open ridge, thus supporting the Indian claims. For a summary report of this study, see McDonald, et al., "The Cheyenne Outbreak Revisited: The Employment of Archaeological Methodology in the Substantiation of Oral History," 265–69.

78. Grinnell, *Fighting Cheyennes*, 421, 426.

79. Marquis, *Cheyenne and Sioux*, 22.

80. Fort Robinson Hospital Records, Jan. 9, 1879, Eli S. Ricker Manuscript Collection, tablet 43, reports 2–8.

81. Grinnell, *Fighting Cheyennes*, 421–422.

82. Marquis, *Cheyenne and Sioux*, 22–23.

83. Wessells, "Hard Military Service," 604.

84. Wessells, interview, 2.

85. *Army and Navy Journal*, Jan. 18, 1879.

86. Grinnell, *Fighting Cheyennes*, 426.

87. *Senate Report 708*, 13.

88. Board of Officers, 81.

89. Bronson, *Reminiscences*, 177–78.

90. Grinnell, *Fighting Cheyennes*, 422.

91. Board of Officers, 29, 66–67, 138.

92. *New York Herald*, Jan. 14, 1879.

93. Interview with Sgt. Carter P. Johnson, 5.

94. Board of Officers, 69.

95. Grinnell, *Fighting Cheyennes*, 422.

96. *New York Herald*, Jan. 14, 1879.

97. Bronson, *Reminiscences*, 178.

98. Grinnell, *Fighting Cheyennes*, 426.

99. For an evaluative analysis, see Grange, "Treating the Wounded," 273–94.

100. *Army and Navy Journal*, Jan. 18, 1879.

101. Statement of Miles Seminole, Jan. 16, 1951, John Stands in Timber Papers, Father Peter John Powell Collection.

102. *Army and Navy Journal*, Jan. 18, 1879.

103. Board of Officers, 29.

104. Grinnell, *Fighting Cheyennes*, 423.

105. Wessells, interview, 2.

106. Big Beaver to Grinnell, Aug. 10, 1911, Grinnell Field Notebooks.

107. In the popular literature, this daughter is referred to as "the Princess" (Bronson is the source). This might have been a name for her given by Captain Wessells, as he had become fond of her prior to January 9, 1879. Powell places some validity on the claim of George Bent, in Bent to Hyde, December 11, 1912, that her name was "probably" Walking Woman. See *People of the Sacred Mountain*, 2: 1205, 1394 n. 23. Powell also states that Dull Knife's wife who escaped with him was "Pawnee Woman" (Little Woman?), but other sources contend that Little Woman was killed by a stampeding horse prior to the captivity at Fort Robinson.

108. Grinnell, *Fighting Cheyennes*, 422.

109. Bronson identified this man as Bull Hump, Dull Knife's son. Cheyenne testimony verifies Bull Hump's survival in the bluffs with his father. Powell believes this man to be Little Hump. See Powell, *People of the Sacred Mountain*, 2: 1394 n. 22.

110. Bronson, *Reminiscences*, 181–83.

111. Board of Officers, 169.

112. Ibid., 132–33, 147–48.

113. All three of the officers attested to this incident. See Board of Officers, Lt. Simpson, 112–13; Lt. Hardie, 132–33; Lt. Crawford, 147.

114. Ibid., 150–51; 166. Old Crow testified that he was taken out in a wagon the morning following the breakout and saw the bodies of twenty-two women and children at that time. See *Senate Report 708*, 23.

115. Wessells, interview, 2.


CHAPTER 7

1. Board of Officers, 167.

2. Ibid., 135.

3. Ibid., 167–70.

4. Ibid., 161–65.

5. Ibid., 170–72.

6. Bronson, *Reminiscences*, 187–90.

7. Fort Robinson Hospital Records, 1879, report 10.

8. Bronson, *Reminiscences*, 190–91.

9. Board of Officers, 116.

10. Marquis, *Cheyenne and Sioux*, 23.

11. Ibid.

12. Big Beaver to Grinnell, Aug. 10, 1911, Grinnell Field Notebooks; Grinnell, *Fighting Cheyennes*, 423–24.

13. Ibid., 424.

14. Interview with Sgt. Carter P. Johnson, 5.

15. A couple of testimonies given by the Board of Officers in February 1879 suggest that Orr was killed on January 12, 1879.

16. Fort Robinson Hospital Records, report 11, Board of Officers, 31–33, *Army and Navy Journal*, Jan. 18, 1879.

17. Grinnell, *Fighting Cheyennes*, 425.

18. Ibid., Fort Robinson Hospital Records, report 12.

19. Board of Officers, 117–18.

20. Ibid., 68.

21. Ibid., 68–69, *Army and Navy Journal*, Jan. 18, 1879.

22. Interview with John Shangreau, Allen, S.D., Nov. 6, 1906, Eli S. Ricker Manuscript Collection, tablet 9, microfilm reel no. 2, microfilm copy located in Denver Public Library (hereafter referred to as Shangreau's Account).

23. Ibid.; Board of Officers, 116.

24. Fort Robinson Hospital Records, 1879, report 13.

25. Shangreau's Account.

26. *Army and Navy Journal*, Jan. 18, 1879.

27. McGillycuddy, *McGillycuddy Agent*, 98–99.

28. *Senate Report 708*, 251.

29. Shangreau's Account.

30. Wessells IV, "Hard Military Service," 604.

31. Ibid.; *Army and Navy Journal*, Feb. 1, 1879. The actual location of the last stand of Little Finger Nail's party of Northern Cheyennes has been disputed over the years. Edgar Beecher Bronson (who was not present) places it "at a point on the Hat Creek Bluffs, near the head of "War Bonnet" (Hat) Creek (*Reminiscences*, 195). Because of the availability of Bronson's memoirs, many writers of recent generations have assumed that the stand was *in the bluffs*. Scout Shangreau and Sgt. Carter P. Johnson (who were present), however, place the historic stand on the plain below the bluffs, on a dry fork of Antelope Creek. A recent National Park Service

investigation supports Shangreau's and Johnson's account by locating the site in Sioux County, Nebraska, twenty-one miles north of Harrison and east of County Road 29.

32. *New York Journal*, Jan. 24, 1879.

33. Ft. Robinson Hospital Records, 1879, report 20.

34. Wessells, interview, 3.

35. Board of Officers, 173; *New York Journal*, Jan. 24, 1879

36. The officers' reports of this fighting are found in Board of Officers, 42–46, 70–73, 121–23, and 173–74. Specific casualty reports are from Ft. Robinson Hospital records, 1879, Reports 16–19.

37. Francis H. Hardie to Joseph C. Hardie, Sept. 21, 1889, Manuscript Collection, Dept. of Anthropology, American Museum of Natural History.

38. *New York Journal*, Jan. 24, 1879.

39. Johnson, "Statement Regarding the Cheyenne Outbreak," Eli S. Ricker Manuscript Collection, 19–20, n.d.

40. Ft. Robinson Hospital Records, 1879, report 20.

41. Ibid., Report 15.

42. Interview with Sgt. Carter P. Johnson, 6.

43. Johnson, "Statement Regarding the Cheyenne Outbreak," 19–20; Board of Officers, 46.

44. Bronson, *Reminiscences*, 196.

45. *Army and Navy Journal*, Feb. 1, 1879.

46. Board of Officers, 3, 208; Johnson, "Statement Regarding the Cheyenne Outbreak," 20.

47. Hardie to Hardie, Sept. 21, 1889. Today the Little Finger Nail Ledger Book may be found in the Hall of the Plains Indian, American Museum of Natural History in New York City.

48. Board of Officers, 138.

49. Ibid., 208–210. The adjutant general's office reported 32 Northern Cheyennes killed and 71 recaptured between January 10 and January 22, 1879. The total of 103 is inconsistent with the more that 140 Northern Cheyennes who were held prisoner at Fort Robinson. See AGO, *Chronological List of Actions*, 69.

50. Reconstructed from Moseley's hospital records in Grange, "Treating the Wounded," 291–92.

51. Ibid., 285–89.

52. *Ft. Robinson Post Returns*, NARA, RG 393, Special Files: Cheyenne Outbreak, Jan., 1879.

53. Board of Officers, 81. At the same time, Wessells testified that prior to the breakout the Cheyennes had been without water for barely over twenty-four hours.

54. Schubert, *Buffalo Soldiers*, 21.

55. Potter, "The Pageant Revisited," 217–29.

56. Board of Officers, 210.

## CHAPTER 8

1. William Rowland to George B. Grinnell, Oct. 27, 1896, George B. Grinnell Field Notebooks. See also Big Beaver to Grinnell, Aug. 10, 1911.

2. Bronson, *Reminiscences*, 196–97.

3. McDermott in Malinowski, ed., *Notable Native Americans*, 134.

4. Wessells, interview, 5.

5. Board of Officers, 137.

6. Marquis, *Cheyenne and Sioux*, 24.

7. Ibid., n. 24.

8. Little Wolf to Grinnell. Oct. 8, 1898, Grinnell Field Notebooks; Board of Officers, 188–89; Powell, *People of the Sacred Mountain*, 2: 1185.

9. Scott, *Some Memories of a Soldier*, 100.

10. Black Horse to Grinnell, Aug. 24, 1909, Grinnell field Notebooks. Black Horse's account is the exception to the lack of communication with whites regarding Indian foraging raids on civilians.

11. Powell, *People of the Sacred Mountain*, 2: 1249.

12. Black Horse to Grinnell, Aug. 24, 1909.

13. Ibid. According to John Stands In Timber, the wounding of Black Horse occurred when he went into the cellar of the house where the white man was hiding. See Stands In Timber and Liberty, *Cheyenne Memories*, 234.

14. *New York Times*, Feb. 9, 1879; *Omaha Daily Bee*, Feb. 11, 1879; *Omaha Weekly Bee*, Feb. 19, 1879.

15. Ibid., *Omaha Daily Bee*, Feb. 11, 1879. For a chronological list of these raids, see Mari Sandoz Papers, box 28, folder 2, 1.

16. Shell to Grinnell, Oct. 12, 1898, Grinnell Field Notebooks. See also Marquis, *Cheyenne and Sioux*, 20–21. For a synopsis of the differing versions of Black Coyote's crime, see Powell, *People of the Sacred Mountain*, 2: 1399 n. 18.

John Stands In Timber related that it was Red Robe who was killed and that Black Coyote was not banished. In Wooden Leg's verions, the shooting occurred over an argument in which Black Crane objected to Black Coyote's riding a horse while women walked. After killing Black Crane, Wooden Leg claimed in another version of the story, Black Coyote fled the camp and never returned. See Stands In Timber and Liberty, *Cheyenne Memories*, 45–47, and Marquis, *Wooden Leg*, 328.

17. Stands In Timber and Liberty, *Cheyenne Memories*, 234.
18. Marquis, *Wooden Leg*, 327.
19. Frazer, *Forts of the West*, 82.
20. Cullum, *Biographical Register*, 115. See also ACP File of William P. Clark, NARA, RG 94, 9W4/7/9/D/box 4.
21. Clark's movements and final capture of Little Wolf's people are well chronicled in his official report, "Fort Keogh, Mt., April 2, 1879, Pursuit and Capture of Little Wolf's Band: Report of Lieutenant Clark" (hereafter referred to as Clark's Report), published as an appendix to *Senate Report 708*, 246–50.
22. Ibid., 246–47.
23. In addition to Clark's Report, for a slightly more dramatic perspective, see W. P. Clark and Little Wolf, *Frank Leslie's Illustrated Newspaper*, 48 (June 28, 1879): 239, 277; and "Bill Jackson's Capture," *Forest and Stream* 49 (August 7, 1897): 102–103. Jackson claims that he spent the night in Little Wolf's tent and escaped, as did the others, by slitting the tent with a knife. The number of "tents" Little Wolf's people possessed at this stage of the odyssey is problematic.
24. Clark's Report, 248.
25. Ibid., 249.
26. Ibid., 249–50.
27. *Army and Navy Journal*, May 3, 1879.
28. Clark's Report, 250.
29. John Stands In Timber speaks of a man named Vanishing Heart (Wolf) in association with Black Coyote at this time.
30. *New York Times*, Feb. 22, 1879; Mari Sandoz Papers, box 28, folder 2, 1.
31. Stands In Timber and Liberty, *Cheyenne Memories*, 241.
32. *Army and Navy Journal*, Apr. 19, 1879; AGO, *Chronological List of Actions*, 69.
33. Ibid. Officially, Glover captured eight Northern Cheyennes in Black Coyote's party. See AGO, *Chronological List of Actions*, 69.
34. G. N. Whistler to Asst. Adj. General, Dept. of Dakota, NARA RG 393, Apr. 17, 1879. See also Roberts, "The Shame of Little Wolf," 42.
35. Stands In Timber and Liberty, *Cheyenne Memories*, 241.
36. *Bismarck Tribune*, July 19, 1879.
37. W. P. Clark to Adj. General, Dept. of Dakota, NARA, RG 393, Special Files: Little Wolf Papers, Apr. 6, 1879.
38. Ibid.
39. *Bismarck Tribune*, Apr. 19, 1879.

## CHAPTER 9

1. Miller and Snell, "Some Notes on Kansas Cowtown Police," 383, 392–93.

2. George R. Peck to George Anthony, Dec. 17, 1878, Governor's Papers: Letters of Gov. George T. Anthony.

3. Board of Officers, 2, 4–10, 18.

4. Schuyler to Crook, Jan. 16, 1879, *Senate Misc. Doc. No. 64*, 26.

5. Board of Officers, 204.

6. For a synthesis of the changing mood of the army versus the anger of civil authorities in Kansas, see Johnson, "Cheyennes in Court," 6–12.

7. *Senate Misc. Doc. No. 64*, 17.

8. Ibid.

9. *Leavenworth (Kansas) Daily Times*, Feb. 12, 1879.

10. *Dodge City Times*, Feb. 15, 1879.

11. *Leavenworth (Kansas) Daily Times*, Feb. 16, 1879.

12. Ibid.

13. *Topeka Commonwealth*, Feb. 16, 1879.

14. *Dodge City Times*, Feb. 22, 1879.

15. Ibid.

16. Collins, *The Indians' Last Fight*," 261.

17. Indictment for murder in the first degree, State of Kansas, *County of Ford, v. Wild Hog, et al.*, June Term, 1879, CR (Court Record) 663. Douglas County Clerk's Office, Sept. 6, 1879; Atchison Champion, June 29, 1879.

18. *Dodge City Times*, Feb. 22, 1879; *Atchison Champion*, June 29, 1879.

19. CR 663, documents of June 24, 25, Oct. 1, 1879.

20. *Ford County Globe*, July 1, 1879.

21. Epp, "*State of Kansas v. Wild Hog, et al.*," 142–43.

22. CR 663, various documents, Aug. 19–Sept. 8, 1879.

23. Douglas County District Court Journal J, Lawrence: 4th District Court of Kansas, microfilm roll 5–6, Sept. 30, 1879, 469.

24. Epp, "*State of Kansas v. Wild Hog, et al.*," 143. See also Wilson, "Reflections on Mike Sutton," 277–78.

25. *Kansas Tribune*, Oct. 16, 1879

26. Douglas County District Court Journal J, Oct. 13, 1879, roll 5–6, 470.

27. Epp, "*The State of Kansas v. Wild Hog, et al.*," 146

28. *Senate Report 708*, 1.

29. *Kansas Session Laws*, 1879, 216–18. Governor's Papers, Gov. John P. St. John, 1879–83. Letter Book 14, 102.

30. Kansas State Historical Society, *Eighteenth Biennial Report*, 31; R. E. Stevenson to John P. St. John, Governor of Kansas, July 1, 1879, Topeka: Records of the Governor's Office, Gov. John P. St. John 1879–83, Correspondence Received, Dept. of State, Claim file: folder 6, box 2.

31. Kansas State Historical Society, *Eighteenth Biennial Report*, 31.

32. Ibid., 211

33. Claims, Indian Raid folders 18–21, 1878. These and other claims are surveyed in Powers, "Kansas Indian Claims Commission," 208–210.

34. For information on the convoluted red tape leading to these federal payments, see Powers, "Kansas Indian Claims Commission," 205–207, 210.

35. Collins, *The Indians' Last Fight*, 311; Frazer, *Forts of the West*, 136.

36. Tongue River Cantonment became Fort Keogh in November, 1878, a month before Little Chief's band arrived in Indian Territory.

37. Collins, *Indians' Last Fight*, 313–14.

38. *Cheyenne (Wyoming) Leader*, Aug. 24, 1878.

39. House, *Annual Report, Commissioner of Indian Affairs (1879)*, 57.

40. Ibid., Collins, *Indians' Last Fight*, 315–16.

41. Carroll, ed., "Experiences of Major Mauck," in *Papers of the Order of the Indian Wars*, Sept. 30, 1928, 6.

42. Collins, *Indians' Last Fight*, 317–18. The unidentified officer who wrote his recollections in 1828 claimed that mixed-blood George Bent mediated the tension on the North Canadian, but Bent was a Southern Cheyenne, not a member of Little Chief's band. The officer describes how Bent laid his rifle at Mauck's feet and all of his family followed suit. If Bent was a scout or interpreter with the expedition at this point, it is doubtful his family was with him. This inidentified officer also claims that Amos Chapman was the chief scout and interpreter, when in fact it was Ben Clarke.

43. House, *Annual Report , Commissioner of Indian Affairs*, 1879, 57–59.

44. Grinnell, *Fighting Cheyennes*, 401.

45. House, *Annual Report, Commissioner of Indian Affairs*, 1879, 58–59.

46. House, *Annual Report, Commissioner of Indian Affairs*, 1881, 41.


# CHAPTER 10

1. Dusenberry, "Northern Cheyenne," 30–31.

2. Johnson, "Statement Regarding the Cheyenne Outbreak," 26.

3. House, *Annual Report, Commissioner of Indian Affairs*, 1880, 160–61.

4. House, *Annual Report, Commissioner of Indian Affairs, 1881*, 49–50.

5. House, *Annual Report, Commissioner of Indian Affairs, 1883*, 30–39.

6. Svingen, *Northern Cheyenne Indian Reservation*, x, 23. Svingen's administrative history of the Northern Cheyenne Indian Reservation between 1877 and 1900 picks up where this study ends. It is a significant analysis of the northerners' struggle against ranching interests and bureaucrats to unite their people in Montana.

7. McDermott in Malinowski, ed., *Notable Native Americans*, 134.

8. For an excellent human interest account of the Dull Knife descendents, see Starita, *The Dull Knifes of Pine Ridge*.

9. Dull Knife Memorial College, Lame Deer, Mo. Website home page: <www.montana.edu/~wwwai/DKMC.html>.

10. Marquis, *Wooden Leg*, 331–32. For an excellent survey of Little Wolf's crime, see Roberts, "The Shame of Little Wolf," 43–48. See also Stands In Timber and Liberty, *Cheyenne Memories*, 47–48.

11. Letters Received, Office of the Adj. General, Dept. of Dakota, NARA, RG 393, Dec. 14, 1880.

12. Marquis, *Wooden Leg*, 332.

13. Ibid.

14. Roberts, "The Shame of Little Wolf," 45–46.

15. This information about the chiefs' renewal of 1992 was given by a man named High Forehead, who was present at the killing of Starving Elk, in K. N. Llewellyn and E. Adamson Hoebel, *The Cheyenne Way: Conflict and Case Law in Primitive Jurisprudence*, 85–86. See also Stands In Timber and Liberty, *Cheyenne Memories*, 47–48.

16. George Bird Grinnell to R. S. Ellison, Oct. 1, 1925, Robert S. Ellison Manuscript Collection, Papers and Letters of George Bird Grinnell, doc. 29.

17. Dusenberry, "Northern Cheyenne," 23–24. The cemetery is located east of Dull Knife Memorial College, at the intersection of Montana State Highway 39 and U. S. 212.

18. Stands In Timber and Liberty, *Cheyenne Memories*, 234.

19. Cullum, *Biographical Register*, 116.

20. Wessells IV, "Hard Military Service," 602.

21. *Senate Report 708*, 251.

22. Brininstool, *Dull Knife*, 5.

23. *Crawford Tribune*, Mar. 25, 1898.

24. Buecker, *Fort Robinson*, 192.

25. *Billings Gazette*, Apr. 7, 1935. See also "The Messiah Preacher," in Marquis, *Cheyennes of Montana*, 124–36.

26. Boye, *Holding Stone Hands*.
27. Dusenberry, "Northern Cheyenne," 23–24.
28. Marquis, *Cheyenne and Sioux*, 24–26.

# BIBLIOGRAPHY

## GOVERNMENT DOCUMENTS

### Kansas

*Indian Raid of 1878. The Report of the Commission Appointed in Pursuance of Senate Joint Resolution No. 1, Pertaining to Losses Sustained by Citizens of Kansas by the Invasion of Indians during the Year 1878,* Topeka: George W. Martin Publishing House, 1879.

Kansas Session Laws. Topeka, 1879.

Records of the Governor's Office, Topeka. Papers of John P. St. John, 1879–1883.

——. Papers of George T. Anthony, 1878.

Records of the Department of State. Commission to Examine Claims: Indian Raid of 1878. Topeka, 1879.

### United States

*Annual Reports of the Commissioner of Indian Affairs, 1878–1883.* In U.S. Serials as:

1878: *House Ex. Doc. No. 1,* 45th Cong., 2d sess. (Serial 1850).

1879: *House Ex. Doc. No. 1,* 46th Cong., 2d sess. (Serial 1910).

1880: *House Ex. Doc. No. 1,* 46th Cong., 3d sess. (Serial 1959).

1881: *House Ex. Doc. No. 1,* 47th Cong., 1st sess. (Serial 2018).

1883: *House Ex. Doc. No. 1,* 48th Cong., 1st sess. (Serial 2191).

*Annual Report of the Secretary of War, 1878, House Ex. Doc. No. 1,* 45th Cong., 2d sess. (Serial 1872).

"Resolution of Removal of Cheyenne Indians." *Senate Miscellaneous Document 65,* 45th Cong., 3d sess. (Serial 1833).

"The Select Committee on the Removal of the Northern Cheyennes: Testimony Submitted to the Committee." *Senate Report 708,* 46th Cong., 2d sess. (Serial 1899).

## LEGAL RECORDS

Douglas County (Kansas) District Court, Journal J, Douglas County Clerk's Office, Lawrence, Kans., 1879.

*State of Kansas, County of Ford v. Wild Hog, et al.,* June Term, 1879, Court Record 663, Douglas County Clerk's Office, Lawrence, Kans., Sept. 6, 1879.

## MANUSCRIPT COLLECTIONS

Bent, George. Correspondence to George Hyde. William Robertson Coe Collection. Beinecke Manuscript Library, Yale University, New Haven, Conn.

Bourke, John G. Diary of John Gregory Bourke. vol. 19. U. S. Military Academy Library, West Point, N.Y.

Camp, Walter Mason. Manuscript Collection. University of Indiana Library, Bloomington, Ind.

Campbell, Walter S. Walter S. Campbell Papers. Western History Collection. University of Oklahoma, Norman, Okla.

   Report of Capt. W. E. Wedemeyer on Cheyenne Depredations to the Asst. Adj. Gen., Military Division of the Missouri, Ft. Leavenworth, Kans.

Constable, Claude. "History of Rawlins County [Kansas]." Kansas State Historical Society, Topeka, Kans., n.d.

Decatur County Museum, Oberlin, Kans.

   Anonymous officer. "The Great Cheyenne Chase: A Truthful Account by a Dragoon Who Participated in It." Fort Reno [Indian Territory], Dec. 24, 1878.

   Laing, Rev. Robert. "A Tale of Horror: The Narrative of the Massacre of the Laing Family as Told by a Brother of one of the Victims," n.d.

Nellans, George, ed., Interview with Billy O'Toole, n.d.

Sutton, E. S. "More About the Dull Knife Raid," 1901.

Wallsmith, Fred. "Centennial, 1878–1978: Last Indian Raid and Battle in Kansas," 1978.

Dodge, Richard Irving. Papers of Richard Irving Dodge. Everett D. Graff Collection. Newberry Library, Chicago, Ill.

Ellison, Robert S. Ellison Manuscript Collection. Denver Public Library, Denver Colo.

Johnson, Carter P. Interview with Sgt. Carter P. Johnson, Sept. 9, 1913.

Wessells, General. Outbreak of the Cheyennes at Fort Robinson: Interview with Henry W. Wessells, n.d.

Grinnell, George. Papers and Letters of George Bird Grinnell.

————. Field Notebooks. George B. Grinnell Papers. Southwest Museum, Los Angeles, Calif.

Hardie, Francis H. Letter to Joseph C. Hardie, Sept. 21, 1889, accompanying the Little Finger Nail Ledger Book. Manuscript Collection, Dept. of Anthropology, American Museum of Natural History, New York, N.Y.

Keenan, Jack. "They Fought Crook and Custer." Wyoming Works Projects Administration, 1937. Wyoming State Archives and Historical Department, Cheyenne, Wyo.

Marquis, Thomas B. Indian Diaries, 1919–1935. National Library of Medicine, Bethesda, Md.

Ricker, Eli S. Ricker Manuscript Collection. Nebraska State Historical Society, Lincoln, Nebr.

Johnson, Carter P. "Statement Regarding the Cheyenne Outbreak from Fort Robinson," n.d.

Fort Robinson Hospital Records, Jan. 10, 1879.

Shangreau, John. Interview with John Shangreau. Allen, S.D., Nov. 6, 1906.

Sandoz, Mari. Mari Sandoz Collection, Pt. 2: Research Files. University of Nebraska Libraries, Lincoln, Nebr.

Scott County (Kansas) Clippings Scrapbook. Vol. 1, 1888–1967. Kansas State Historical Society, Topeka, Kans.

Seminole, Miles. Statement of Miles Seminole, Jan. 16, 1951. John Stands In Timbers Papers, Father Peter John Powell Collection, Newberry Library, Chicago, Ill.

Street, William D. "Incidents of the Dull Knife Raid. Notes of William D. Street," Kansas State Historical Society, Topeka, Kans., n.d.

## NATIONAL ARCHIVES AND RECORDS
## ADMINISTRATION (NARA)

Adjutant General's Office. *Chronological List of Actions, &c., With Indians from January 15, 1837 to January, 1891*, facsimile copy, Fort Collins: The Old Army Press, 1979.

Old Military Records Division, Washington, D.C. Records of the Adjutant General's Office, 1780–1917. RG 94.

William P. Clark, 330 ACP File, 1877.

William H. Lewis, ACP File, 1878.

Henry W. Wessells Jr., ACP File, 1891.

————. Enlistment Papers.

Letters Received and Sent, Departments of Dakota, the Missouri, the Platte, 1878–1879.

Proceedings of a Board of Officers, Department of the Platte, Special Orders no. 8.

————. Records of the United States Army Continental Commands, 1821–1920. RG 393.

Records of Fort Dodge, Kans., 1878.

Records of Fort Robinson, Neb., 1870–1879.

Special Files: Cheyenne Outbreak; Little Wolf Papers


## NEWSPAPERS AND NEWS PERIODICALS

*Army and Navy Journal*

*Atchison (Kansas) Champion*, June 29, 1879.

*Billings Gazette*, April 7, 1935.

*Bismarck Tribune*

*Crawford (Nebraska) Tribune*, Mar. 25, 1898.

*Daily Nebraska State Journal*, Oct. 26, 1878; Nov. 1, 1878.

*Dodge City Times*, Sept. 14, 1878; Nov. 2, 1878; Feb. 15, 1879; Feb. 22, 1879.

*Emporia (Kansas) Times*, July 26, 1956; July 26, 1959.

*Ford County (Kansas) Globe*, July 1, 1879.

*Frank Leslie's Illustrated Newspaper*

*Harper's New Monthly Magazine*

*Harper's Weekly*

*Hays (Kansas) Daily News*, Nov. 20, 1966.

*Kansas City Star*, Feb. 24, 1938; Sept. 23, 1962.

*Kansas City Times*, May 28, 1939.

*Kansas Tribune*, Oct. 16, 1879.

*Leavenworth (Kansas) Daily Times*, Feb. 12, 1879; Feb. 16, 1879.
*Leslie's Illustrated News*
*National Tribune*, Oct. 19, 1911.
*New York Herald*, Oct. 10, 1878; Jan. 14, 1879; Feb. 14, 1879.
*New York Journal*, Jan. 24, 1879.
*New York Times*, Feb. 9, 1879; Feb. 22, 1879.
*New York Tribune*
*Oberlin (Kansas) Times*, Sept. 10, 1909.
*Omaha Daily Bee*, Oct. 16, 1878; Feb. 11, 1879.
*Omaha Weekly Bee*, Feb. 19, 1879.
*Omaha Weekly Republican*, Nov. 22, 1878.
*Rocky Mountain News*
*Russell (Kansas) Reformer*, Feb. 4, 1898.
*Topeka Capitol*, Jan. 3, 1910.
*Topeka Commonwealth*, Feb. 16, 1879.
*Wichita Weekly Beacon*, Sept. 25, 1878.
*Winners of the West*, Sept. 30, 1928.


ARTICLES


Berryman, J. W. "Early Settlement of Southwest Kansas." *Kansas Historical Collections* 17 (1926–1928): 561–70.
"Bill Jackson's Capture by Cheyennes." *Forest and Stream* 49 (Aug. 7, 1897): 102–103.
Brown, George W. "Life and Adventures of George W. Brown." *Kansas Historical Collections* 17 (1926–1928): 99–138.
Buecker, Thomas R., and R. Eli Paul. "Cheyenne Outbreak Firearms." *The Museum of the Fur Trade Quarterly* 29 (summer 1993): 2–12.
Colcord, Charles F. "Reminiscences of Charles F. Colcord." *Chronicles of Oklahoma* 12 (Mar. 1934): 5–18.
Covington, James Warren. "Causes of the Dull Knife Raid." *Chronicles of Oklahoma* 26 (spring 1948): 13–22.
Crockett, Bernice Norman. "Health Conditions in Indian Territory from the Civil War to 1890." *Chronicles of Oklahoma* 36 (spring 1958): 21–35.
Dusenberry, Verne. "The Northern Cheyenne: All They Have Asked Is to Live in Montana." *Montana: The Magazine of Western History* 5 (winter 1955): 23–40.
Epp, Todd. "*The State of Kansas v. Wild Hog, et al.*" *Kansas History* 5 (1982): 139–46.

Foster, L. M. "The Last Indian Raids in Kansas, September, 1878." *Brand Book of the Denver Posse of the Westerners* (19th Annual Edition 1963): 140–50.

Goodale, Roy, ed. "A Civilian at Fort Leavenworth and Fort Hays, 1878–1879: Extracts From a Diary of Ephriam Goodale." *Kansas Historical Quarterly* 33 (summer 1967): 138–39.

Grange, Roger T., Jr. "Treating the Wounded at Fort Robinson." *Nebraska History* 45 (Sept. 1964): 273–94.

Greene, Jerome A., and Peter M. Wright, eds. "Chasing Dull Knife: A Journal of the Cheyenne Campaign of 1878 by Lieutenant George H. Palmer." *Heritage of Kansas: A Journal of the Great Plains* 12 (winter 1971): 25–36.

Halaas, David Fridtjof. "Beecher Island Re-examined." *Colorado Heritage* (summer 1993): 45–46.

Johnson, Barry C. "Cheyennes in Court: An Aftermath of the Dull Knife Outbreak of 1878." *English Westerners Brand Book* 4 (Sept. and Oct. 1962): 6–12.

Jordan, Weymouth T., Jr., ed. "A Soldier's Life on the Indian Frontier, 1876–1878: Letters of 2d Lt. C. D. Cowles." *Kansas Historical Quarterly* 38 (summer 1972): 129–55.

Keith, A. N. "Dull Knife's Cheyenne Raid of 1878." *Nebraska History* 7 (Oct.-Dec. 1924): 116–19.

Lockard, F. M. "The Battle of Achilles." *Kansas Magazine* 2 (July 1909): 26–30.

Marquis, Thomas B. "Red Pipe's Squaw." *Century Magazine* (June 1929): 201–209.

McDonald, Douglas, A. L. McDonald, Bill Tallbull, and Ted Risingson. "The Cheyenne Outbreak Revisited: The Employment of Archaeological Methodology in the Substantiation of Oral History." *Plains Anthropologist* 34 (Aug. 1989): 265–69.

Miller, Nyle H., and Joseph W. Snell. "Some Notes on Kansas Cowtown Police Officers and Gun Fighters—Continued." *Kansas Historical Quarterly* 27 (autumn 1961): 383–447.

Patzki, J. H. "Fort Fetterman, Wyoming Territory." *Annals of Wyoming* 4 (Jan. 1927): 361–62.

Pickering, I. O. "The Administration of John P. St. John." *Transactions of the Kansas State Historical Society* 9 (1905–1906): 380–89.

Potter, James E. "The Pageant Revisited: Indian Wars Medals of Honor in Nebraska, 1865–1879." In *The Nebraska Indian Wars Reader, 1865–1877*, edited by Eli R. Paul. Lincoln: University of Nebraska Press, 1998.

Powers, Ramon. "Why the Northern Cheyenne Left the Indian Territory in 1878: A Cultural Analysis." *Kansas Historical Quarterly* 3 (fall 1971): 72–81.

———. "The Northern Cheyenne Trek Through Western Kansas in 1878: Frontiersmen, Indians and Cultural Conflict." *The Trail Guide* 17 (Sept. 1972): 2–33.

———. "The Kansas Indian Claims Commission of 1879." *Kansas History* 7 (autumn 1984): 199–211.

Roberts, Gary L. "The Shame of Little Wolf." *Montana: The Magazine of Western History* 27 (July 1978): 36–61.

Street, William D. "Cheyenne Indian Massacre on the Middle Fork of the Sappa." *Transactions of the Kansas State Historical Society* 10 (1907–1908): 368–73.

Twitchell, Philip G., ed. "Camp Robinson Letters of Angeline Johnson." *Nebraska History* 77 (summer 1996): 89–96.

Wessells, Henry W. IV. "Hard Military Service: Two Officers in the Nineteenth Century West." *AB Bookman's Weekly* 102 (Oct. 5, 1998): 601–605.

West, Elliot. "Contested Plains." *Montana: The Magazine of Western History* 48 (summer 1998): 2–15.

Wilson, Paul E. "Reflections on Mike Sutton." *Journal of the Kansas Bar Association* 45 (winter 1976): 275–80.

Wright, Peter M. "The Pursuit of Dull Knife from Fort Reno." *Chronicles of Oklahoma* 46 (summer 1968): 141–54.

## BOOKS

Altshuler, Constance Wynn. *Cavalry Yellow and Infantry Blue: Army Officers in Arizona Between 1851 and 1886.* Tucson: Arizona Historical Society, 1991.

Boye, Alan. *Holding Stone Hands: On the Trail of the Cheyenne Exodus.* Lincoln: University of Nebraska Press, 1999.

Bratt, John. *Trails of Yesterday.* Lincoln: University of Nebraska Press, 1921.

Brininstool, E. A. *Dull Knife (A Cheyenne Napoleon): The Story of a Wronged and Outraged Indian Tribe, and the Most Masterful and Stubborn Resistance in the History of the American Indian.* Hollywood, Calif.: E. A. Brininstool, 1935.

Bronson, Edgar Beecher. *Reminiscences of a Ranchman.* Lincoln: University of Nebraska Press, 1962.

Buecker, Thomas R. *Fort Robinson and the American West, 1874–1899.* Lincoln: Nebraska State Historical Society, 1999.

Carroll, John M., ed. *The Papers of the Order of the Indian Wars*. Fort Collins: The Old Army Press, 1975.

Chalfant, William Y. *Cheyennes at Dark Water Creek: The Last Fight of the Red River War*. Norman: University of Oklahoma Press, 1997.

Cherokee Strip Volunteer League. *Battle of Turkey Springs, I. T. 1878*. Alva, Oklahoma. Brochure commemorating the one hundredth anniversary of the Battle of Turkey Springs, Sept. 30, 1978.

Collins, Dennis. *The Indians' Last Fight, or the Dull Knife Raid*. Girard, Kans.: Press of the Appeal to Reason, 1915.

Cullum, George W. *Biographical Register of the Officers and Graduates of the U.S. Military Academy at West Point, New York From Its Establishment in 1802 to 1890*. 2 vols. Boston: Houghton Mifflin, 1891.

Cutler, William G. *History of the State of Kansas*. Chicago: A. T. Andreas, 1883.

Dale, Edward Everett, ed. *Frontier Trails: The Autobiography of Frank M. Canton*. Norman: University of Oklahoma Press, 1966.

Dodge, Col. Richard Irving. *33 Years among Our Wild Indians*. New York: Archer House, 1959.

Dorsey, George A. *The Cheyennes*. 2 vols. Chicago: Field Columbian Museum Anthropological Series, 1905.

Eastman, Charles. *Heroes and Great Chieftans*. Boston: Little, Brown, 1918.

Frazer, Robert W. *Forts of the West: Military Forts and Presidios and Posts Commonly Called Forts West of the Mississippi River to 1898*. Norman: University of Oklahoma Press, 1965.

Grange, Roger T., Jr. *Fort Robinson: Outpost on the Plains*. Lincoln, Nebraska: State Historical Society, 1978.

Greene, Jerome A., ed. *Battles and Skirmishes of the Great Sioux War, 1876–1877: The Military View*. Norman: University of Oklahoma Press, 1993.

———, ed. *Lakota and Cheyenne: Indian Views of the Great Sioux War, 1876–1877*. Norman: University of Oklahoma Press, 1994.

Grinnell, George B. *The Cheyenne Indians: Their History and Ways of Life*. 2 vols. New Haven: Yale University Press, 1923.

———. *By Cheyenne Campfires*. New Haven: Yale University Press, 1962.

———. *The Fighting Cheyennes*. Norman: University of Oklahoma Press, 1982.

Hammer, Kenneth, ed. *Custer in '76: Walter Camp's Notes on the Custer Fight*, Provo: Brigham Young University Press, 1976.

Hayden, Ruth. *The Time That Was: The Courageous Acts and Accounts of Rawlins County Kansas, 1875–1915*. Colby, Kans.: Colby Community College, 1973.

Heitman, Francis B. *Historical Register and Dictionary of the United States Army from 1789–1903.* 2 vols. Washington, D.C.: Government Printing Office, 1903.

Hoebel, E. Adamson. *The Cheyennes: Indians of the Great Plains.* New York: Holt, Rinehart & Winston, 1960.

Hoig, Stan. *The Peace Chiefs of the Cheyennes.* Norman: University of Oklahoma Press, 1980.

Hyde, George F. *Spotted Tail's Folk: A History of the Brulé Sioux.* Norman: University of Oklahoma Press, 1961.

————. *The Life of George Bent Written From His Letters.* Edited by Savoie Lottinville. Norman: University of Oklahoma Press, 1968.

Jablow, Joseph. *The Cheyenne in Plains Indian Trade Relations 1795–1840.* Lincoln: University of Nebraska Press, 1994.

Kansas State Historical Society. *Eighteenth Biennial Report of the Board of Directors of the Kansas State Historical Society for the Biennial Period, July 1, 1910–June 30, 1912.* Topeka, 1912.

Kappler, Charles J. *Indian Affairs, Laws and Treaties.* 2 vols. Washington, D.C.: Government Printing Office, 1904.

Llewellyn, K. N., and E. Adamson Hoebel. *The Cheyenne Way: Conflict and Case Law in Primitive Jurisprudence.* Norman: University of Oklahoma Press, 1941.

Lockard, F. M. *The History of the Early Settlement of Norton County, Kansas.* Norton, Kans.: Champion Press, 1894.

Malinowski, Sharon, ed. *Notable Native Americans.* Detroit: Gale Research, 1995.

Marquis, Thomas B. *Wooden Leg: A Warrior Who Fought Custer.* 1931. Reprint, Lincoln: University of Nebraska Press, 1986.

————. *Cheyenne and Sioux: The Reminiscences of Four Indians and a White Soldier.* Edited by Ronald H. Limbaugh. Stockton, Calif.: Pacific Center for Western Historical Studies, University of the Pacific, 1973.

————. *The Cheyennes of Montana.* Edited with an introduction by Thomas D. Weist. Algonac, Mich.: Reference Publications, 1978.

Mather, William D. "The Revolt of Little Wolf's Northern Cheyennes." Master's thesis, Wichita University, Wichita, Kans., 1956

McDermott, John D., ed. *Papers of the Dull Knife Symposium.* Sheridan, Wyo.: Fort Phil Kearny/Bozeman Trail Assoc., 1989.

McGillycuddy, Julia B. *McGillycuddy Agent: A Biography of Dr. Valentine T. McGillycuddy.* Stanford: Stanford University Press, 1941.

Miles, Nelson A. *Personal Recollections and Observations of General Nelson A. Miles.* Chicago: Werner, 1896.

Miner, Craig. *West of Wichita: Settling the High Plains of Kansas 1865–1890*. Lawrence: University Press of Kansas, 1986.

Monnett, John H. *Massacre at Cheyenne Hole: Lieutenant Austin Henely and the Sappa Creek Controversy*. Niwot, Colo.: University Press of Colorado, 1999.

Paul, R. Eli, ed. *The Nebraska Indian Wars Reader, 1865–1877*. Lincoln: University of Nebraska Press, 1998.

Powell, Peter John. *Sweet Medicine: The Continuing Role of the Sacred Arrows, the Sun Dance, and the Sacred Buffalo Hat in Northern Cheyenne History*. 2 vols. Norman: University of Oklahoma Press, 1969.

————. *People of the Sacred Mountain: A History of the Northern Cheyenne Chiefs and Warrior Societies, 1830–1974, With an Epilog, 1969–1974*. 2 vols. San Francisco: Harper & Row, 1981.

Sandoz, Mari. *Cheyenne Autumn*. New York: McGraw Hill Books, 1953.

Schubert, Frank N. *Buffalo Soldiers, Braves and the Brass: The Story of Fort Robinson, Nebraska*. Shippensburg, Pa.: White Mane Publishing, 1993.

Scott, Hugh Lenox. *Some Memories of a Soldier*. New York: Century, 1928.

Seeger, John Homer. *Early Days Among the Cheyenne and Arapahoe Indians*. Edited by Stanley Vestal. Norman: University of Oklahoma Press, 1934.

Sheridan, Gen. P. H. *Records of Engagements with Hostile Indians within the Division of the Missouri from 1868 to 1882: Compiled at Headquarters Military Division of the Missouri from Official Records*. Washington, D.C.: Government Printing Office, 1882.

Stands In Timber, John and Margot Liberty. *Cheyenne Memories*. New Haven: Yale University Press, 1967.

Starita, Joe. *The Dull Knifes of Pine Ridge: A Lakota Odyssey*. New York: G. P. Putnam's Sons, 1995.

Svingen, Orlan J. *The Northern Cheyenne Indian Reservation 1877–1900*. Niwot, Colo.: University Press of Colorado, 1993.

West, Elliott. *The Contested Plains: Indians, Goldseekers and the Rush to Colorado*. Lawrence: University Press of Kansas, 1998.

Wheeler, Homer. *Buffalo Days: Forty Years in the Old West: The Personal Narrative of a Cattleman, Indian Fighter and Army Officer*. Indianapolis: Bobbs-Merril, 1925.

## INTERNET SOURCES

These Web sites contain information of interest concerning the odyssey of the Northern Cheyennes and the lands they traveled.

<www.montana.edu/~wwwai/DKMC.html>
<www.ukans.edu/carrie/kancoll/books/cutler>

# INDEX